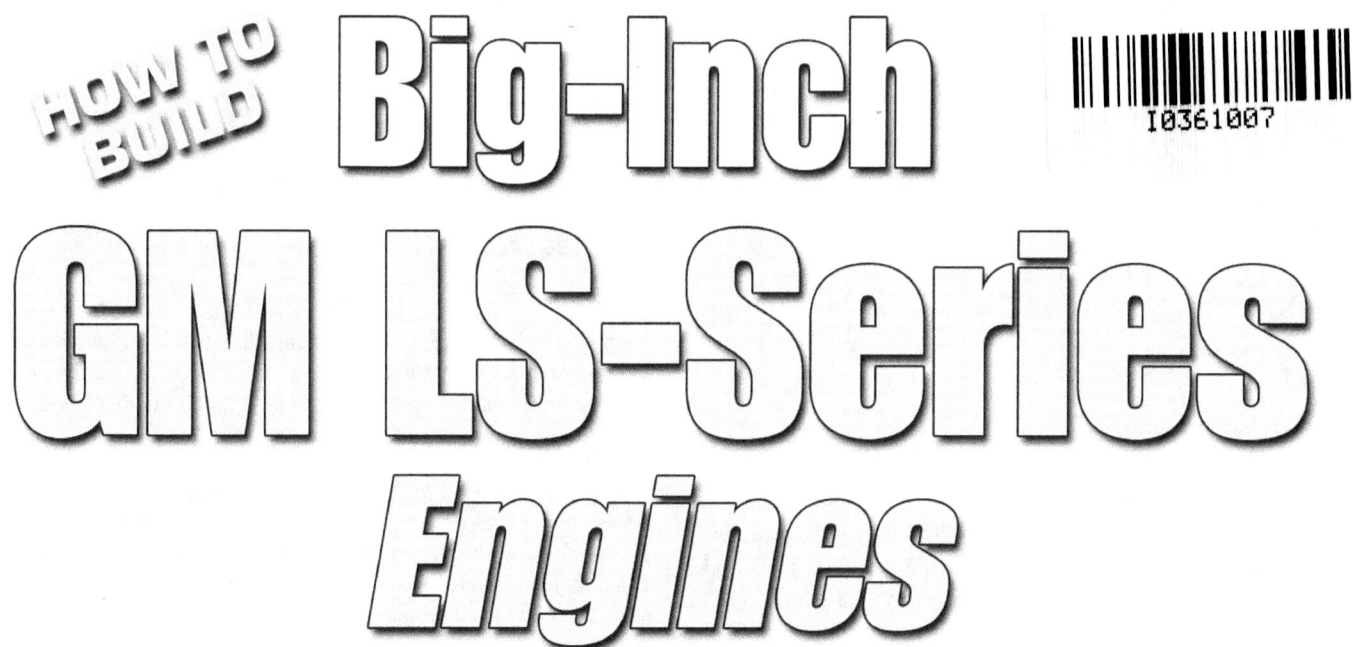

How to Build Big-Inch GM LS-Series Engines

Stephen Kim

CarTech®

CarTech®

CarTech®, Inc.
39966 Grand Avenue
North Branch, MN 55056
Phone: 651-277-1200 or 800-551-4754
Fax: 651-277-1203
www.cartechbooks.com

© 2011 by Stephen Kim

All rights reserved. No part of this publication may be reproduced or utilized in any form or by any means, electronic or mechanical, including photocopying, recording, or by any information storage and retrieval system, without prior permission from the Publisher. All text, photographs, and artwork are the property of the Author unless otherwise noted or credited.

The information in this work is true and complete to the best of our knowledge. However, all information is presented without any guarantee on the part of the Author or Publisher, who also disclaim any liability incurred in connection with the use of the information and any implied warranties of merchantability or fitness for a particular purpose. Readers are responsible for taking suitable and appropriate safety measures when performing any of the operations or activities described in this work.

All trademarks, trade names, model names and numbers, and other product designations referred to herein are the property of their respective owners and are used solely for identification purposes. This work is a publication of CarTech, Inc., and has not been licensed, approved, sponsored, or endorsed by any other person or entity. The Publisher is not associated with any product, service, or vendor mentioned in this book, and does not endorse the products or services of any vendor mentioned in this book.

Edit by Paul Johnson
Layout by Monica Seiberlich

ISBN 978-161325-164-5
Item No. SA203

Library of Congress Cataloging-in-Publication Data

Kim, Stephen.
 How to build big-inch GM LS-series engines / Stephen Kim.
   p. cm.
 ISBN 978-1-934709-44-3
 1. General Motors automobiles—Motors. I. Title.
 TL215.G4K56 2011
 629.25'04—dc22
                                    2010052885

Printed in USA

Title Page:
The entire rotating assembly is pieced together.

Back Cover Photos

Top Left:
Main bearing clearances should always be set with the main caps torqued to spec. Compared to the Gen I small-block, the thrust bearing on LS motors has been relocated to the number-3 main cap.

Top Right:
A longer stroke pulls the pistons farther down the bore at BDC, decreasing the clearance between the counterweights and the piston skirts. Making sure there are no interference issues is a balancing act between counterweight height, piston skirt design, and connecting rod length.

Middle Left:
Most aftermarket rods employ cap screws that thread directly into the rod itself rather than stock-style bolts that use a separate nut. This means that no part of the rod protrudes into the shoulder, which improves rod bolt clearance around the camshaft. Aftermarket cap screws and bolts are available in tensile strength ratings ranging from 190,000 to 280,000 psi.

Middle Right:
Most aftermarket pistons utilize 1/16-inch first and second ring grooves, and a 3/16-inch oil ring groove. This arrangement provides excellent cylinder seal.

Bottom Left:
The factory L92/LS3 heads are impressive. With nothing more than a 225-at-.050 cam, Gen IV enthusiasts are picking up an additional 65 hp. Some hot rodders feel that the 260-cc intake runners on these heads are far too large to use on small-displacement stroker engines, but that simply isn't the case.

Bottom Right:
To feed oil to the VVT system's phaser assembly, oil is routed from a groove cut into the number-2 cam journal to the oil control valve that bolts inside the cam snout. This simple arrangement allows supplying hydraulic pressure to actuate the system without any modifications to the block, which makes it very easy to retrofit VVT to non-VVT engines.

CONTENTS

Preface 4
Acknowledgments 4

Chapter 1: Advent of the GM LS Engine 5
Design Features 5
Pushrod Power 6
Explosive Potential 8

Chapter 2: Stroking Options 10
Efficiency 12
Displacement Defined 14
Pushing the Envelope 15
Clearancing 16
The Power of Cubic Inches 17

Chapter 3: The LS Engine Family 20
LS1 20
LS2 20
LS3/L92/L99 21
LS4 22
LS6 22
LS7 23
LS9 23
LSA 24
LQ4/LQ9 25
LY6 25
L76 25
Vortec 4800 25
Vortec 5300 26

Chapter 4: Engine Blocks 27
Getting Bored 28
Factory Aluminum Blocks 29
Factory Iron Blocks 32
Aftermarket Blocks 33
Machine Work 37

Chapter 5: Crankshafts 44
Stroking for Displacement 44
Factory Crankshafts 45
Cast vs. Forged vs. Billet 46
Strength 47
Metallurgy 48
Overlap 49
Twist vs. Non-Twist Forging 50
Heat-Treating the Crankshaft 50
Knife-Edging the Crankshaft
    Counterweights 50

Balancing the Crankshaft 50
Crankshaft Weight 51
Dampeners 51
Manufacturer Choices 52

Chapter 6: Connecting Rods 54
Stock Rods 54
Forging Materials 56
Rod Shape 58
Rod Length 59
Manufacturer Choices 60

Chapter 7: Pistons 62
Factory Pistons 62
Alloys 62
Skirts 63
Gas Porting 64
Wrist Pins 65
Compression Height 65
Dishes and Domes 66
Power Adder Pistons 67
Custom Pistons 69
Coatings 69
Weight 70
Manufacturer Choices 70

Chapter 8: Oiling System 72
Lubrication Basics 73
Pressure vs. Volume 73
Oil Pumps 74
Stock Pans 75
Aftermarket Pans 76
Dry Sump Systems 77
Oil Coolers 77

Chapter 9: Cylinder Heads 78
Appetite for Air 79
Port Volume 80
Flow vs. Velocity 81
Valve Angle 82
Angle of Attack 83
Valve Seat Angle 84
Combustion Chambers 84
Factory Cathedral-Port Heads 85
Factory Rectangle-Port Heads 87
Aftermarket Heads 90

Chapter 10: Camshafts 98
Cam Effects 100
Lobe Profile 101

Duration 101
Overlap 102
Measuring Duration 103
Lift 104
Piston-to-Valve Clearance 104
Valve Events 105
Timing Tricks 107
Variable Valve Timing 108
Single- vs. Dual-Pattern 109

Chapter 11: Valvetrain 110
Valvetrain Dynamics 110
Fighting Float 112
Lifters 112
Solid Rollers for the Street 114
Valvesprings 114
Retainers 116
Rocker Arms 116
Rocker Ratio 117
Pushrods 118
Timing Sets 119
Timing Covers 119

Chapter 12: Induction 120
Intake Dynamics 120
Early Stock Intakes 121
Stock Rectangle-Port Intakes 122
LS6-Style Aftermarket Intakes ... 124
Aftermarket Rectangle-Port
    Intakes 125
Carbureted Intakes 126
Throttle Bodies 127

Chapter 13: Fuel and Spark 129
Electronic Fuel Injection 129
Fuel Pump and Injector Sizing 134
Carburetors 135
Ignition 135

**Chapter 14: Proven Stroker
    Combinations** 136
Full-Race Screamer LSX 136
Wee Beast LS1 137
Big Daddy LS2 138
Welterweight Brawler LS3 138
Brazilian Stock Car LS3 Motor ... 140

Source Guide 143

PREFACE

Like most traditionalists, I wasn't quite sure what to make of the LS1 small-block when it first debuted in the 1997 Corvette. Naturally, I was a bit skeptical as to how much GM could have possibly improved upon the most prolific engine to ever compete in both amateur and professional racing, the small-block Chevy. This wasn't so much a knock against GM's engineering talents, but rather a deferential homage to the legacy the small-block Chevy had built over a span of more than four decades.

By the turn of the millennium, the LS1 hot rodding scene was in full swing, and Gen III–powered Corvettes and F-bodies quickly asserted their dominance on the street and at the track. I watched firsthand as LS1 Camaros with nothing more than a set of long-tube headers, a high-stall torque converter, and a shorter ring-and-pinion set ripped 11-second ETs. That's right; near-stock LS1s with only a few bolt-on mods were destroying stroked Gen I and II small-blocks.

It didn't take long for the muscle car crowd to get in on the action, too. As GM began phasing the Gen III small-block into more of its cars and trucks—and core motors became more plentiful—the small-block found its way into retrofit applications, and the engine was no longer the exclusive turf of late-model EFI enthusiasts.

With the staggering pace of parts development for the LS-series small-block, trying to keep up with it all is quite a challenge. All-new cylinder head castings and aftermarket cylinder blocks seemed to pop up each day. That's why when the opportunity presented itself to write this book, I didn't hesitate to sign up. Although all engines are nothing more than glorified air pumps, and the theories and concepts behind building stroker motors are somewhat universal, there's a plethora of information specific to the LS-series platform that only a comprehensive book on the subject matter can adequately cover. Through years of research and many nights of painstakingly working into the wee hours of the morning, it's my goal to outline the process of building a big-inch LS-series small-block as thoroughly as possible.

ACKNOWLEDGMENTS

Although there's only one author listed on the cover of this book, putting it all together was a tremendous undertaking that required the assistance of countless engine shops and aftermarket manufacturers. Make no mistake, they're the real experts. My job was to simply gather information from a multitude of sources and present it in a coherent and cohesive fashion. I'd be remiss to take all the credit, so it's only appropriate to acknowledge everyone who helped make this book a reality.

First and foremost, I thank Judson and Linda Massingill of the School of Automotive Machinists. They own and operate the most well-respected vocational school in the racing industry, and they were always willing to let me take over their shop to take photos and gather information. Right down the street from SAM in Houston, Texas, is HK Racing Engines, one of the top LS-series engine builders in the country. Owner Erik Koenig is a virtual encyclopedia of information in all things LS, and he was always available to answer questions and open up his shop's doors.

By far, the most challenging topic to cover while writing this book was cylinder head theory and design. Fortunately, I had access to the greatest minds in the business. Special thanks go out to Tony Mamo of Air Flow Research, Darin Morgan of Reher-Morrison, Kevin Feeney of Racing Head Service, Judson Massingill of SAM, and Al Noe of Trick Flow Specialties for their willingness to take the time to explain an extremely complex subject matter in a way that most people can understand. Cylinder head design is truly an art form, much of which is shrouded in secrecy, so it was somewhat miraculous to get such a brilliant group of head porters to divulge their trade secrets.

On behalf of all LS enthusiasts, I thank the GM engineers who developed and continue to refine such an outstanding engine platform. The impact the LS-series small-block has had on the hot rodding community in a little over a decade is beyond comprehension. GM conceived what became the original default engine for swap applications in 1955 with the Gen I small-block Chevy, and it has done it again with the Gen III/IV small-block. Considering how much better the LS platform is than its forebear, the prospect of what its legacy will someday become is very exciting.

CHAPTER 1

Advent of the GM LS Engine

Not long after its debut in the 1997 Corvette, General Motor's LS-series V-8 established itself as the gold standard of performance. Sure, other engine platforms can be built to match it in terms of sheer horsepower output, but none of them offer the LS small-block's balance of performance, simplicity, low mass, durability, compact size, affordability, and outstanding fuel mileage.

Design Features

With the immense power potential of the Gen III design, bulking up the bottom end to meet OE longevity requirements was imperative. At the same time, engineers sought to decrease weight for improved fuel economy. The result was a deep-skirt aluminum block with six-bolt main caps and enlarged cam bores. The innovative deep-skirt design extends the sides of the block around the main caps. This effectively cradles the sides of the main caps and allows securing each cap to the block skirts using a pair of cross bolts.

In addition, engineers insisted upon enlarging the cam bores and positioning them higher up in the block. Larger cam bores can accommodate larger cam journals, which are more resistant to flex when subjected to aggressive lobe profiles and stiff valvespring pressures. With future growth in mind, the camshaft has been positioned higher up in the block as well. This increases clearance between the cam, and the crankshaft counterweights and connecting rods, making it easier to install a longer-stroke crankshaft.

Despite these improvements in performance and durability, the Gen III weighs approximately 100 pounds less than its Gen I forbear while boosting fuel mileage by 10 percent. When the Gen III platform made its debut in the form of the original 5.7L LS1 in 1997, it was rated at 345 hp. That figure climbed to 505 by 2006 with the introduction to the 7.0L LS7 before being topped again by the 638 hp LS9 in 2009. Having nearly doubled in horsepower in a little more than a decade, the LS small-block's legacy is just getting started.

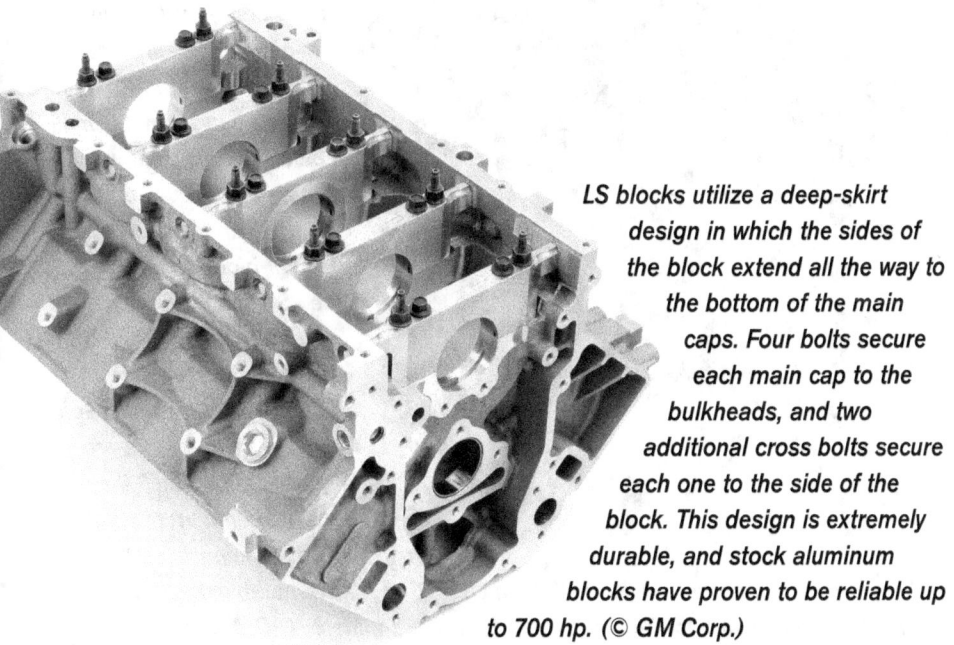

LS blocks utilize a deep-skirt design in which the sides of the block extend all the way to the bottom of the main caps. Four bolts secure each main cap to the bulkheads, and two additional cross bolts secure each one to the side of the block. This design is extremely durable, and stock aluminum blocks have proven to be reliable up to 700 hp. (© GM Corp.)

CHAPTER 1

The single greatest contributing factor to the Gen III/IV small-block's outstanding power potential is its cylinder heads. In contrast to the Gen I heads that cram the two center intake ports between a pair of pushrods, LS cylinder heads feature replicated intake ports that are evenly spaced. This allows for uncompromised port geometry and excellent airflow. Stock LS1 castings flow 240 cfm, which is enough to put many ported Gen I castings to shame. (© GM Corp.)

Pushrod Power

Many casual enthusiasts measure the merit of an engine by the number of valves it has and the RPM it turns rather than by the tally it posts in the horsepower column. By those standards, with just two valves per cylinder, actuated by an in-block camshaft via pushrods, the Gen III/IV small-block is a veritable relic. However, those who know a thing or two about building engines are well aware that a highly refined pushrod design can handily trounce a poorly executed dual overhead cam (DOHC) design. Modern innovations in valvetrain technology enable pushrod engines to rev as freely as many of their DOHC contemporaries. It won't be long before pushrod NHRA Pro Stock engines eclipse the 12,000-rpm mark, which is about 3,000 rpm more than you'd ever want to turn on the street. Combined with the staggering airflow that's capable these days with a single intake valve per cylinder, most of the pushrod engine's past maladies are no longer applicable. That means engine swappers can enjoy all of the advantages of a pushrod small-block without any of its past shortcomings.

Chief among the advantages are the simplicity, low cost, and compact size. Together, they make the OHV Gen III/IV small-block practical to build and extremely easy to install, even into the smallest of engine bays. In fact, LS engines will drop right into the diminutive chassis of Pontiac Fieros and Mazda Miatas without much fuss. On the other hand, positioning a pair of camshafts directly over the valves necessitates very tall and wide cylinder heads, especially on a V-8. Consequently, trying to retrofit certain domestic DOHC V-8s into an otherwise commodious engine compartment can be a huge challenge, and it often requires cutting out the shock towers.

Perhaps the most significant contributing factor to the Gen I small-block's success and popularity was GM's ability to mass produce it in countless iterations and displacements for a multitude of applications using one common architecture. This led to an interchangeability of components never before seen in any production motor, which reduced costs and promoted aftermarket parts development. The same applies to the Gen III/IV small-block, as the platform powers everything from Corvettes and Camaros to trucks, SUVs, and family sedans. Almost all the hardware among the different LS variants is interchangeable, and except for the smallest (4.8L) and largest (7.0L) motors in the LS lineup, all share the same 3.622-inch stroke. In most instances, the cylinder heads, camshafts, crankshafts, and intake manifolds can all be mixed and matched among different LS motors. This makes it much more appealing for aftermarket manufacturers to develop parts, promoting incessant technical innovations, an extremely diverse catalog of products from which

Unlike the Gen I small-block, LS-series motors were designed from the very beginning as corporate GM power plants, so referring to them as small-block Chevys or Mouse motors is inaccurate. Since the first variant of the Gen III small-block was named the LS1, many use "LS1" as a generic name for all Gen III/IV engines. Adding to the confusion is that while Gen III and IV truck motors are usually labeled "Vortec," they share the exact same architecture and many of the same parts as their "LS" counterparts. So whether you call them LS1s, Gen III/IV small-blocks, or LS motors, you are referring to the same great family of engines. (© GM Corp.)

6   HOW TO BUILD BIG-INCH GM LS-SERIES ENGINES

ADVENT OF THE GM LS ENGINE

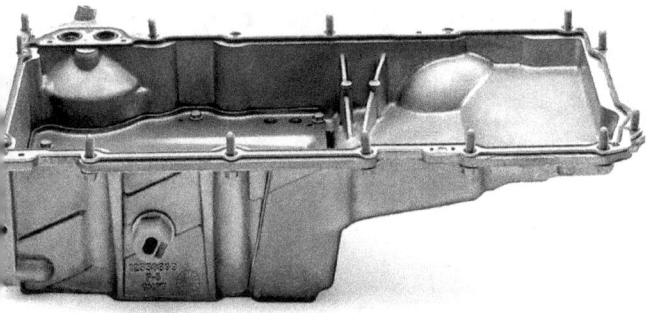

The LS small-block's cast-aluminum oil pan isn't just an oil container. It serves as a stressed member of the block that helps reduce noise and vibration. Like the rest of the block, it features structural strengthening ribs on the inside and outside of the oil pan. (© GM Corp.)

Part of what made the Gen I small-block so successful was an extensive interchangeability of parts among engines with different displacements. The same is true of the LS platform. Except for the 7.0L LS7 and 4.8L Vortec truck motor, all Gen III/IV small-blocks use 3.622-inch crankshafts. (© GM Corp.)

to choose, and more competitively priced parts.

In addition to parts interchangeability, GM further simplified the Gen III design by reducing the number of moving parts and streamlining the production process on the assembly line. For hot rodders, the result is an engine that's even easier to assemble than the Gen I small-block. For instance, LS motors feature plates that seal the intake manifold off from the lifter valley. Not only does this prevent hot oil from splashing onto the intake and heating up inlet air temperatures, it also allows for the removal and reinstallation of the intake manifold without having to run a bead of silicone on the block. Reusable rubber gaskets integrated around each intake runner eliminate the need to replace them each time the intake manifold is removed. Likewise, removing the camshaft in a Gen III small-block can be accomplished

Four Generations of Small-Blocks

In terms of sheer volume and overall popularity, the Gen I small-block Chevy is the most prolific engine platform ever produced. Introduced in 1955, more than 90 million copies were built over a 48-year production run in displacements ranging from 265 to 400 ci. Nicknamed the "Mouse" motor, or simply referred to as the small-block Chevy, the engine's 350-ci configuration was by far the most popular. Although it was conceived during an era when Chevrolet's GM rivals—Buick, Oldsmobile, Pontiac, and Cadillac—each built their own V-8s, the 350 Chevy became the standard corporate GM V-8 powerplant. When the Corvette was due for a power upgrade in 1992, the 350 was revamped. By fitting new fast-burn aluminum cylinder heads, reverse-flow cooling, an optical ignition system, and a high-flow intake onto the 350, GM created the 300-hp Gen II small-block dubbed the LT1. The Gen II was also installed in fourth-gen Camaros, Firebirds, and Impalas. In 1996, a bigger camshaft and improved cylinder heads and intake manifold were added to the Gen II to create the LT4, which boosted output to 330 hp. Production of the Gen II small-block ceased in 1997.

Although GM continued manufacturing the Gen I engine alongside the Gen II, it determined the only way to meet the power and emissions requirements of the coming decades was to create a brand-new platform from the ground up. The Gen III small-block was a revolutionary departure from the Mouse motor, featuring an all-new aluminum deep-skirt block, aluminum 15-degree cylinder heads, and a high-flow composite intake manifold. First introduced as the 345-hp LS1 in the 1997 Corvette, it was later installed in various GM trucks, SUVs, sports sedans, and coupes. By 2005, GM phased in minor revisions to create the 400-hp Gen IV LS2. Differences between the Gen III and the Gen IV are very minor, with Gen IV engines having provisions for active fuel management, variable valve timing, and relocated cam and knock sensors. Much like the Gen II small-block, the Gen IV is based on the exact same architecture and platform as the Gen III.

without pulling out the lifters, as they ride in a plastic bucket that hold them into the block. Although Gen I engines have several oil passages on the back of the block that need to be plugged, LS motors use a single plate to seal them.

Explosive Potential

Thanks to the hard work of GM engineers, enthusiasts immediately recognized the untapped performance potential of the Gen III small-block. In stock trim, it frequently pushed C5 Corvettes and fourth-generation Camaros to 12-second passes down the quarter-mile. Simple cam swaps had LS1s putting out 450 hp, and stroker combos routinely produced power in excess of 600 hp. What makes these accomplishments even more impressive is that they were achieved within five years of the LS1's launch in 1997. This was well before the first aftermarket cylinder head castings and blocks were unveiled to the public, and several years before GM introduced the big-bore Gen IV LS2. Since that time, a multitude of aftermarket manufacturers have stepped up with cylinder head and block designs of their own. Additionally, the 24-plus variants of the original LS1 that

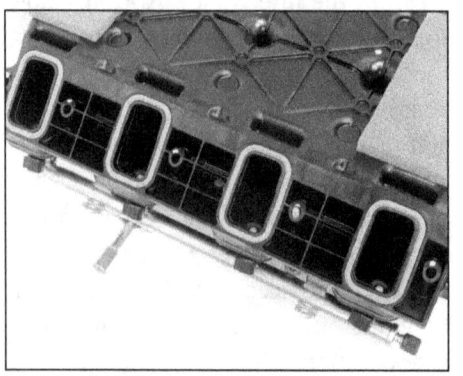

With reusable rubber gaskets that fit into the intake itself and seal each runner, the manifold can be removed and installed without having to replace the gaskets. This not only saves money, but it also eliminates the risk of blocking off the intake runners due to gasket misalignment.

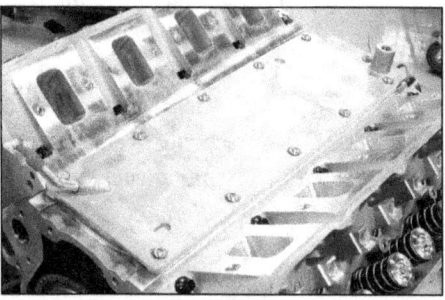

In addition to superb power potential, LS small-blocks are far easier to work on than their Mouse predecessors. A lifter plate seals oil inside the lifter valley, which prevents it from splashing on the bottom of the intake manifold and heating it up. This means that the intake doesn't need to be glued down to the block with silicone every time it's removed and installed.

The overwhelming popularity of the LS small-block has pushed the aftermarket to develop parts at an astonishing rate. There are now several aftermarket blocks and more than a dozen cylinder head castings at an engine builder's disposal. This crate motor from GM Performance Parts features an LSX block, forged pistons, and L92-style rectangle-port cylinder heads. (© GM Corp.)

They don't do much for aesthetic value, but Gen III/IV small-blocks have a separate coil pack for each spark plug mounted on the valve covers. This provides a much more powerful spark to ignite the air/fuel mixture, and it eliminates the need for a distributor, as the coils receive instructions directly from the engine management computer.

Fourth-generation Camaros and Firebirds are cursed with tiny engine compartments, yet it's still possible to shoehorn a 500-ci tall-deck LS2 inside one. Even with the increase in deck height, the motor still clears the shock towers with room to spare.

GM has released over the years means that Gen III/IV small-blocks can be built in an infinite number of configurations using both aftermarket and production parts. As deck heights keep growing, cylinder walls keep thickening, and crank throws keep orbiting farther and farther away from their mains, to make it all fit, cam bores are creeping closer to the deck, and oil pan rails continue spreading outward. To make sense of all the options at your disposal, this book's objective is to answer the myriad questions that come up along the way with any stroker Gen III/IV engine build.

As displacement figures continue to grow, the aftermarket is stepping up with serious cylinder heads that flow enough air to feed all those hungry cubic inches. These LSX-DR castings from GMPP are capable of flowing 430 cfm through the intake ports and 280 cfm on the exhaust side. That's enough to embarrass most big-block heads. (© GM Corp.)

An interesting footnote in the development of the Gen III small-block is that the 1997 Corvette served as the guinea pig for the entire LS engine program. At the time the Gen III was conceived, GM was building more than 1 million trucks and SUVs per year, so its primary objective was to design an all-new family of engines to replace the Gen I small-block in GM's truck fleet. First releasing the Gen III in the low-volume Corvette enabled GM to establish a performance image for its new V-8 as well as solve any potential teething issues during the manufacturing process before ramping up production. The Gen III was then introduced in GM's truck line in 1999. (© GM Corp.)

Perhaps the ultimate validation of the Gen III/IV's race-bred design is the new Chevy R07 NASCAR Sprint Cup V-8. Like the LS engine family, it's a clean-sheet design that uses evenly spaced intake and exhaust ports. It also features an intake valve angle of about 12 degrees, just like in the LS7. (© GM Corp.)

First introduced in the L92, the variable valve timing system used in select LS motors can advance the camshaft up to 5 degrees and retard it up to 45 degrees, resulting in a remarkably broad powerband. It features a phaser assembly, integrated into the cam gear, that's actuated by hydraulic pressure. With an aftermarket controller, the system is fully tunable for performance applications. (© GM Corp.)

CHAPTER 2

STROKING OPTIONS

Displacement is king. Whether it's in NASCAR Sprint Cup, NHRA Pro Stock, or Formula One, professional race teams always build the biggest motors that their respective rule books allow. This universal quest for maximizing displacement is hardly a coincidence. Internal-combustion engines are nothing more than glorified air pumps, and, as such, the engine that moves the most air in and out of its cylinders and combustion chambers will make the most power. Obviously, there's far more to optimizing an engine combination than displacement alone. Cylinder head airflow, intake manifold design, compression ratio, camshaft selection, valvetrain setup, cylinder wall finish, and the weight of the rotating assembly are just a few of the myriad factors that ultimately determine an engine's horsepower output. Nonetheless, having a greater volume of space inside the cylinder bores to cram full of air and fuel yields a competitive advantage few engine builders and hot rodders are willing to sacrifice. Increasing displacement by building a stroker motor is one of the easiest ways to boost performance, and thanks to the recent influx of affordable aftermarket crankshafts and connecting rods, it's now cheaper than ever.

Understanding why big cubic inches reign supreme requires examining the relationship between horsepower, torque, and displacement. All other factors being equal, bigger engines generate more torque than their smaller counterparts, as they can ingest more air and fuel into their larger cylinders at any given RPM. Torque is the rotational force an engine's crankshaft produces, measured in foot-pounds (ft-lbs). This force is the product of the expanding air/fuel mixture pushing down on the pistons during the combustion process. The connecting rods and crankshaft convert the reciprocating motion of the pistons into rotating motion. If a 1-pound weight is placed at the end of a 1-foot-long lever, the twisting force it exerts would be equivalent to 1 ft-lb. Expanding upon this example, an engine that generates 500 ft-lbs of torque produces the same amount of force as a 500-pound weight hanging off the end of a 1-foot lever.

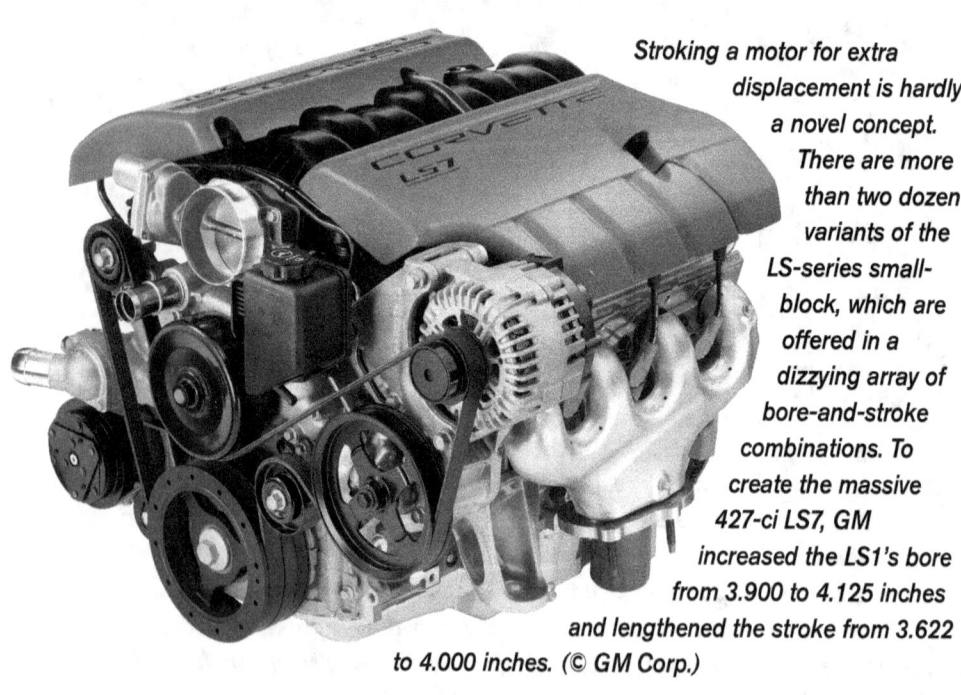

Stroking a motor for extra displacement is hardly a novel concept. There are more than two dozen variants of the LS-series small-block, which are offered in a dizzying array of bore-and-stroke combinations. To create the massive 427-ci LS7, GM increased the LS1's bore from 3.900 to 4.125 inches and lengthened the stroke from 3.622 to 4.000 inches. (© GM Corp.)

10   HOW TO BUILD BIG-INCH GM LS-SERIES ENGINES

STROKING OPTIONS

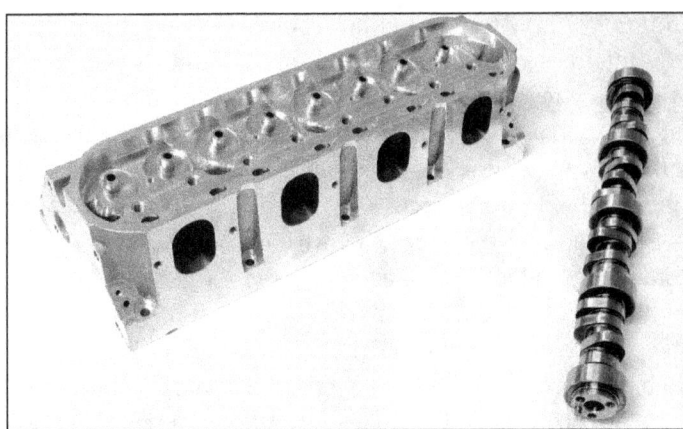

It wasn't too long ago when building a stroker motor involved scrounging a crankshaft from a junkyard, reconditioning a set of factory connecting rods, and hoping that there's an off-the-shelf piston for your desired combination of parts. With the influx of affordable cranks and rods that have hit the market in the last decade, acquiring a stroker rotating assembly is cheaper and easier than ever. Dozens of manufacturers offer stroker kits that include the crankshaft, rods, pistons, rings, and bearings in convenient pre-bundled packages for $2,500.

Having lots of cubic inches means nothing without adequate airflow. Because no single engine component impacts power production and power potential more than the cylinder heads, investing in a set of quality castings will pay enormous dividends. Cylinder heads must be paired with the right camshaft to optimize the shape of the power curve for your intended application.

However, torque is a static measurement that doesn't accurately express the total amount of work an engine can accomplish over a given duration of time. Recognizing this problem, eighteenth-century Scottish engineer James Watt developed a formula for horsepower to calculate the amount of work his newly invented steam engine could accomplish. He concluded that the average horse was capable of performing 33,000 ft-lbs of work per minute, and he coined his new unit of measure "horsepower." To covert the linear value of 33,000 ft-lbs to accurately represent the rotational motion of a crankshaft, Watt divided that figure by 6.28 to establish a mathematical constant of 5,252. That's because the circumference of a circle with a 1-foot radius is 6.28 feet. In other words, since the end of a 1-foot lever attached to a crankshaft would travel 6.28 feet per each revolution of the crankshaft, dividing 33,000 ft-lbs by 6.28 yields a constant of 5,252. This figure, which converts linear motion to rotating motion, is a key component in Watt's horsepower formula:

$$HP = Torque \times RPM \times 33{,}000 / 2\pi$$
$$HP = Torque \times RPM / 5{,}252$$

Using this formula, we can calculate that an engine that produces 500 ft-lbs of torque at 6,000 rpm will make 571 hp (500 x 6,000 / 5,252). Furthermore, Watt's formula offers several important revelations

Thanks to its 717-hp engine, which consists of a 500-ci LS2 short-block topped with LS7 heads, the School of Automotive Machinists' 3,700-pound 1998 Camaro rips the quarter-mile in 9.96 seconds at 135 mph. When fitted with cylinder heads that flow serious air, big-inch stroker motors produce outstanding horsepower and torque while retaining excellent street manners.

Building a potent and reliable engine combination starts with quality machine work. A typical stroker buildup requires boring, honing, and decking the block, in addition to balancing the rotating assembly. Throw in align honing the main caps, magnafluxing for cracks, and sonic testing the cylinder walls for thickness, and the machining bill can easily top $1,000. Although that may seem pricey, it's money well spent.

HOW TO BUILD BIG-INCH GM LS-SERIES ENGINES

CHAPTER 2

in terms of how torque and horsepower are interrelated. Torque is multiplied with every revolution of the crankshaft, and horsepower is simply the total cumulative torque an engine produces in one minute. In other words, horsepower is nothing more than the rate at which torque is produced. Consequently, the only way to boost horsepower is to increase torque output or RPM. Both are viable options, but there is a practical limit to how many RPM a motor can turn. Even the healthiest of small-blocks will rarely make usable power beyond 7,500 rpm, and most street/strip motors live in the 1,000- to 6,500-rpm range. Given this small window of RPM in which a typical street/strip motor operates, the most practical way to bulk up horsepower curves is by maximizing torque, which is what building a big-inch stroker motor is all about.

Granted, long-duration camshafts and big-port heads can shift the bulk of the torque curve higher up in the RPM band, which can yield tremendous gains in horsepower, but it comes at the expense of compromised idle quality and decreased low-speed torque. Likewise, taking full advantage of a large cam requires turning more RPM. This not only mandates the use of exotic valvetrain hardware that's expensive and more prone to failure, it often results in compromised reliability and poor drivability that even the most hardcore of enthusiasts couldn't bear to endure. Furthermore, a high-winding engine combo needs shorter rear-end gearing, which increases cruising RPM and adversely affects gas mileage. Ultimately, it's all about personal preference, and an engine combination that one person deems radical and unstreetable is perceived as docile and well-mannered to someone else. The beauty of a big-inch stroker is that it can make more power than a smaller motor without having to turn as many RPM. And regardless of your personal tastes or tolerance level for cam lope and low-RPM surge, cubic inches are your friend.

Efficiency

Chevrolet reached a huge milestone in 1957 when it managed to wring out 1 hp per cubic inch (hp/ci) from its 283-ci fuelie small-block. The horsepower-per-cubic-inch metric has been used to gauge efficiency for decades, and the fuelie was one of the first mass-produced engines to reach that mark. Even today, making 1 hp/ci is nothing to balk at. When the 346-ci LS1 first made its debut in the 1997 Corvette, its 345-hp rating was right at 1 hp/ci. However, since hot rodders aren't burdened with the same design constraints as factory engineers, the efficiency of a motor can be dramatically improved with the addition of high-flow cylinder heads, more aggressive camshafts, and a big helping of cubic inches. Due to the staggering airflow capabilities of LS-series cylinder heads, it's not uncommon for a stroker Gen III/IV engine combo to effortlessly reach the 1.5- hp/ci mark while retaining acceptable street manners. In the wake of LS small-blocks, 408-ci stroker motors belting out 600 hp are a dime a dozen. The fact that they produce peak power at a perfectly streetable 6,000- to 6,200-rpm

Good things can come in small packages. One of the easiest and most affordable stroker LS engine combos you can build is a simple 383 that combines a 3.905-inch bore and a 4.000-inch stroke. This can be achieved with either a 5.7L LS1 block or a 5.3L iron unit. Fitted with a camshaft with 230 to 240 degrees of intake duration at .050-inch lift and 300-cfm cylinder heads, a little 383 can easily produce 550-plus hp.

Big displacement and high RPM needn't be an either/or proposition. Built by SAM, this otherworldly 429-ci combo includes a GM Performance Parts LSX block, a monstrous 278/302-at-.050 solid roller cam, a custom sheet metal intake manifold, a 15.5:1 compression ratio, and ported C5R heads that flow 410 cfm. Its epic 1,002 hp peaks at 9,000 rpm, and the 434 revs to a jaw-dropping 9,600 rpm. In a 3,500-pound 1999 Camaro, the 434 powers the car to 8.52-second quarter-mile times at nearly 160 mph.

range is even more impressive. More radical combinations can easily surpass 1.5 hp/ci, with all-out race engines approaching and sometimes exceeding 2 hp/ci.

Surely, enthusiasts who grew up building Gen I small-block Chevys may have a hard time believing these outstanding efficiency numbers. However, such skepticism is merely a testament to how good the LS1 platform is from the factory. With nothing more than a larger camshaft, with roughly 220 to 230 degrees of intake duration at .050-inch lift, a stock 346-ci LS1 easily makes 475 hp. That works out to 1.37 hp/ci, which is still considered very respectable for a stroker Gen I motor. Nonetheless, efficiency alone only gets you so far. It takes a motor with both big-time efficiency and big-time displacement to make the most of the LS small-block's impressive hp-per-cube capabilities. You don't need to be a professional engine builder to realize that for any given level of efficiency—1.5 hp/ci, for instance—a bigger motor makes more power than a smaller one.

That's not to say that small motors can't make serious power. NASCAR Sprint Cup engines measure just 358 ci, yet churn out 850 hp. The 500 ft-lbs of torque a Cup motor produces at its 9,000-rpm horsepower peak isn't any more than that of a healthy stroker LS motor, but the fact that it turns so many RPM is the reason it can make so much power. However, not only are the astronomical engine speeds of a Cup motor impractical for a street motor, due to cost, reliability, and drivability issues, NASCAR engines are a perfect example of why RPM is the single biggest limiting factor of how much power small motors can produce. The current limit of steel valvesprings is 83 to 85 cycles per second, which translates to roughly 10,000 rpm in a four-stroke engine. For motors that run for any appreciable length of time, 9,000 rpm is as high as you want to go.

Since horsepower is nothing more than torque multiplied by RPM, and smaller motors produce less torque, they must turn more RPM to match the power output of larger motors. Consequently, considering the limits of current valvespring technology, it's impossible for even an all-out race engine to exceed the 9,000- to 10,000-rpm threshold. If engine builders at NASCAR shops could wring another 1,000 rpm out of their motors, horsepower output would skyrocket accordingly. Unfortunately, this isn't feasible.

Similarly, whether it's due to budget, reliability, maintenance concerns, or how large of a camshaft you can tolerate, there are only so many RPM an engine can turn. Additional cubic inches helps combat this problem, since bigger motors produce more torque, and increasing displacement reduces the RPM at which peak power is produced. For example, if you unbolted the cylinder heads and camshaft from a stroker motor and installed it on a stock-displacement short-block, the smaller motor would produce less torque and similar peak horsepower, but at a higher RPM. Putting this theory to practice, let's examine two very similar real-world LS engine combinations built by HK Racing Engines in Houston, Texas.

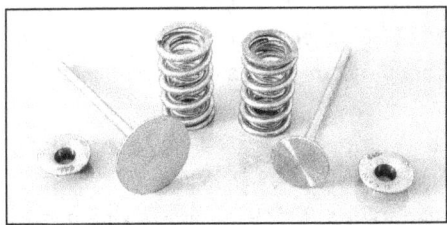

Motors that routinely turn in excess of 8,500 rpm—such as SAM's 434—require very lightweight, exotic, and expensive valvetrain hardware. These Del West titanium valves cost $2,000 for a set of 16, and the beefy 1.640-inch Manley springs exert 920 pounds of seat pressure and cost $1,000 for 16. The titanium retainers tack on another $400 to the total.

Although it weighs about 80 pounds more than an aluminum block, a factory Gen III/IV iron block is a very popular choice among hot rodders. Compared to aluminum blocks, iron units are stronger and can be bored up to .060 inch over without aftermarket cylinder sleeves.

The beauty of GM's LS-series small-block is that it crams a lot of displacement into a relatively compact package. As with the Gen I small-block Chevy, this has made the LS platform extremely popular with engine swappers. Although Gen III/IV small-blocks are finding their way into more muscle cars, they're also being swapped into Mustangs, BMWs, Mazdas, Hondas, Porsches, and even Jaguars.

CHAPTER 2

Unwanted harmonics can quickly destroy an expensive short-block, so a stroker build must always be properly balanced. With today's lightweight connecting rods and pistons, material is usually removed from the crankshaft's counterweights.

The first is a 346-ci motor with Air Flow Research 205-cc heads, a FAST intake manifold, a 238/242-at-050 cam, and an 11.9:1 compression ratio. This stout mill puts out 590 hp at 6,600 rpm and 524 ft-lbs of torque at 4,800 rpm. The second motor is a 408-ci combo with Air Flow Research 205-cc heads, a FAST intake manifold, a slightly larger 244/250-at-.050 cam, and 11.5:1 compression. On the dyno, the 408 kicks out 604 hp at 6,100 rpm and 568 ft-lbs at 4,500 rpm.

As camshaft duration is increased, an engine's compression ratio must be increased in order to retain cylinder pressure at low RPM. This is because long-duration camshafts hold the intake valves open until after BDC on the compression stroke, which bleeds off cylinder pressure until engine speeds pick up. Dish piston (left), flat-top piston (center), and D-shaped piston (right) are shown.

The differences in dyno numbers between these two engine combos are quite revealing. With the exception of the 408's slightly larger cam, these motors are nearly identical on paper. As expected, the larger motor produced an additional 44 ft-lbs of torque at peak, which is 300 rpm lower than that of the 346 and 14 more hp while turning 500 fewer rpm. So while the 346 posts a very impressive 1.70 hp/ci compared to the 1.48-hp/ci mark of the 408, the stroker motor boasts more streetable torque and power curves. Not only is this easier on valvetrain parts, which improves reliability, it also yields a combo that requires less rear-end gearing for more relaxed freeway cruising and better gas mileage. Furthermore, the extra cubic inches of the 408 effectively increases its appetite for air, which means that it can swallow up a substantially larger camshaft while still retaining drivability characteristics similar to that of the 346. The difference is that if the 408 had a camshaft large enough to extend its peak power to 6,600 rpm, the difference in horsepower would blow the 346 into the weeds.

Perhaps the greatest advantage of a stroker motor has less to do with science and more to do with parts availability. Small motors must turn lots of RPM to make big power, but they are ultimately limited by the maximum cycles per second that modern steel valvesprings can handle. On the other hand, by nature,

Increasing the stroke of a crankshaft involves moving the rod journals farther outward from the crankshaft centerline. This decreases strength, which is why most aftermarket LS-series crankshafts are built from rugged 4340 forged steel.

larger motors have a greater demand for airflow at any given RPM compared to their smaller-displacement counterparts. Although attempts to extend the RPM limit of valvesprings are moving forward at a deliberate pace, there's no shortage of monstrous cylinder heads to feed the voracious appetite of big-inch stroker motors. As displacement figures continue to grow with more commodious aftermarket blocks and longer-stroke crankshafts, the aftermarket is more than happy to keep up with the demand with bigger and better-flowing cylinder heads. AFR released the first aftermarket LS1 cylinder heads in 2004, and within five years, intake port volumes have already grown from 205 cc to 265 cc. Should the need arise for more cavernous ports, rest assured that the aftermarket will deliver.

Displacement Defined

Even soccer moms know that engines come in different shapes and sizes, but since the subject at hand is how to increase the displacement of a motor, it's prudent to define exactly what displacement is and how to calculate it. The two dimensions that determine an engine's displacement are the diameter and height

Bore spacing is the distance from the center of one cylinder to the center of an adjacent cylinder. This and the cylinder wall thickness determine the maximum bore diameter that a block can accommodate. Like the Gen I small-block, the LS-series engine features a bore spacing of 4.400 inches.

of its cylinders, which are referred to as bore and stroke, respectively. As we learned in high school geometry class, the volume of a cylinder is calculated using this formula: $V = \pi r^2 h$. In other words, a cylinder's volume is equivalent to its radius squared, multiplied by pi (3.1415), multiplied by its height. The final step is multiplying that product by eight, since the GM LS-series small-block distributes its total displacement over eight cylinders. Putting this formula into practice, the displacement of a GM LS7 small-block—which features a 4.125-inch bore and a 4.000-inch stroke—can be easily calculated as follows:

$$\text{Volume} = \pi r^2 h$$
$$\text{Volume} = 3.1415 \times 2.0625 \times 2.0625 \times 4$$
$$\text{Volume} = 53.45$$
$$\text{Displacement} = 53.45 \times 8$$
$$\text{Displacement} = 427.6 \text{ ci}$$

This formula can be simplified even further to bore x bore x stroke x .7854 x 8. For example, plugging in the LS3's 4.065-inch bore and 3.622-inch stroke dimensions yields: 4.065 x 4.065 x 3.622 x .7854 x 8 = 376 ci.

Now that we've established how to calculate displacement, it's easy to conceptualize how it can be increased by enlarging the bore and increasing the stroke. In geometric terms, this means that both the diameter and height of the cylinders are being increased. What makes this possible is the fact that every motor has some "spare capacity" in its architecture to accommodate additional cubic inches. An engine block is merely the envelope in which its cylinders are housed. In fact, every different iteration of the Gen III and Gen IV family of engines, and their varying displacements, is simply the product of combining different bore-and-stroke dimensions. For instance, the original LS1 utilizes a 3.900-inch bore and a 3.622-inch stroke to achieve a displacement of 346 ci. Its LS2 successor uses the same 3.622-inch stroke, but combines it with a larger 4.000-inch bore, for a total of 364 ci. Likewise, the massive LS7 matches up a 4.125-inch bore with a 4.000-inch stroke, which equates to 427 ci.

That said, it's important to clarify that when increasing the stroke of a motor, the actual height of the cylinder is not being changed. Instead, a longer-stroke crankshaft merely increases the distance the pistons travel between top dead center (TDC) and bottom dead center (BDC). Consequently, displacement, in automotive terms, refers to the piston-swept volume of the cylinders. In other words, although the height of the actual cylinder in an LS1 is greater than its stroke of 3.622 inches, the volume of air it can draw into each cylinder is limited by how far the pistons travel down the bores. Therefore, the effective displacement—or piston-swept displacement—of a four-stroke internal-combustion engine is determined by bore diameter and stroke length, not the actual height of the cylinder itself. Furthermore, unlike the bore diameter, the length of the cylinder sleeves is built into the block and can't be altered without casting a brand-new block.

Pushing the Envelope

The maximum displacement attainable in an engine block is dependent on a multitude of factors, including bore spacing, deck height, cylinder wall thickness, camshaft location, piston design, connecting rod length, and the distance between the oil pan rails. Of these, a block's bore spacing and deck height are the most important factors in determining displacement potential.

Bore spacing is simply the distance from the center of one cylinder to the center of an adjacent cylinder. Larger bore spacing can accommodate larger bore diameters inside the block. Like its legendary Mouse motor forebear, the LS engine family features a 4.400-inch bore spacing. This offers an engine package with relatively compact external dimensions, from front to back, that still has plenty of internal real estate to support lots of cubic inches. An aluminum LS-series block with aftermarket cylinder sleeves can handle up to a 4.200-inch bore. However, as the diameter of the bore increases, the thickness of the cylinder walls decreases. This can potentially weaken the block, which is why it's imperative to sonic check the cylinder walls prior to machining to ensure that there's adequate wall thickness for your desired bore diameter. Ultimately, both bore spacing and cylinder wall thickness determine the maximum bore that a block can handle.

Deck height, on the other hand, is the distance between the centerline of the crankshaft and the deck of the block. All production Gen III and IV small-blocks have a deck height of 9.240 inches, and since the block must have sufficient space inside to house the crankshaft and connecting rods, only a portion of the total deck height can be dedicated to cylinder height. A stock LS-series block

The distance from the crankshaft centerline to the block deck is known as the deck height. Taller-deck blocks can accommodate longer strokes, and, therefore, more cubic inches. All Gen III/IV small-blocks have a deck height of roughly 9.024 to 9.026 inches.

CHAPTER 2

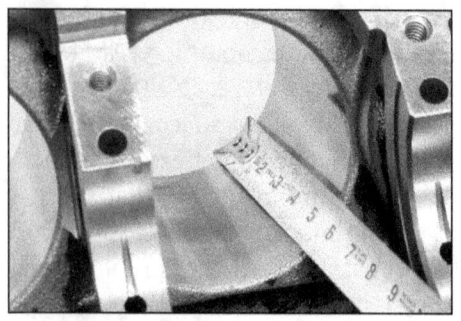

The length of the cylinder sleeves determines how much stroke a block can handle. A 4.000-inch crank fits inside a production LS block without much fuss. A 4.125-inch-stroke crank can be made to fit, but it often requires custom pistons.

can swallow up a 4.000-inch-stroke crankshaft without much fuss. In fact, the stock cylinder sleeves are long enough to accommodate a 4.125-inch stroke, but at that point, careful attention must be paid to the piston and connecting rod selection to prevent the pistons from hanging too far down the bore at BDC. Several aftermarket block offerings—from companies such as RHS, GM Performance Parts, ERL, and World Products—incorporate taller deck heights. This allows stuffing in a 4.500-inch or longer crank for engine combinations of nearly 500 ci.

Clearancing

Since the basic tenant of stroking an engine involves taking advantage of unused space inside the block, it's imperative to make sure that there's adequate clearance between the various moving components. This isn't difficult, but it does require paying close attention to parts selection and carefully clearancing any potential problem areas when necessary.

Lengthening a crankshaft's stroke involves increasing the distance between the crank centerline and connecting rod journals. Doing so moves the crankshaft counterweights farther outward, which means that the clearance between the counterweights and the oil pan rails become much tighter. Most aftermarket stroker cranks have profiled counterweights in order to prevent them from coming in contact with the block. However, since different blocks within the LS engine lineup have different internal dimensions, checking for clearance is a mandatory step in any stroker buildup. Using a die grinder to remove metal from the problem areas of the block is a very common procedure. Furthermore, the crank counterweights can potentially come in contact with the oil pan, which requires massaging the inside of the pan with a mallet for extra clearance, or grinding it out if the pan is built from cast aluminum. One of the primary advantages of aftermarket blocks is that most have larger crankcases and additional space between the oil pan rails to more easily fit longer-stroke cranks.

Another consequence of longer-stroke crankshafts is that they increase the angularity of the connecting rods as they swing from side to side in the block. This is simply due to the fact that a longer stroke pulls the pistons farther down the cylinder bores. The drawback is that this causes the connecting rods to come into much closer proximity of both the bottom of the cylinder sleeves and the crankcase. Again, the easy fix is to grind metal off areas where the connecting rods or bolts contact the block, a procedure that has already been performed with most aftermarket blocks.

Many aftermarket blocks offer taller deck heights for additional displacement capacity. ERL Performance takes this concept to the extreme with its Super Deck II block. By attaching a slug of billet aluminum to a stock LS2 deck surface, then re-sleeving the block, ERL increases deck height to 10.200 inches. Taking advantage of the block's taller deck with a 4.500-inch crankshaft, the Super Deck II is good for 500 ci when that stroke is combined with a 4.200-inch bore.

Callies offers 4.500-inch forged crankshafts for applications running tall-deck blocks where ultimate displacement is the goal. One of the drawbacks of extreme-displacement combinations is that their rotating assemblies can get rather heavy. This isn't a huge deal, because large motors don't need to turn high RPM to make power. However, it does make balancing the rotating assembly difficult, and it can require adding several slugs of heavy metal to the crankshaft counterweights.

STROKING OPTIONS

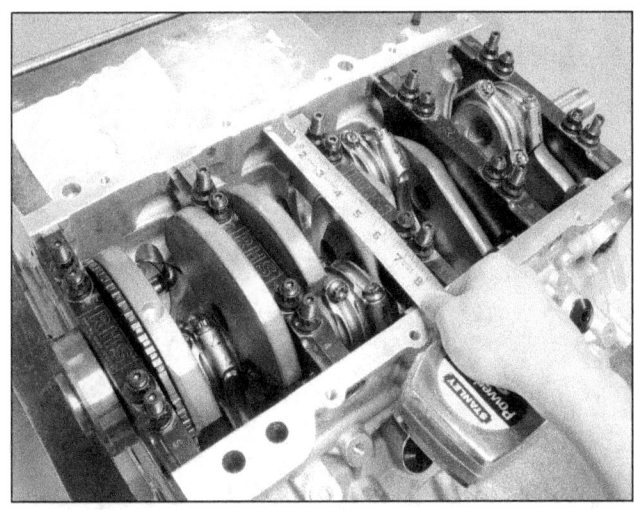

As long-stroke crankshafts pull the pistons farther down the bores, the connecting rods come into closer proximity of the crankcase. To combat potential clearance issues between the rotating assembly and crankcase, most aftermarket blocks incorporate oil pan rails that are spread farther apart.

Increases in stroke and rod angularity also push the connecting rods closer to the camshaft as their respective pistons approach TDC. The most effective solution is to grind down the connecting rod shoulders where necessary, and using a camshaft with small base circle lobes. In fact, many aftermarket rods feature profiled shoulders for this purpose, and countless off-the-shelf camshafts are offered with small base circle lobes. Perhaps the most effective method of increasing rod-to-camshaft clearance is to raise the cam location, a feature offered in many aftermarket blocks.

The Power of Cubic Inches

Nothing illustrates the benefits of building a big-inch stroker motor more than real-world dyno and dragstrip testing. To make the point resoundingly clear, let's take a look at a pair of LS engine combos built by the School of Automotive Machinists (SAM) in Houston, Texas. As part of a class project, SAM's students and instructors pulled the stock 346-ci LS1 out of their 1998 Camaro shop car and increased its displacement to 375 ci. This was accomplished by re-sleeving the stock LS1 block, boring it out to 4.060 inches, retaining the original 3.622-inch crankshaft, and matching it up with a set of Eagle steel rods and Wiseco 10.8:1 forged pistons. Working in concert with a Competition Cams 252/264-at-.050 solid roller camshaft, factory LS1 cylinder heads ported to flow 290 cfm, and a FAST intake manifold, the 375-ci small-block produced an impressive 570 hp and 496 ft-lbs of torque. Despite a chunky race weight of 3,700 pounds, the motor propelled SAM's Camaro down the quarter-mile in 10.58 seconds at 127 mph.

Although the 375 is no slouch, the crew at SAM decided to step it way up. By utilizing an ERL Performance tall-deck LS2 block, SAM combined a 4.202-inch bore with a massive 4.500-inch stroke crank for a total of 500 ci. The crank was matched with Carrillo rods and 10.8:1 Wiseco pistons. Since big displacement calls for big airflow, a set of

Even within the confines of a production block, a very large crankshaft can still fit with the right prep work. By removing metal from the bottom of the cylinder sleeves and into the bottom of the crankcase to make room for the rod bolts, a builder can make this LS2-based ERL block accommodate a 4.500-inch-stroke crank.

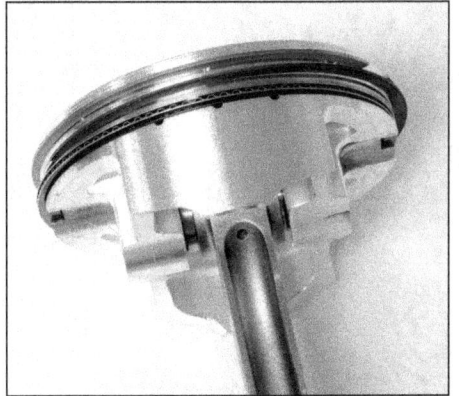

Another consequence of pulling the pistons farther down the bores is that the piston skirts can actually hit the crankshaft counterweights at BDC. Many pistons are offered with narrower skirts to provide extra clearance. The counterweights can also be turned down on a lathe, if necessary.

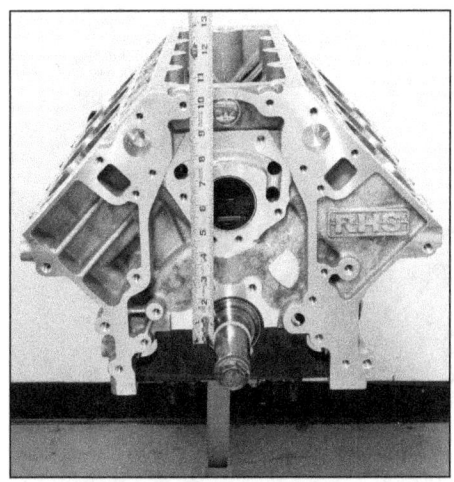

As a piston approaches TDC, a stroker crank pushes the connecting rod closer to the bottom of the camshaft. Aftermarket blocks, such as this RHS unit, reposition the camshaft higher up to create additional rod-to-camshaft clearance.

HOW TO BUILD BIG-INCH GM LS-SERIES ENGINES

lightly massaged GM LS7 cylinder heads and a stock LS7 intake were bolted atop the short-block. A very conservative Comp Cams 248/254-at-.050 hydraulic camshaft was installed to actuate the valvetrain. On the dyno, the 500-ci mill churned out 717 hp and 630 ft-lbs of torque. After pulling out the 375 and dropping in the 500, SAM's 1998 Camaro

SAM 375-ci LS1

RPM	TQ	HP	RPM	TQ	HP
4,600	476	417	6,000	483	551
4,700	480	430	6,100	475	551
4,800	481	440	6,200	470	555
4,900	486	453	6,300	468	561
5,000	486	463	6,400	463	564
5,100	490	476	6,500	458	567
5,200	490	485	6,600	452	568
5,300	491	496	6,700	446	569
5,400	496	510	6,800	440	570
5,500	492	515	6,900	434	569
5,600	491	524	7,000	425	566
5,700	487	529			
5,800	488	539	Average HP: 522		
5,900	486	546	Average TQ: 473		

SAM 500-ci LS2

RPM	TQ	HP	RPM	TQ	HP
4,200	564	451	5,600	618	659
4,300	570	466	5,700	614	667
4,400	582	488	5,800	611	675
4,500	600	514	5,900	609	684
4,600	615	538	6,000	608	694
4,700	622	557	6,100	605	703
4,800	626	572	6,200	601	709
4,900	628	586	6,300	595	713
5,000	629	599	6,400	588	716
5,100	630	612	6,500	579	717
5,200	629	623			
5,300	627	633	Average HP: 620		
5,400	625	643	Average TQ: 608		
5,500	622	651			

A peek through the cam bores reveals exactly how close the rods come to contacting the cam when the engine has a stroker crank. Even without the luxury of an aftermarket block with raised cam bores, careful parts selection can help you avoid potential clearance issues.

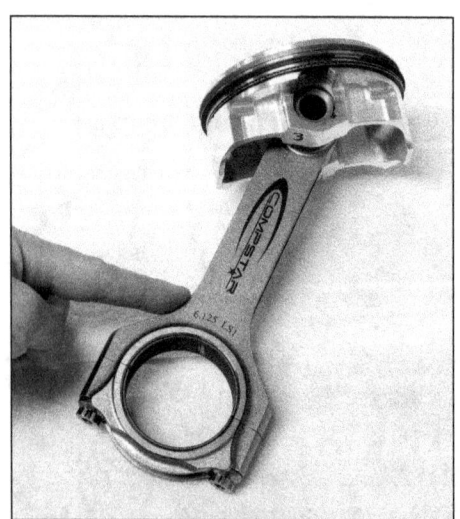

Most aftermarket connecting rods feature profiled shoulders to help them clear the camshaft. If the rods still contact the cam, they can be clearanced with a die grinder without compromising strength.

The smaller the base circle of the camshaft, the more clearance there is between it and the connecting rods. Cam manufacturers can grind your desired cam specs onto small base circle lobes upon request, and, additionally, many off-the-shelf cams are offered that way.

ran 9.96 seconds at 135 mph in the quarter-mile. That's an improvement of more than six tenths of a second and 8 mph, despite a smaller camshaft!

These results are quite revealing. Even more impressive than the 500's additional horsepower and torque output over the 375 is how it goes about producing it. Not only is the 500's 248/254-at-.050 camshaft less substantial than the 375's 252/264-at-050 unit, its hydraulic roller design means that its lobes aren't nearly as steep as the solid roller lobes found on the smaller motor. As you'd expect, the 500 doesn't need to turn as many RPM to reach peak power. It hits its peak of 717 hp by 6,500 rpm, while the 375 doesn't hit its peak of 570 hp until 6,800 rpm. Thanks to an additional 125 ci, the 500 stomps its smaller counterpart by 147 hp and 134 ft-lbs, and does so while producing more street-friendly power and torque curves. Since it doesn't need to turn as many RPM, the 500 can get away with using lighter valvespring pressure and hydraulic lifters, which reduces maintenance and extends both valvetrain longevity and reliability.

The biggest highlight when comparing the two motors, however, is how much extra power potential the bigger-inch motors offer. The greater the displacement of a motor, the greater its airflow demands. Match that appetite for air with some high-flow cylinder heads, and the result is serious, yet streetable, horsepower. Although there's no debating that bolting the 375's heads on the 500 would only yield a slight gain in horsepower, combining a 500-ci short-block with LS7 heads that flow an astounding 400 cfm yields tremendous gains in horsepower and torque while actually improving streetability. Furthermore, with slightly more cam duration, the 500 could easily produce another 50 to 60 hp while still retaining acceptable street manners.

Popular Displacement Combinations

Bore (inches)	Stroke (inches)	Displacement (cubic inches)	Bore (inches)	Stroke (inches)	Displacement (cubic inches)
3.780	3.622	325	4.155	4.000	434
3.900	3.622	346	4.125	4.125	441
3.905	4.000	383	4.155	4.125	447
3.905	4.125	395	4.125	4.250	454
4.000	3.622	364	4.125	4.375	468
4.000	4.000	402	4.200	4.000	443
4.030	4.000	408	4.200	4.125	457
4.060	4.000	414	4.200	4.250	471
4.000	4.125	415	4.200	4.375	485
4.030	4.125	421	4.200	4.500	499
4.060	4.125	427	4.250	4.000	454
4.065	3.622	376	4.250	4.125	468
4.065	4.000	415	4.250	4.250	482
4.065	4.125	428	4.250	4.375	497
4.125	4.000	427	4.250	4.500	511

If a piston is pulled too far down the cylinder bore, it has a tendency to rock from side to side at BDC. This not only accelerates wear, but it also causes the rings to lose contact with the cylinder wall, which severely compromises oil control. In such applications, custom pistons with tapered skirts are required.

SAM's gargantuan 500-ci LS2 is the poster child for big-inch performance. It produces 717 hp and 630 ft-lbs of torque with a relatively mild 248/254-at-.050 camshaft. Its operating range of 1,000 to 6,500 rpm is about as user-friendly as it gets.

CHAPTER 3

THE LS ENGINE FAMILY

With more than two dozen variants of the LS engine platform already in existence, choosing the right one for your stroker build can seem quite daunting. The Gen III/IV family covers the gamut, from plebian 4.8L truck motors to the beastly 638-hp supercharged LS9. Each has its pros and cons when asked to serve as the basis of a big-inch engine build. Some LS motors boast greater displacement potential, while others feature superior cylinder head castings. As is often the case, the most desirable members of the Gen III/IV motors are the rarest and most expensive, but several run-of-the-mill alternatives are cheap, plentiful, and pack some serious power potential. To help you select the ideal LS engine for your performance goals, the following run-down includes the critical specs of every Gen III/IV small-block ever built by GM, along with a synopsis of their strengths and shortcomings in the wake of stroker buildups.

LS1

Although the one that started it all is already a relic, no one could have predicted the impact the original Gen III LS1 would have on the hot rodding public. The LS1's greatest asset is its revolutionary 15-degree cylinder heads, which are capable of flowing more than 320 cfm in the hands of a skilled porter. So good were these castings, in fact, that it took the aftermarket more than five years to even attempt to top the factory design. Simply massaging the stock heads and swapping in a larger cam had LS1s easily approaching the 550-hp mark in no time. Furthermore, bone-stock LS1s routinely pushed F-bodies into 12-second quarter-mile times. Although F-body LS1s were rated at 40 hp less than their Corvette-spec brethren, they essentially produced the same power, despite slight differences in cam specs. All 2001 to 2004 LS1s were upgraded from the factory with the same valvesprings and high-flow intake manifold as found in the LS6.

One of the biggest drawbacks of the LS1 is its thin iron cylinder liners that can only be bored about .010 inch over, which, when combined with a 4.000-inch crank, limits displacement to 383 ci. Anything larger requires re-sleeving the block with aftermarket liners, which isn't cheap, but doing so enables displacement figures well in excess of 400 ci. Additionally, the standard 3.900-inch bore isn't compatible with the latest-and-greatest GM L92 cylinder heads.

Nonetheless, as long as a 400-plus-ci build isn't in the cards, the original LS1 provides more than enough power potential for the vast majority of hot rods.

LS2

The 400-hp LS2 was unveiled in the 2005 Corvette, and it represents the first of the Gen IV small-blocks. Compared to its LS1 and LS6 forebears, it boasts a larger 4.000-inch bore while retaining a 3.622-inch stroke, which bumps displacement to an even 6.0 liters. Making the large bore size possible are siamesed cylinder walls, which eliminate coolant passages between the cylinders. At its core, the LS2 resembles an enlarged LS6. It utilizes LS6 cylinder heads, as well as a 2001-spec LS6 camshaft. Subtle differences include a larger 90-mm throttle body (75 mm on LS1/LS6), a higher 10.9:1 compression ratio, and a different intake manifold. Interestingly, the LS2 intake manifold features slightly greater plenum volume and re-contoured runners, which actually flows less than the LS6 intake. For hot rodders, one of the key advantages the LS2 has over its smaller-bore counterparts is its compatibility with the highly desirable rectangle-port GM L92 cylinder heads.

LS3/L92/L99

Covering the LS3's history chronologically first requires examining the L92. This trick Gen IV mill made its debut in the 2007 Cadillac Escalade and is rated at 403 hp. Its outstanding output is largely attributable to a set of revolutionary rectangle-port cylinder heads, which borrow their basic port design from the LS7. Unlike the LS1 and LS6 heads, which are hampered by a relatively low intake port entrance, the L92 castings incorporate raised intake runners to take full advantage of their flat 15-degree valve angle. These architectural tweaks equate to 330

LS1 Specifications

Displacement: 346 ci
Block: Cast aluminum
Heads: Aluminum 15-degree cathedral-port
Bore/Stroke: 3.900 x 3.622 inches
Compression: 10.0:1
Camshaft (2001+ F-body): 196/207-at-.050; .467/.479-inch lift; 116-degree LSA
Output: 305-350 hp and 335-375 ft-lbs
What It's In: 1998-2002 F-body, 1997-2004 Corvette, 2004 GTO
GMPP PN: 17801267

Although its small 3.900-inch bore limits maximum displacement to 383 to 396 ci, the LS1 is still capable of producing tons of power. Simply porting the heads and installing a 230-at-.050-duration camshaft can easily boost horsepower past the 550 mark. (© GM Corp.)

LS2 Specifications

Displacement: 364 ci
Block: Cast aluminum
Heads: Aluminum 15-degree cathedral-port
Bore/Stroke: 4.000 x 3.622 inches
Compression: 10.9:1
Camshaft: 204/211-at-.050; .525/.52-inch lift; 116-degree LSA
Output: 400 hp and 400 ft-lbs
What It's In: 2005-2007 Corvette, 2005-2006 SSR and GTO, 2006-2007 CTS-V, 2006-2009 Trailblazer SS
GMPP PN: 19156261

With the introduction of the Gen IV LS2, almost all aluminum LS blocks transitioned to a siamesed-bore design. This allows for thicker cylinder walls and larger bore diameters. The LS2 block is the most affordable siamesed casting, making it a very popular block to re-sleeve for big-bore stroker combinations. (© GM Corp.)

LS3 Specifications

Displacement: 376 ci
Block: Cast aluminum
Heads: Aluminum 15-degree rectangle-port
Bore/Stroke: 4.065 x 3.622 inches
Compression: 10.7:1
Camshaft (LS3): 204/211-at-.050; .551/.525-inch lift; 116-degree LSA
Output: 400-430 hp and 410-428 ft-lbs
What It's In: 2008+ Corvette, 2010 Camaro, 2008+ G8 GTP (LS3), 2007+ Escalade, Tahoe, Silverado, Yukon, Sierra, Hummer H2 (L92), 2010 Camaro automatic (L99)
GMPP PN: (LS3): 19201992

The variable valve timing feature, first utilized in the L92, offers an unparalleled balance between low-end torque and top-end horsepower. The system advances the cam at low RPM and gradually retards valve timing as RPM increases to boost high-RPM breathing. Using aftermarket engine management software, the system is fully adjustable for use in hot rod applications. (© GM Corp.)

CHAPTER 3

cfm of flow out of the box, and the heads are available for just $800 fully assembled from GM Performance Parts. (All prices represent 2011 market values.)

Blurring the line between GM's car and truck lines of engines, the L92 was the first Vortec motor with an aluminum block and the first GM small-block ever to utilize variable valve timing. The bump in displacement to 6.2L over the LS2 and Vortec 6000 comes courtesy of a larger 4.065-inch bore. By dropping the L92's variable valve timing capabilities and using a lower-profile intake manifold, GM created the LS3 to serve as the base motor in the 2008-and-up Corvette. In addition to having a slightly stronger block than the LS2, the LS3 is fitted with a 2001 LS6 cam that's been modified with a smidgen more intake lobe lift. The result is 430 hp and 428 ft-lbs. As with prior generations, the base Corvette motor also powers the top-of-the-line fifth-gen Camaro. However, automatic-equipped SS Camaros have an L99 under their hoods, which is a slightly detuned LS3 with active cylinder deactivation that produces 400 hp and 410 ft-lbs.

LS4

The oddball of the LS family, the Gen IV LS4 was designed specifically for transverse mounting in front-wheel-drive Impalas and Monte Carlos. To accomplish this, GM shortened the LS4's overall length—from crankshaft to flexplate—by 13 mm and streamlined the accessory drive. Furthermore, it shares the same 3.780- x 3.622-inch bore-and-stroke dimensions as Vortec 5300 truck motors, but it is based on an aluminum block and topped with LS6 cylinder heads. Despite their displacement handicap, LS4s are relatively stout for their size, producing between 290 and 303 hp. However, they're almost as expensive as LS1s and LS6s on the second-hand market and have very limited displacement potential, so it's of little value to muscle car buffs seeking a swap candidate.

LS6

For the 1999 model year, GM expanded the Corvette lineup by adding a stripped-down, lightweight, more stiffly sprung version of the C5 dubbed the fixed-roof coupe. When it proved to be a sales flop, GM squeezed an extra 40 hp out of the LS1 to create the LS6, and Chevrolet dropped it into the hardtop chassis in 2001, renaming the car Z06. The Gen III LS6 is basically a hopped-up version of the LS1. In fact, it shares much more in common with the LS1 than the LS2, LS3, or LS4.

LS4 Specifications

Displacement: 325 ci
Block: Cast aluminum
Heads: Aluminum 15-degree cathedral-port
Bore/Stroke: 3.780 x 3.622 inches
Compression: 10.0:1
Output: 290-303 hp and 325 ft-lbs
What It's In: 2006+ Impala SS, 2006-2007 Monte Carlo SS, 2005-2008 Grand Prix GXP, 2008+ LaCrosse

Illustrating the versatility of the Gen III/IV platform, the LS4 is basically a smaller version of the LS2 that has been modified for transverse mounting in front-drive applications. Although it is equipped with high-flow LS6 cylinder heads, its small 3.780-inch bores and thin cylinder walls make it an unappealing candidate for a stroker build. (© GM Corp.)

LS6 Specifications

Displacement: 346 ci
Block: Cast aluminum
Heads: Aluminum 15-degree cathedral-port
Bore/Stroke: 3.900 x 3.622 inches
Compression: 10.5:1
Camshaft (2001): 204/211-at-.050; .525/.525-inch lift; 116-degree LSA
Camshaft (2002+): 204/218-at-.050; .555/.551-inch lift; 117.5-degree LSA
Output: 385-405 hp and 385-400 ft-lbs
What It's In: 2001-2004 Corvette Z06, 2004-2005 CTS-V
GMPP PN: 17801268

The alpha-numeric codes designated to each LS variant can be confusing, because GM released them out of sequence. Launched four years after the LS1, the LS6 is actually a Gen III small-block, and the LS2, LS3, and LS4 are Gen IVs. (© GM Corp.)

THE LS ENGINE FAMILY

Compared to the LS1, the LS6 boasts improved cylinders heads, a larger camshaft, a better-flowing intake manifold, a more durable valvetrain, a bump in compression, and stronger main bearing bulkheads. Furthermore, the LS6 head design features a raised port floor and a smoother transition at the short-turn radius for improved flow. The exhaust ports were also altered from an oval- to a D-shaped design. These mods bumped horsepower to 385 in 2001 and to 405 in 2002, thanks to an even larger cam. There was a time when factory LS6 heads were the hot ticket for enthusiasts, but the design has long been superseded by superior factory and aftermarket offerings. Like the LS1, the non-siamesed LS6 block must be re-sleeved for bore diameters exceeding 3.910 inches.

LS7

Although it falls 133 hp shy of the LS9's staggering output, which is substantial in anyone's book, in many respects the 505-hp LS7 is an even more impressive engineering feat. Without the assistance of a factory-installed blower, the Gen IV LS7 gets the job done the old-fashioned way with lots of cubic inches and airflow. In essence, it's the ultimate factory stroker motor. The Le Mans-winning factory Corvette racing program heavily influenced the design of the LS7, and, as such, it's stuffed with loads of bona fide race-bred hardware.

To achieve its epic 427 ci of displacement, the LS7 incorporates press-fit iron cylinder liners in lieu of the cast-in sleeves found in lesser Gen III/IV small-blocks, which enables boring the block out to 4.125 inches. The short-block is further fortified with a 4.000-inch forged steel 4140 crank, titanium rods, 11.0:1 hypereutectic pistons, and doweled steel main caps. With nearly .600 inch of lift, the 211/230-at-.050 cam is huge for stock, and the dry sump oil system is simply unheard of for a production motor.

Displacement is just half of the battle, and the LS7's cylinder heads are equally as impressive. These CNC-ported, 12-degree castings feature 2.20/1.61-inch valves (the intakes are titanium), and they flow an astounding 370 cfm. That's enough to put most big-block heads to shame. Best of all, factory LS7 heads flow enough to feed the largest and hungriest of stroker combinations, and they are available from GM Performance Parts (GMPP) for about $2,500. The end product is a motor that revs freely to 7,000 rpm and spits out 505 hp, which makes it the baddest naturally aspirated small-block ever built.

LS9

The big hoss in LS land is the factory-supercharged 638-hp small-block

---

LS7 Specifications

Displacement: 427 ci
Block: Cast aluminum
Heads: Aluminum 12-degree rectangle-port
Bore/Stroke: 4.125 x 4.000 inches
Compression: 11.0:1
Camshaft: 211/230-at-.050; .591/.591-inch lift; 120.5-degree LSA
Output: 505 hp and 470 ft-lbs
What It's In: 2006+ Corvette Z06
GMPP PN: 17802397

Few muscle car purists are likely to agree, but the LS7 small-block is arguably a more impressive piece of engineering than the 454-ci big-block LS7 of the 1970s after which it's named. Considering that the Gen IV LS7 is rated using stringent SAE net testing standards, it probably makes more power than its legendary big-block forebear. (© GM Corp.)

LS9 Specifications

Displacement: 376 ci
Block: Cast aluminum
Heads: Aluminum 15-degree rectangle-port
Bore/Stroke: 4.065 x 3.622 inches
Compression: 9.1:1
Camshaft: 211/230-at-.050; .562/.558-inch lift; 122.5-degree LSA
Output: 638 hp and 604 ft-lbs
What It's In: C6 Corvette ZR1
GMPP PN: 19201990

Big displacement and forced-air induction make for a potent combination. The 350 ft-lbs of torque that the supercharged LS9 produces at 1,000 rpm is more than the 343 ft-lbs that the Ferrari F430's high-tech 4.3L DOHC V-8 produces at its 5,250-rpm peak. (© GM Corp.)

CHAPTER 3

that powers the sixth-generation Corvette ZR1. Not only is the Gen IV LS9 the most powerful engine ever conceived by GM, it easily produces the fattest torque curve of any Chevrolet motor in history. Although its torque peak of 604 ft-lbs at 3,800 rpm is very impressive, the fact that it belts out 350 ft-lbs at just 1,000 rpm is downright breathtaking.

At its core, the LS9 shares more in common with the LS3 and L92—found in base Corvettes and Cadillac Escalades, respectively—than the LS7. To enhance block rigidity, GM passed on the LS7's 4.125-inch bore dimensions for the thicker cylinder walls afforded by smaller 4.065-inch holes. Furthermore, the block is cast from 319-T7 aluminum and features larger bulkheads, which makes it substantially stronger than previous LS units. It encases a steel crank, titanium rods, and forged 9.1:1 pistons.

With a remarkably efficient 2.3L Eaton blower huffing out 10.5 psi through a dual-core intercooler, the exotic race-ported 12-degree LS7 cylinder heads were deemed unnecessary. Instead, GM opted for 15-degree rectangle-port castings that are very similar in design to the L92 and LS3 heads, but built from more durable A-356T6 aluminum.

GMPP offers complete LS9 crate motors (PN 19201990) for about $22,000. Granted, that isn't cheap, but it's still a heck of a lot less than trying to replicate a motor of this caliber that's also emissions legal and capable of lasting 100,000 miles. Although they can be hard to find, the rugged LS9 block is an excellent foundation for LS stroker buildups.

LSA

The LSA is essentially the LS9's detuned little brother. Even so, the LSA's 556 hp and 551 ft-lbs have helped make the 2009 Cadillac CTS-V the quickest four-door sedan to ever lap Germany's famed Nürburgring road course. Major differences between it and the LS9 are the use of hypereutectic pistons instead of forged slugs, and powdered metal connecting rods instead of titanium units. Although the LSA also utilizes an Eaton blower, it's slightly smaller at 1.9L and produces 1.5 fewer psi of boost. It's a very impressive setup, indeed, but the limited production numbers of Cadillac's top dog means there are very few LSAs to extract from your local boneyard.

LQ4/LQ9 Specifications

Displacement: 364 ci
Block: Cast iron
Heads: Aluminum or iron 15-degree cathedral-port
Bore/Stroke: 4.000 x 3.622 inches
Compression: 9.4:1-10.0:1
Camshaft (1999-2000 LQ4): 191/190-at-.050; .457/.466-inch lift; 114-degree LSA
Camshaft (2001-2004 LQ4 and LQ9): 196/207-at-.050; .467/.479-inch lift; 116-degreee LSA
Output: 300-347 hp and 360-380 ft-lbs
What It's In: 1999-2004 Silverado, Suburban, Yukon, and Hummer H2 (LQ4); 2002-2006 Escalade, 2003-2007 Silverado SS and Sierra (LQ9)
GMPP PN (LQ9): 19156262

Smart shopping can score a used Vortec 6.0L motor for $1,000 to $1,500. This makes it one of the most affordable and capable foundations for a stroker project. Its big 4.000-inch bores and thick cylinder walls are capable of supporting more than 400 ci. Additionally, the 6.0L's LS6-style cylinder heads flow enough air to produce more than 600 hp. (© GM Corp.)

LSA Specifications

Displacement: 376 ci
Block: Cast aluminum
Heads: Aluminum 15-degree rectangle-port
Bore/Stroke: 4.065 x 3.622 inches
Compression: 9.1:1
Output: 556 hp and 551 ft-lbs
What It's In: 2009+ CTS-V

One of the most surprising aspects of the LSA is that it uses hypereutectic pistons instead of more rugged forgings. An advanced engine management system that can retard ignition timing almost instantaneously at the slightest hint of detonation makes this possible. (© GM Corp.)

THE LS ENGINE FAMILY

LQ4/LQ9

As the LS6 was being developed inside GM, engineers were so enamored with its performance that they decided to adapt some of its technology to the truck engine line. By bolting LS6-style heads to a big 4.000-inch-bore iron block, GM created the LQ4. Offered as the top-of-the-line gasoline engine in full-size pickups and SUVs, the LQ4 was rated at a stout 300 hp and 360 to 370 ft-lbs. In 2002, Cadillac wanted a piece of the action, too, and it added a bigger cam and more compression to boost output to 347 hp.

Due to their rugged iron blocks, generous bore diameters, and excellent cylinder heads, the LQ4 and LQ9 are among the most coveted Gen III/IV motors on the second-hand market. With the exception of their larger combustion chambers, the LQ4/LQ9 heads are virtually identical to the LS6 castings. Furthermore, their 4.000-inch bores enable them to be paired with GM L92 cylinder heads. By bolting a set of these budget $800 rectangle-port castings to a stock 6.0L short-block, you can make some serious power for peanuts. Unless you're excessively fastidious about saving a few pounds, it makes little sense to pass up on an LQ4/LQ9 for a comparably priced LS1 or LS6.

LY6

When it came time to improve upon the venerable LQ4 in 2007, GM bolted on a set of L92 heads and increased the compression ratio to create the LY6. These simple changes increased output to 352 hp. The addition of variable valve timing helps broaden the powerband. The LY6 is currently offered for heavy-duty hauling applications in 3/4-ton pickups and SUVs. Although it's too new to be filling up boneyards just yet, expect it to be a very popular choice among engine swappers in a couple of years.

L76

Used primarily in light-duty trucks, the L76 is essentially an aluminum-block variant of the LY6. Major differences include a higher compression ratio and a slightly larger cam, which boosts output to 366 hp and 376 ft-lbs. Like the LY6, the L76 utilizes variable valve timing, but ups the ante even further with active cylinder deactivation. Interestingly, the L76 also powered the 2008–2009 Pontiac G8 GT. The car version of the L76 drops variable valve timing and features an LS3 intake manifold, which sacrifices some horsepower while picking up some torque.

Vortec 4800

The smallest of the Gen III/IV platform is also the least desirable. Although

LY6 Specifications

Displacement: 364 ci
Block: Cast iron
Heads: Aluminum 15-degree rectangle-port
Bore/Stroke: 4.000 x 3.622 inches
Compression: 9.67:1
Output: 352 hp and 382 ft-lbs
What It's In: 3/4-ton 2007+ Silverado, Sierra, Suburban, and Yukon

The LY6 is essentially an LQ9 with rectangle-port cylinder heads and variable valve timing. With a relatively conservative 9.67:1 compression ratio, the engine is an excellent candidate for forced induction. (© GM Corp.)

L76 Specifications

Displacement: 364 ci
Block: Cast aluminum
Heads: Aluminum 15-degree rectangle-port
Bore/Stroke: 4.000 x 3.622 inches
Compression: 10.4:1
Output: 366 hp and 376 ft-lbs (trucks); 361 hp and 385 ft-lbs (cars)
What It's In: 2007+ Silverado, Sierra, Suburban, Yukon, Avalanche, and G8 GT

At one time, Vortec truck motors could easily be distinguished by their iron blocks, but that changed with the all-aluminum L92 released in the Cadillac Escalade. Further blurring the lines is the L76, which is used in both cars and trucks. (© GM Corp.)

CHAPTER 3

they're very capable mills for their intended application and can power stock Silverados to respectable 14-second ETs, their lack of cubes makes them unlikely candidates for engine swaps. This assessment is only reinforced by the fact that they're just as expensive as the 5.3L at the wrecking yard. The Gen III LR4 was built from 1999–2006 for full-size trucks and SUVs, and it was replaced in 2007 by the Gen IV LY2. Other than tweaks universal to all Gen IV motors, the difference between Gen III and Gen IV 4.8L small-blocks is negligible.

Vortec 5300

Many consider the 5.7L LS1 as "the new 350 Chevy," but that title more accurately goes to the 5.3L Vortec truck motor. As the bread-and-butter small-block from 1999 onward, GM installs the 5.3L in the vast majority of its full-size trucks and SUVs. Considering that GM has built way more trucks than cars in the past 10 years, the 5.3L is far more plentiful and cheaper than its 5.7L, 6.0L, 6.2L, and 7.0L big brothers. At roughly $500 at your local boneyard, complete 5.3L motors can be had for a fraction of the price of an LS1 or an LS6. Price alone, however, isn't what makes the 5.3L the biggest sleeper in the Gen III/IV camp. Its cylinder heads flow just as well in ported trim as 5.7L LS1 castings. In fact, in the early days of Gen III tweaking, before aftermarket heads became widely available, many enthusiasts preferred 5.3L heads to 5.7L LS1 heads due to the slight bump in compression that their smaller combustion chambers afforded.

For those who see the 5.3L's smaller displacement as a drawback, it has sufficient cylinder wall thickness to easily accommodate the same 3.900-inch bore diameter as the 5.7L. Throw a 4.000-inch stroker crank in a punched-out 5.3L block, and you've got yourself a nice 383-ci short-block. The added durability of an iron block is tough to beat, as well.

From 1999–2007, GM built several versions of the Gen III Vortec 5300, of which the LM7 is the most common. The LM4 and L33 are aluminum-block variants of the LM7, while the L59 is a flex-fuel spinoff. GM began phasing in Gen IV 5.3Ls in 2005 with the launch of the all-aluminum LH6, which replaced the LM4 in mid-size SUVs. Then in 2007, the iron-block, 320-hp LY5 was introduced as an update to the stalwart LM7 for use in full-size trucks and SUVs. Also that year, the LMG and LC9 were unveiled as flex-fuel versions of the LY5 and LH6, respectively. Finally, the LH8 is a slightly detuned 300-hp 5.3L that powers the 2009-and-up Chevy Colorado pickup.

Vortec 4800 Specifications

Displacement: 293 ci
Block: Cast iron or aluminum
Heads: Iron or aluminum 15-degree cathedral-port
Bore/Stroke: 3.780 x 3.267 inches
Compression: 9.5:1
Output: 270-295 hp and 285-305 ft-lbs
What It's In: 1999-2006 Silverado, Tahoe, Yukon, and Sierra (LR4); 2007+ Silverado, Tahoe, Yukon, and Sierra (LY2)

Displacing just 293 ci, the 4.8L Vortec truck motor is an unlikely candidate for a stroker combo. However, when its small 3.780-inch bores are opened up to 3.900 inches and a 4.125-inch crank is installed, the engine's displacement becomes a respectable 396 ci. (© GM Corp.)

Vortec 5300 Specifications

Displacement: 325 ci
Block: Cast iron or aluminum
Heads: Iron or aluminum 15-degree cathedral-port
Bore/Stroke: 3.780 x 3.622 inches
Compression: 9.5-10.0:1
Output: 285-320 hp and 325-340 ft-lbs
What It's In: 1999-and-newer mid/full-size trucks and SUVs
GMPP PN: 19165628

In terms of quantity, the 5.3L Vortec truck motor is the most abundantly produced engine of all Gen III/IV small-blocks. That means you can pick one up at your local junkyard for less than $500. If maximum displacement isn't a necessity, then the 5.3L represents one of the least expensive ways to build a stroker LS motor. (© GM Corp.)

CHAPTER 4

ENGINE BLOCKS

Engine builders compare an engine block to the foundation of a house so frequently that the analogy has become a vapid cliché. There's good reason for this, however, as every component on an engine is attached to the block. The stresses of internal combustion can lead to block distortion, poor ring seal, and power loss; in more severe situations, they can actually split a block in half. Fortunately, factory LS blocks are extremely stout and can handle plenty of abuse with very little modifications. Conceived from the very beginning as an aluminum design, GM engineers employed several innovations to ensure the block's durability. When a Gen III block is placed beside a Gen I block, the improvements to the Gen III design are dramatic. Most noticeable are reinforcement ribs that run the length of the block and oil pan. Likewise, six-bolt main caps secure the crankshaft in place, and the head bolts thread into the main webs, further reducing block flex.

As far as GM engineers are concerned, these design elements were incorporated to minimize cylinder distortion, thereby maximizing fuel economy and durability while reducing

The Gen III/IV small-block shares the same 4.400-inch bore spacing, 90-degree cylinder-bank angle, and .843-inch lifter bores as the Gen I engine, but the similarities end there. LS blocks have taller decks and raised cam bores, to accommodate longer strokes. The longest stroke GM ever used in a production small-block Chevy was 3.750 inches; by comparison, GM was able to stuff a 4.000-inch crank in the Gen IV LS7. (© GM Corp.)

In addition to containing the violent forces associated with internal combustion, a block must also resist the stress imparted on its exterior by the engine mounts as it rocks from side to side under acceleration, deceleration, and in corners. Stock and aftermarket LS blocks incorporate stiffening ribs between the engine mount bosses to minimize deflection.

HOW TO BUILD BIG-INCH GM LS-SERIES ENGINES

emissions. As far as hot rodders are concerned, a strong block provides an excellent foundation for making reliable horsepower. All factory LS blocks share a common 4.400-inch bore spacing, 9.240-inch deck height, and 2.559-inch main bearing diameter.

In the past few years, we have witnessed the introduction of several iron, aluminum, and even billet aftermarket blocks. In addition to offering unparalleled strength, many of the latest aftermarket castings boast raised cam locations, spread oil pan rails, and extra-thick cylinder walls that up the displacement ante and simplify the process of building a big-inch stroker motor. Nonetheless, for the average street/strip engine build, it's always tempting to try to score that perfect block out of the junkyard, and this chapter outlines what to look for. Some of the best values in engine blocks are offered directly from GM Performance Parts, as the factory uses several big-bore aluminum and iron blocks in passenger cars and trucks. Selecting the right block for your application is just step one, This chapter also outlines short-block machining procedures that are critical to every performance build.

Getting Bored

Stroking an engine for extra displacement is a two-pronged approach that involves increasing the diameter of the bore and lengthening the stroke of the crankshaft. That said, the bulk of the displacement increase comes from installing a long-arm crank, and enlarging the bore has a less substantial impact. For instance, a 6.0L Vortec truck motor utilizes a 4.000-inch bore and a 3.622-inch stroke. Enlarging the bore to 4.030 inches, while retaining the stock stroke, bumps displacement from 364 to 370 ci. On the other hand, a stock 4.000-inch bore combined with a 4.000-inch stroker crankshaft yields a displacement figure of 402 ci. That's not to undermine the importance of a bigger bore, but its benefits play a crucial role in overall engine dynamics that go far beyond marginal increases in displacement.

As the intake valve opens, it comes closer and closer to the outer half of the cylinder wall. Consequently, air entering the bore from the intake port has a tendency to stack up against the cylinder wall, which can impair airflow. The flat valve angles used in the Gen III/IV archi-

Bolts are fine for production motors, but quality main studs are a good idea for any performance engine build. The stock bolt holes are 7/16 inch, but they can be enlarged to 1/2 inch if bigger studs are on the agenda.

tecture negate some of this effect, but it's an important consideration nonetheless. Although there is a point of diminishing returns, larger bores generally help de-shroud the intake valves, which in turn improve airflow through the cylinder heads. Moreover, since larger bores increase the distance between the cylinder wall and the face of the valve, they enable the fitment of larger valve diameters, further increasing airflow at high lift points.

Ultimately, the cylinder wall thickness and bore spacing of a block limit maximum bore size. Although the

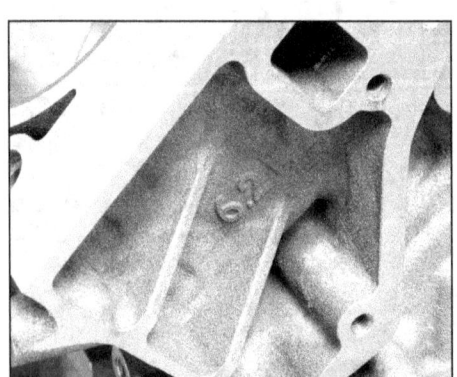

Factory aluminum and iron blocks are easily identified by marks, cast into the front or back of the block, that denote their displacement. Shown here is a 6.2L block. Small-bore iron blocks are labeled "4.8L/5.3L," because they're used in 4800 and 5300 Vortec motors.

With the exception of the LS7 and LS9, production blocks use powdered metal main caps. One disadvantage of a deep-skirt block design is that it impedes the flow of crankcase pressure from bay to bay. To improve flow, GM designed breathing windows into the sides of the main caps.

Stock powdered metal main caps are remarkably strong and can safely handle more than 1,000 hp. For extra insurance beyond that point, companies, such as Pro-Gram and Callies, offer billet caps for about $500.

ENGINE BLOCKS

distance between a block's bore centers can't be changed, both factory and aftermarket LS blocks are offered with varying cylinder wall thickness. Generally, blocks with thicker walls that can accommodate a larger bore come with a higher price tag to match. Even so, opting for the biggest bore your wallet can afford usually pays dividends in horsepower.

Factory Aluminum Blocks

A testament to the stunning pace of LS engine development, the Gen III small-block is no longer in production, and the Gen IV has already superseded it. Mechanically, the two generations of blocks are 99 percent similar, and almost every component is interchangeable between them. With the exception of the 5.3L block, the primary difference between them is that Gen IV blocks utilize siamesed cylinder walls, which can accommodate larger bore diameters.

Although GM manufactures nearly twice as many LS-series motors out of iron than aluminum, there is still a plethora of aluminum-block variants out there. Since 1997, GM has produced 5.3L, 5.7L, 6.0L, 6.2L, and 7.0L versions of aluminum LS small-blocks. One common thread among all aluminum LS blocks is their excellent durability. Although traditionalists raised on iron Mouse motors may have some reservations regarding the strength of these units, aluminum LS blocks can easily handle 700-plus hp. Many factory blocks have been pushed past that mark.

LS1/LS6

Cast from 319-T5 aluminum using a semi-permanent mold process, the original 5.7L LS1 represented a dramatic departure from its Gen I forebear. Like most production aluminum engines, Gen III/IV small-blocks incorporate iron sleeves that are either cast or pressed into their cylinder bores. This provides a solid surface for the pistons to slide upon, because aluminum is too soft and would wear out very quickly without liners. Unfortunately, this limits maximum overbore to about .010 inch. With the small 3.900-inch bore used in LS1 and LS6 blocks, even with a 4.125-inch stroke this limits displacement to 396 ci. Prior to GM's release of the 4.000-inch siamesed-bore

The oil passages on the back of a Gen I small-block need to be blocked with an assortment of plugs. To simplify the assembly process, factory LS motors use a single block-off plate instead. Aftermarket blocks usually come with their own application-specific plates.

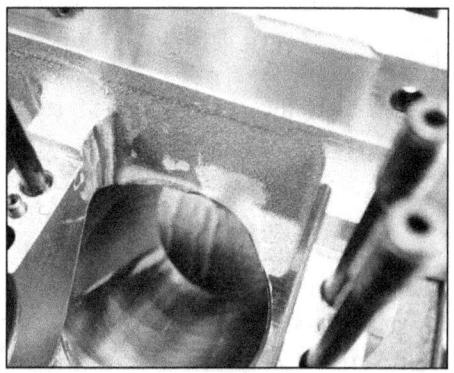

Stroker cranks increase the angularity of the connecting rods as they swing from side to side in the cylinder bores. This can cause the rod bolts to come in contact with the block right below the cylinders. Aftermarket blocks have much more space in this area, but with production blocks, some metal must be removed with a die grinder to create sufficient clearance.

Although it's very difficult to break the stock main caps, they start moving around at the 1,000-hp mark. To combat this, LS7 and LS9 blocks incorporate a sleeve positioned inside the two inner main bolt holes.

The dowel sleeves used on the LS7 and LS9 work reasonably well, but they are not as reliable as solid dowel pins on the bulkheads. The process of installing them involves drilling a small hole between the inner and outer bolt holes and then press-fitting each dowel into place. The cost for doing this, including an align-hone, is about $500.

Main bearing clearances should always be set with the main caps torqued to spec. Compared to the Gen I small-block, the thrust bearing on LS motors has been relocated to the number-3 main cap.

LS2 block, the only option for bumping up displacement beyond 400 ci was to install larger sleeves into the block. Although this allows running bore diameters as large as 4.125 inches, the sleeving process is extremely time consuming and expensive. It involves removing the stock sleeves (and sometimes portions of the aluminum block that hold the sleeves in place), heating up the block, and then pressing larger sleeves into place. Moreover, the procedure tends to distort the block, so it must be stress-relieved afterward. The biggest downside to re-sleeving a block is cost, as price of parts and labor can exceed $2,500.

Additionally, the specialized technique required to re-sleeve an aluminum block is not something that all machine shops can handle, and if not executed properly, it can lead to serious reliability problems. In the early days of building stroked LS1s and LS6s, re-sleeved blocks often suffered coolant leaks and blown head gaskets as a consequence of poor cylinder seal. Although a properly re-sleeved block can reliably support plenty of horsepower, GM's introduction of big-bore Gen IV factory blocks in 2005 has made re-sleeving an LS1/LS6 casting very uncommon, uneconomical, and impractical. For about the same price as re-sleeving an LS1/LS6 block, hot rodders can purchase a 4.125-inch-bore LS7 block directly from GM Performance Parts. Likewise, a 4.000-inch LS2 block lists for $1,100. If you stumble upon a very cheap LS1 or LS6 core and don't plan on cracking the 400-ci mark for your stroker project, then it might be practical to build it up. If maximum cubic inches is your goal, however, there are far more reasonably priced blocks from both GM and the aftermarket.

LS2

Enthusiasts collectively rejoiced when GM launched the Gen IV LS2 block in the 2005 Corvette. Like the 400 Gen I small-block, the LS2 features a siamesed-bore design that eliminates coolant passages between adjacent cylinders. This allows for the fitting of a larger cylinder sleeve into the block, resulting in an increase in bore diameter from 3.900 to 4.000 inches. Combined with a 4.000-inch stroke, the LS2 block nets 402 ci. Increasing the stroke further yet to 4.125 inches boosts displacement to 415 ci. Although it's labeled as a Gen IV block, very little distinguishes it from the Gen III design. Changes include revised oil galleries to accommodate active cylinder deactivation, knock sensors that have been moved from the lifter valley to the side of the block, and relocation of the camshaft position sensor from the back of the motor to the front timing cover.

Adding to the appeal of the LS2 block is the fact that its bore diameter is large enough to be compatible with GM's rectangle-port L92 cylinder heads. It didn't take hot rodders long to figure out that pairing an LS2 block with L92 heads created an engine package that's affordable and easy to build with outstanding power potential. Available for just $1,100 from discount GMPP distributors, the LS2 block offers big cubic inch potential at a reasonable price. The LS2 block is also used in the L76, so it's more accurate to refer to it as a 6.0L aluminum production block. For applications that call for a re-sleeved aluminum GM block, a used LS2 is the ideal candidate, as it's the least expensive siamesed-bore block and can be found in junkyards for less than $500. Thanks to recent innovations in sleeving technology, an LS2 block can accommodate a 4.190-inch bore with a set of Darton dry sleeves, and a 4.200-inch bore with Darton wet sleeves.

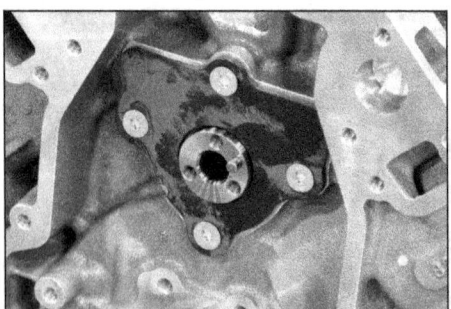

Gen I small-blocks rely on a cam button or limiter wedged between the cam gear and the camshaft snout. This prevents the cam from moving forward at high RPM. GM started using retainer plates in the LT1 and LT4, and that trend has carried over to the Gen III/IV design.

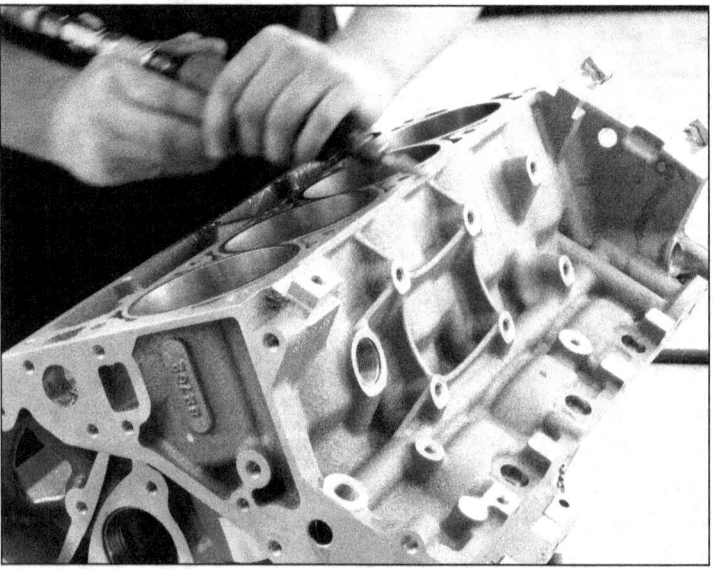

De-burring the sharp edges of a block isn't a mandatory step for most street engines, but it does stress-relieve parts of the block to help prevent the formation of cracks. Fewer sharp edges also means fewer cuts and scrapes on your hands.

ENGINE BLOCKS

6.2L

In the wake of aluminum LS blocks, dollar for dollar, it's tough to beat the factory GM 6.2L unit. Taking the virtues of the LS2 block one step further, the 6.2L boasts the same siamesed cylinder wall design but with a larger 4.065-inch bore. When matched with a 4.125-inch stroke, this big-bore block brings the displacement tally to 428 ci. Throw in the fact that it can be had brand new for a very reasonable $1,400 through GMPP, and it's not surprising that the 6.2L block is one of the most popular foundations for an LS stroker motor. The block was introduced in the 2007 Cadillac Escalade's L92, but it has since been installed in LS3-powered C6 Corvettes, as well as both LS3- and L99-powered fifth-gen Camaros.

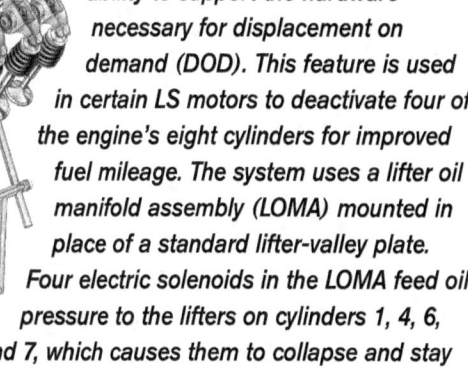

The biggest difference between the Gen IV block and the earlier Gen III block is the Gen IV's ability to support the hardware necessary for displacement on demand (DOD). This feature is used in certain LS motors to deactivate four of the engine's eight cylinders for improved fuel mileage. The system uses a lifter oil manifold assembly (LOMA) mounted in place of a standard lifter-valley plate. Four electric solenoids in the LOMA feed oil pressure to the lifters on cylinders 1, 4, 6, and 7, which causes them to collapse and stay shut as the cam lobes move across the lifters. The revised oil passages and extra space required by the LOMA prompted relocating the knock sensors from the lifter valley to the sides of the block and moving the camshaft position sensor from the back of the motor to the front. (© GM Corp.)

LS7

For those who seek maximum displacement packed in a lightweight aluminum envelope, the LS7 block is the hot ticket. By using press-fit iron cylinder liners instead of cast-in sleeves, GM was able to increase the LS7's bore to 4.125 inches. Even in stock trim, that big of a bore combined with a 4.000-inch stroke nets a big-block-like 427 ci. Stroke the block further to 4.125 inches, and you have a cool 441 ci. Further fortifying the LS7 block are doweled billet steel main caps. However, the LS7 block's attributes come with a stiff price tag, as it sells for $3,000 through GMPP distributors. Furthermore, although it's capable of supporting 700 hp, there is a risk of cracking the thin cylinder liners once that figure is exceeded. If you insist on running a 4.125-inch or larger bore in an aluminum block at that power level, a more durable alternative is to re-sleeve a 6.0L or 6.2L block with aftermarket ductile iron liners, which are nearly three times stronger than the GM gray-iron sleeves.

LS blocks feature a traditional six-bolt bellhousing bolt pattern, but with a slight twist. On production LS blocks, the bolt hole in the upper right-hand corner (arrow) is absent, and it is replaced with another hole at the very top of the pattern that's not present in Gen I blocks. Consequently, transmissions designed for either engine bolt up to both LS motors and Mouse motors, but with one of the bolts missing. Aftermarket blocks, like the GMPP LSX, typically have all seven holes drilled and tapped.

Opening up the bore not only increases displacement, it also creates extra space for larger valves and improves cylinder head flow by moving the cylinder wall farther away from the valves. In order to fit cylinder heads having large 2.165-inch intake valves, as in the L92 castings, GM had to increase the bore to 4.065 inches.

LS9/LSA

At 638 hp, the supercharged LS9 is the most powerful GM engine ever produced. To endure the rigors of forced induction, engineers determined that the thin cylinder walls of the LS7 block wouldn't meet their durability standards. The solution was to beef up the existing 6.2L block used in the L92 and LS3, whose thicker cylinder walls offered more inherent rigidity. To further reduce block distortion, the LS9 block is cast from a stronger 319-T7 aluminum alloy and features larger bulkheads. Since the Corvette ZR1 the LS9 is built to power is produced

CHAPTER 4

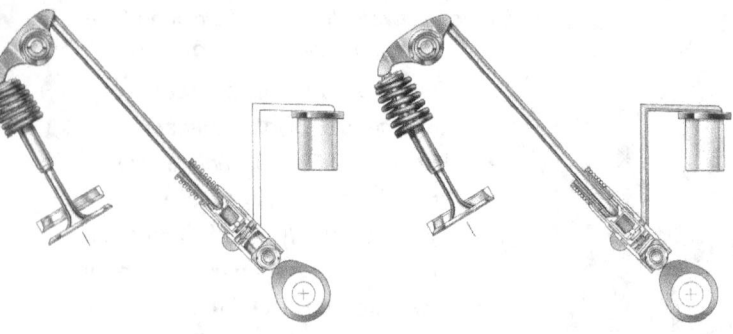

The lifter assembly used in DOD engines consists of a two-piece body where the inner portion of the lifter slides inside the outer portion. During normal operation, a spring-loaded pin locks the inner body in place. When DOD is activated (left), solenoids mounted in the LOMA unlock the pin via oil pressure, and the force of the valvespring causes the inner portion of the lifter to collapse. Once DOD and oil pressure from the solenoids is deactivated (right), springs on the top and bottom of the lifter's inner sleeve push it back up, and the spring-loaded pin locks it back in place. It is possible to swap cams in DOD motors, as long as valve lift is limited to .550 inch. To install a bigger cam, DOD can be eliminated entirely with an LS2 lifter-valley cover and standard LS lifters. (© GM Corp.)

in relatively low volumes, finding an LS9 block on the second-hand market is unlikely. However, it is offered through GMPP for $3,300. LSA blocks used in the Cadillac CTS-V are very similar to the LS9, but have iron main caps instead of billet steel units. GM rates the LSA block at 100 hp less, and it sells for $2,400.

C5R

If money is no object, the C5R block is the ultimate aluminum GM casting. Designed for GM's factory-backed C5R endurance racing program, this block has proven its durability at prestigious venues, such as LeMans and Daytona. Although its $7,000 price is enough to make anyone gasp, that money buys a block that can safely support more than 900 hp. It's cast from 356-T6M aluminum alloy using a hot isostatic pressure process in which the block is placed in a vacuum chamber to remove porosity and contaminants, then it is pressurized at 30,000 psi with nitrogen during heat-treating. The result is a block with outstanding material integrity, fatigue life, and strength. Additional reinforcement ribs are cast throughout the block to further stiffen the structure.

Sharing the same deck height, bore spacing, and main journal housing diameter as other LS blocks, the C5R is fully compatible with all standard Gen III/IV hardware. It can accommodate a 4.160-inch bore, which yields 449 ci when paired with a 4.125-inch stroke. Other strengthening measures include doweled billet steel main caps and 4340 steel head studs that are included with the block.

5.3L

Although most 5.3L LS blocks are cast iron, GM manufactures aluminum

Several versions of the LS1/LS6 block were produced, but they are all very similar. GM revised the oil galleries at the rear of the block in 1999, and in 2001, new breathing holes were cast into the main webs to improve bay-to-bay flow of gases through the crankcase. (© GM Corp.)

versions for the LS4, LM4, and L33. Like iron 5.3L blocks, the aluminum units share the same 3.780-inch bore. Unlike its iron counterparts that can be bored to 3.900 inches, the iron liners in aluminum 5.3L blocks can only be opened up .010 inch. This severely limits displacement potential, and, therefore, these are not popular foundations for stroker builds. Furthermore, they cost nearly as much as larger-bore aluminum blocks on the used market, adding yet another reason to avoid them.

Factory Iron Blocks

Granted, it's easy to be seduced by a lightweight aluminum block, but the factory iron castings used in GM trucks and SUVs offer the greatest bang for the buck of all Gen III/IV blocks in existence. Although they're called Vortec motors, GM's truck engines share the same Gen III/IV architecture as their LS-designated stable mates. Consequently, almost all

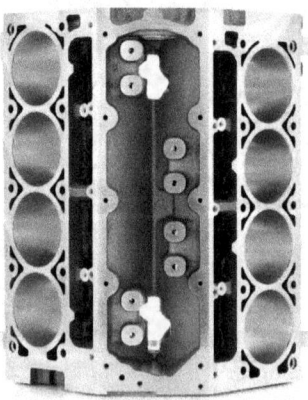

For a big-inch aluminum stroker combo, it's tough to beat the value of the 4.000-inch-bore LS2 block and the 4.065-inch-bore 6.2L block. Both can accommodate well over 400 ci, and their big bores make them compatible with the latest deep-breathing factory and aftermarket cylinder heads. The LS2 sells for $1,000 through GMPP, and the 6.2L block is listed at $1,400. (© GM Corp.)

ENGINE BLOCKS

the components between GM's car and truck motors interchange. The only drawback of iron Vortec blocks is that they weigh about 70 pounds more than aluminum castings. However, they're still 30 pounds lighter than a Gen I small-block, and that extra weight yields a substantially stronger block that's darn near indestructible. Some engine builders contend that Vortec blocks are stronger than the hallowed C5R block, and enthusiasts often push them past the 1,000-hp mark with great success. These factors have made iron Vortec blocks extremely popular in nitrous and forced-induction applications. Best of all, these iron blocks are a fraction of the cost of a comparable aluminum block, as GM manufactures twice as many iron Gen III/IV motors than aluminum motors.

GM builds iron Vortec motors in 4.8L, 5.3L, and 6.0L configurations. The 6.0L block—used in the LQ4, LQ9, and LY6—is the most popular with hot rodders. It features a 4.000-inch bore and can be purchased brand new for $800. It can safely accommodate a 4.030-inch bore and is good for 421 ci when matched with a 4.125-inch stroke. Even so, many hot rodders opt to stick with the standard 4.000-inch bore, which leaves plenty of meat on the cylinder walls for future rebuilds. Most aluminum LS blocks, on the other hand, don't offer this luxury. Further enhancing their value, careful shopping in local junkyards or online can uncover complete second-hand 6.0L long-blocks for $1,000, which is a fraction of the cost of an aluminum LS motor.

For budget-oriented hot rodders who aren't concerned with maximum cubic inches, the 3.780-inch-bore iron block used in 4.8L and 5.3L Vortec engines is an ideal foundation for a low-buck build. Although the block's small cylinders may seem like a huge drawback, they have sufficient wall thickness to open them up to 3.900 inches. That means that the block is compatible with a plethora of off-the-shelf standard-bore LS1 pistons, and it can net 396 ci when combined with a 4.125-inch stroke. Complete 4.8L and 5.3L long-blocks sell for $500 on the used market, and bare blocks can be had for even less. Considering that GM manufactures more 4.8L and 5.3L Vortec motors than any other LS small-block, junkyards will be stocked with these value-priced gems for a very long time.

Aftermarket Blocks

As good as production GM blocks may be, there's a practical limit to how much horsepower and displacement they can support. The need for aftermarket Gen III/IV blocks came early on, as the incessant progress in cylinder head technology meant that block rigidity and a lack of cubic inches were often the limiting factors in power production. Fortunately, companies, such as World Products, Dart, and GM Performance Parts, have all stepped up with aftermarket blocks of their own.

Some of the features aftermarket blocks typically offer include improved casting strength, larger crankcases, extra-thick cylinder walls, priority main oiling passages, longer cylinder sleeves, raised camshaft bores, and taller deck heights. All of that equates to extra clearance for moving parts, enhanced durability, and greater power and displacement potential. Some blocks also have provisions for two extra head bolt holes around each cylinder—at the 12 o'clock and 6 o'clock position—for improved clamping force

Thanks to the LS7's capacious 4.125-inch bore, GM was able to fit the engine with monstrous 2.200-inch intake valves. That large bore comes at the expense of cylinder wall thickness, so if plans call for re-sleeving a factory aluminum block, the LS2 casting is a more affordable alternative. (© GM Corp.)

The billet steel main caps used on the LS7 block have enlarged windows for improved crankcase ventilation, which GM claims reduces pumping losses. GMPP was so pleased with their performance that the company emulated their design in the LSX block. (© GM Corp.)

Some people scratched their heads when GM revealed that the LS9 would be smaller in displacement than the LS7, but engineers determined that the LS7's cylinder walls were too thin to support 638 hp and survive rigorous factory durability testing. The solution was to go with a smaller 4.065-inch-bore block, which allowed for thicker cylinder walls. (© GM Corp.)

and gasket seal when used with six-bolt cylinder heads. Furthermore, aftermarket blocks are typically decked and align-honed prior to shipment, so the only machine work they require are boring (if desired) and a finish hone. In essence, this allows spending your money on hardware instead of labor. For LS engine combinations approaching 500 ci and producing well over 1,000 hp, an aftermarket block is the ideal foundation to hold everything in place.

LSX Bowtie

Designed with the help of NHRA Pro Stock legend Warren Johnson, the GM Performance Parts LSX Bowtie block supports more than 2,500 hp and lists for $2,200. This rugged iron casting can accommodate a 4.250-inch bore and is available in either a 9.260- or a 9.720-inch deck height. The short-deck version can swallow up a 4.250-inch stroke, and the tall-deck version can handle a 4.500-inch stroke, which yields displacement figures of 482 and 511 ci, respectively. Like the LS7 block, the LSX is equipped with doweled billet steel main caps. Other tweaks include a beefed-up cam tunnel, two additional head bolt holes per cylinder, and a priority main oil galleries that sends oil to the main bearings before the lifters and camshaft. In comparison, the stock oil routes oil to the cam and lifters before the mains.

Because producing thousands of horsepower often requires very specialized hardware, the LSX can be adapted for such uses accordingly. Integrated mounting holes allow for the attachment of a front motor plate to the block, and the lifter bores can be enlarged to 1.060 inches for bronze bushings or larger lifters. Likewise, the cam tunnel can be bored out to accommodate a 60-mm cam core, and the head bolt holes can be enlarged for .5-inch studs. Additionally, the front oil feed holes can be blocked or restricted for improved lubrication when running a mechanical cam, and the front of the block can be machined for fitment of a belt-drive timing set.

For maximum end user flexibility in tailoring bore-and-stroke dimensions, the LSX block leaves the foundry with a 3.880-inch bore. This allows engine builders to bore the block out to their desired diameter. That said, GMPP also offers two short-deck versions of the LSX block that come fully bored and honed. These units are available in either a 4.065- or a 4.185-inch bore, and they are decked to 9.240 inches. Compared to a production casting, the only downside to the LSX is weight, with short-deck blocks tipping the scale at 225 pounds and tall-deck units coming in at 250 pounds. On the plus side, if you're making enough horsepower to warrant such a rugged block, a few extra pounds won't hurt performance much at all.

RHS

Many hot rodders were taken by surprise when a company best known for manufacturing aftermarket cylinder heads announced that it was developing a new block casting, but Racing Head Service's LS race block is a very impressive piece of work. Weighing in at 119 pounds, just a hair more than a production LS7 block, the RHS aluminum casting offers exceptional strength in a lightweight package.

Although the company doesn't publish an official horsepower rating, its LS

In the LS family, the Vortec 5.3L aluminum block is often considered the least desirable block for a stroker. It works just fine in the stock vehicles for which it was designed, but its thin cylinder sleeves and tiny bore diameter make it a poor choice as a foundation for a stroker motor. (© GM Corp.)

When it comes to sheer strength, the Vortec 6.0L iron block is the best value among all stock and aftermarket blocks, period. Because the Gen III block was originally designed as an aluminum casting, it features extensive reinforcement ribbing to reduce deflection. Cast that same design in iron, and the result is a block that weighs 70 pounds more but can support more than 1,000 hp. At high power levels, iron blocks typically offer superior ring seal than aluminum blocks. Best of all, a secondhand Vortec 6.0L block can be had for less than $500. (© GM Corp.)

ENGINE BLOCKS

race block has proven to be reliable in engines producing more than 2,000 hp. Available in both 9.240- and 9.750-inch deck heights, the RHS block is cast from A357-T6 aluminum and is extensively reinforced with structural ribbing throughout. Although its maximum bore size is limited to 4.165 inches, the tall-deck version features 6.380-inch-long sleeves, which can accommodate a 4.600-inch stroke and 501 ci. The standard-deck RHS block uses shorter 5.870-inch cylinder sleeves, but it can still support up to 449 ci. For easier fitment of long-stroke cranks, the RHS block has notches cut into the bottom of the crankcase for extra rod bolt clearance, and the cam bores are raised .386 inch. In addition to utilizing priority main oiling, the side oil gallery has been relocated to the outboard of the block. This not only provides extra rod clearance, it also makes it easy to plumb up a dry sump oil system, as the passage is tapped for -12AN feeds.

Bolstering the block's competition-worthy resume are cam bores that can be enlarged to 60 mm, lifter bores capable of accommodating 1.060-inch lifters, billet steel main caps, and provisions for six-bolt cylinder heads. RHS includes ARP main studs with its race block, and, if necessary, the main stud holes can be opened up to .500 inch. To reduce windage, the main cap windows have been revised, and like the LS9 block, the RHS unit can be fitted with piston oil squirters. Well aware that the RHS block would appeal to both street/strip enthusiasts and hardcore racers, engineers fitted it with mounting holes compatible with Gen I/II– and Gen III/IV–style mounts, as well as a motor plate. A casting of this caliber doesn't come cheap, and the RHS block lists for $4,900. It's available as a 4.100-inch bore that requires both boring and honing, a 4.120- or 4.160-inch bore that needs only finish honing, or a completely machined unit in 4.125- or 4.165-inch bores that are ready for final assembly right out of the box.

World Products Warhawk

For decades, World Products has been churning out premium aftermarket blocks, so it was only natural for the company to enter the LS market. The Warhawk block is cast from 357-T6 aluminum in both 9.240- and 9.800-inch deck heights. Tipping the scale at 133 pounds, it provides hot rodders with yet another lightweight alternative for big cubic inches.

With a maximum bore of 4.155 inches, the standard-deck Warhawk can accommodate a 4.125-inch stroke, and the tall-deck variant can be stroked to 4.500 inches. This yields maximum displacement figures of 447 and 488 ci, respectively. Like most aftermarket blocks, the Warhawk employs priority main oiling, doweled billet steel main caps, and two additional head bolt holes per cylinder. Furthermore, Warhawk's cam bores can be enlarged to 60 mm, and its crankcase is pre-notched for up to a 4.250-inch stroke. In order to stay together at the 1,500-hp level at which it's rated, the Warhawk block has substantially stronger cylinder walls than those on stock blocks. Its perimeter-based water jacket design utilizes a .080-inch-thick ductile iron sleeve (at 4.125-inch bore) that's surrounded by .300 inch of block material. A production LS7 block uses .070-inch-thick sleeves encased in .170 inch of block material. The Warhawk block is available in unfinished form with 3.990- and 4.115-inch bores and lists for $4,500. World Products also offers fully machined versions in 4.000-, 4.030-, 4.125-, and 4.155-inch bores with prices starting at $4,900.

One of the biggest advantages of aftermarket blocks over production blocks is their spread oil pan rails. This enables them to swallow up long strokes without a builder's need to grind them for clearance. Even with a 4.500-inch stroke, the connecting rods clear this RHS block with room to spare.

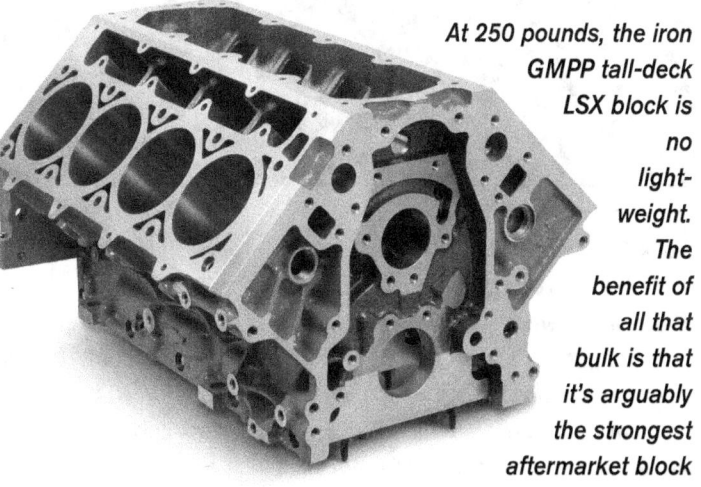

At 250 pounds, the iron GMPP tall-deck LSX block is no lightweight. The benefit of all that bulk is that it's arguably the strongest aftermarket block available. It can handle more than 2,500 hp, and its thick cylinder walls can be bored to 4.250 inches. (© GM Corp.)

CHAPTER 4

ERL

One of the most unique blocks on the market is ERL's Super Deck II LS2. The company starts out with a factory LS2 casting, attaches slugs of billet aluminum on the deck surfaces, then re-sleeves the block with Darton ductile iron liners. This increases deck height from 9.240 to 10.200 inches, which allows for fitment of a 4.500-inch stroke. Combined with a maximum bore of 4.200 inches, the combo yields 500 ci. From a reliability standpoint, wedging a deck plate between the block and heads seems crazy, but the setup has proven to be extremely robust and durable in race applications exceeding 2,000 hp. ERL cut its teeth developing tiny four-cylinder import race motors, many of which produce more than 1,000 hp, so it knows a thing or two about creatively modifying production blocks with deck plates for extra cubic inches.

Darton sleeves that are three times stronger than stock ones and ERL deck plates that cradle them in position are what make pushing that much power through a modified production block possible. The deck plate's design applies clamping pressure right at the top of the cylinder sleeves, instead of the deck surface, and the head bolts are torqued down. This directs pressure to a smaller surface area, which results in greater clamping force. The truss design of the deck plate also transmits loads below the deck surface and between the cylinder bores. Additionally, ERL opens up the head bolt holes to .500 inch, adds dowels to the main bearing bulkheads, and replaces the stock iron main caps with billet steel units. The result of all this is an extremely strong block with excellent strength and head gasket seal. For heavy-duty forced-induction applications, the company recommends running a smaller 4.125-inch bore for added cylinder wall thickness.

The Super Deck II system is sold as a complete turnkey short-block assembly for $14,900. If you provide your own LS2 core, ERL will knock $1,000 off the total. That price includes an ERL block, Callies crankshaft, full internal balancing, Wiseco pistons, rings, bearings, billet main caps, main studs, bushed lifter bores, intake manifold adapter plates, longer head studs and pushrods, and a cam custom ground to your application. All you need to add are cylinder heads, an intake manifold, and an oil pan. ERL offers bore sizes ranging from 4.000 to 4.200 inches and will tailor compression to whatever ratio you chose.

Dart

Without question, Dart's billet-aluminum LS block is the most fascinating and exotic on the market. It's whittled down from a single slug of solid 6061 billet aluminum into the shape of a Gen III/IV block. This equates to a block that's as strong as 7075 aluminum but with an elongation rating that's five times greater than cast aluminum. Since the Dart block is CNC-machined instead of being built from a casting mold, it can be customized in any size deck height, bore, cam tunnel, lifter bore, and main journal housing you need. With the ability to support in excess of 3,000 hp, this block is obviously intended for only the most extreme applications where low mass is paramount and cost is no object. Consequently, depending on how it's optioned, the Dart billet LS block ranges in price from $7,000 to $9,000.

The RHS block boasts exceptional strength in a lightweight aluminum package. For the ultimate in quality control, RHS inspects all of its blocks by using a CT scan prior to shipping them.

Like many competing blocks, the LSX block has two additional cylinder head bolt holes surrounding each cylinder. Some aftermarket heads have bosses that mate up with the two extra holes, but production heads do not. That's not a problem, because it's not mandatory to use the additional holes, and production heads will still bolt up. Another option is to weld tabs onto production heads so that they mate up with the bolt holes.

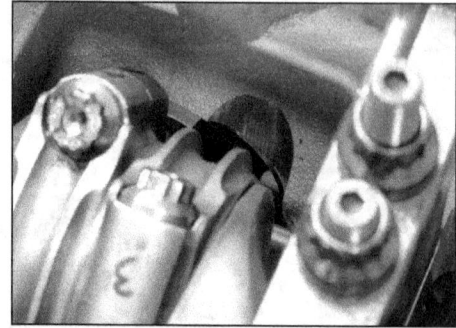

The tall-deck version of the RHS block has very long 6.380-inch sleeves, which can accommodate a 4.600-inch stroke. The bottom of the cylinders comes pre-notched for extra rod bolt clearance. This very much epitomizes the concept of spending money on hardware instead of labor.

Like most aftermarket blocks, the RHS casting has raised cam bores that can be enlarged to 60 mm. The benefit of bigger cam tunnel bores is twofold. First, it allows grinding a cam on a larger-diameter core to reduce cam flex in high-RPM, high-valvespring-pressure applications. Second, it also provides extra space to fit cams with lots of lobe lift.

Machine Work

Bolting premium bottom-end components to a block with shoddy machine work is the best way to ruin the stack of parts. Although proper parts selection is critical in making sure your stroker combo hits your performance objectives, quality machine work is equally important. Consequences of poor machine work range from excessive oil consumption to compromised durability to reduced power production to catastrophic engine failure.

In essence, paying a machinist's bill constitutes laying out cash for labor, as opposed to a tangible product, so enthusiasts are naturally hesitant to do so. However, trying to pinch pennies during the machining phase of a stroker build can sentence the engine to doom before the assembly process begins. There's a good chance that the least expensive machine shop in town doesn't perform the best work, but on the other hand, there are no guarantees that a stiff machining bill buys quality. That's where the experience of your local hot rodding community comes into play to help steer you to a reputable shop. Naturally, knowing what the different machining procedures entail helps you determine which ones are necessary for your engine build, and make paying for them more palatable.

Block Preparation

Aftermarket blocks, brand-new production blocks, and used production blocks all have different machining needs. If you are simply freshening up a motor that you know is otherwise in good shape, or you are starting out with a brand-new block, you can immediately jump into more major operations, such as boring and decking. However, if you've rescued your block out of a junkyard, having it checked for cracks is imperative, unless you're not phased at the prospect of spending thousands of dollars machining a piece of scrap. Two inexpensive, effective ways of ensuring a block is fissure-free are magnafluxing and pressure testing. Magnafluxing involves soaking the block in a luminescent solution that reveals cracks under florescent light. Likewise, sealing off the water jackets and pressure-testing the coolant passages can find internal cracks and porosity issues not easily visible through magnafluxing.

Most factory iron LS blocks can safely handle a .030-inch overbore, and the sleeves in stock aluminum blocks can typically be bored .010 inch without a hitch. Nonetheless, factory casting procedures aren't perfect, so sonic checking the cylinder walls for adequate thickness is always a good idea, especially with blocks that have already been overbored. By sending sonic waves into the bores with a hand-held probe and reading how quickly they reflect back, sonic checkers can determine thickness at any given part of a cylinder wall. The most important areas to check are the major thrust surfaces, which are the inboard wall on the driver-side bank

The World Products Warhawk block is cast from 357-T6 aluminum and weighs 133 pounds. It's offered in 9.240- and 9.800-inch deck heights in a variety of bore diameters. The company rates the block at 1,500 hp. (Photo Courtesy of World Products)

The ERL Super Deck II block starts out as a stock LS2 casting. ERL then removes the stock cylinder walls, presses in a set of Darton wet sleeves, and caps them off with a billet aluminum deck plate that increases deck height to 10.200 inches. ERL perfected this nifty trick on small-displacement four-cylinder import drag motors.

In addition to increasing deck height, the ERL deck plate also reinforces the top of the cylinder bores. Although some may question the durability of a block based on a stock LS2 casting, the Super Deck II has held up just fine in many race motors pushing close to 2,000 hp.

of cylinders and the outboard wall on the passenger side. Aftermarket manufacturers publish maximum-recommended bore diameters for their blocks that should not be exceeded, but since some hot rodders will always roll the dice and try, sonic checking is mandatory for those who choose to ignore their advice.

Once you've determined that the block is solid, giving it a thorough cleaning will not only make it look nice, but make it easier to work on, as well. The most common method of cleaning a block is hot tanking, which submerges or pressure washes the block in a high-alkaline caustic solution to dislodge grease and grime. Most of the time, it works reasonably well, but it doesn't always completely clean water jackets, carbon deposits, rust, or scale in extremely well-worn blocks. In such instances, thermal cleaning—where the block is baked to roughly 700 degrees to burn off all impurities—is a more effective alternative. The next step in thermal cleaning involves media blasting the block to remove all carbon, which also stress-relieves the block. Finally, the block is tumbled to remove all the metal shot, leaving behind a raw cast-iron finish.

Boring

As the miles tack onto a motor, cylinder walls wear out to a shape that's no longer perfectly cylindrical. Fortunately, just about every production block is cast with additional material that can be enlarged, or bored out, to square up the cylinders once again without compromising the block's integrity. Since factory aluminum LS blocks have relatively thin cylinder liners, it's often more practical to simply hone them out .005 inch. Likewise, factory production blocks don't require a cleanup bore and are ready to run after a quick hone job. Aftermarket blocks, on the other hand, come in several different configurations. Some only need a finish hone, others come ready to run out of the box, and unfinished castings have undersized bores that can be enlarged to the size an engine builder desires.

Boring out a block isn't overly complicated, but it still requires good equipment and a skilled set of hands. A boring bar is only as good as its operator, and regardless of whether or not a block is set up straight in the fixture, it bores a hole straight down. With older machines that register off the deck surface, it's critical to check that the surface is completely flat before boring begins. Although there's nothing wrong with them, they do have a higher margin for error. The preferred method is to use a boring machine that registers off the crankshaft centerline by attaching it to the main bearing bores. This ensures that the cylinder bores are perpendicular to the crank.

Cylinders are typically bored to within a few thousandths of an inch of their final bore size, and then they are honed to spec. The Rottler FA boring bar is one of the most popular units in the industry, and the most critical step in the procedure of setting it up is centering the boring bar arm inside the cylinder wall. This is accomplished by equalizing the gap among three fingers that extend from the bar with a feeler gauge. To set the width of the cut, a very precise indexing tool is used to set the depth of the cutter.

Honing

Boring cleans and straightens cylinder walls by removing material, but honing smoothes the bores to provide a smooth surface for the pistons and rings to ride on. The final finish allows the rings to seal properly and also determines the amount of friction exerted on the reciprocating assembly.

Generally, racers, in search of marginal gains in horsepower, prefer a super-smooth finish to reduce ring drag. However, this isn't necessarily the best approach for a street engine. Although a honed bore feels smooth to the touch,

Raising the deck height requires longer head studs, which ERL includes with its blocks. The bolt holes are also enlarged to .500 inch.

Because the cylinder banks are situated at a 90-degree angle, moving the heads upward also moves them farther apart from each other. To compensate for this, ERL provides billet adapter plates that fill the gap that would otherwise exist between the cylinder heads and the intake manifold.

ENGINE BLOCKS

The Ideal Cylinder Wall Finish

The type of finish you choose to put on your block's cylinder walls can literally make or break your entire stroker build. Honing is a lot of science and a little bit of black art, and one particular hone isn't best for all blocks or ring packages. Hot rodders often assume that the smoothest is the best, but that's seldom the case for both street and race engines. Different types of blocks vary on the Rockwell hardness scale. Harder blocks usually perform better with a softer finish, and softer blocks prefer a harder finish. There must be a balance between having enough surface area to properly seal the rings and not so much that it compromises oil retention and ring lubrication. The problem with having too smooth of a finish is that it increases surface area enough to decrease oil retention. Consequently, ring wear and frictional power loss go up significantly. To combat this, racing engines usually have a very deep plateau finish to hold a lot of oil with as little surface area as possible for the rings to ride on. Once mean piston speeds hit 4,500 to 5,000 fps, the difference between the right and wrong hone on a high-end engine is 25 to 30 hp. The power loss from having the wrong hone isn't as noticeable on a street engine, but it does increase ring wear dramatically.

the finish is actually a series of fine peaks and valleys. Because the valleys retain the oil, smoother finishes reduce the depth of the valleys. Most engine wear occurs on cold starts, so street motors that experience routine heat cycles need to sacrifice a bit of smoothness in the name of longevity. This is where your machinist's experience comes into play, as the grit of stones he uses is determined by your motor's intended use.

Once considered exotic, but common practice nowadays, is the process of bolting a torque plate to the deck surface while honing. The process simulates the distortion a block experiences when a cylinder head is bolted into place, and it is just another measure used to make sure the bores are as round as possible.

Another procedure that is becoming more common during street motor building is plateau honing, or honing in multiple stages. As the name suggests, an initial coarse honing stone is used first, and several finer grit stones in different stages follow to flatten the peaks in the finish. The result is a smooth surface with deeper valleys that improve oil retention and lubrication for the pistons and rings. Almost all performance engines these days are plateau honed, and machinists tend to be somewhat secretive about what grit stones they use, which vary from shop to shop.

There is still some debate, however, regarding hot honing. It involves heating up the honing oil to roughly 200 degrees to simulate the expansion a block experiences at operating temperature. As with the use of torque plates, the idea is to get the bores as round as possible, but the jury is mixed regarding whether or not it provides any benefits.

Decking

To promote proper cylinder head sealing, the deck of the block is often surfaced, or decked, to provide a smooth, even surface for the gaskets and cylinder heads to clamp down upon. As with boring, it is critical that the deck is machined perpendicular to the crankshaft centerline. Because the pistons sit below the deck at TDC in most production blocks, the deck height is often reduced to improve quench and raise the static compression ratio. If plans call for

Unlike most blocks that are cast from molds, Dart's 6061 billet block is CNC-machined from a single block of billet aluminum. As a result, its critical dimensions can be sized into just about any configuration.

The rate at which the boring bar cuts depends on how much metal is being removed at one time. With a larger overbore, the bar descends more slowly than with a smaller overbore, and vice-versa. Boring a block .030 over typically takes 40 minutes.

HOW TO BUILD BIG-INCH GM LS-SERIES ENGINES

Tall-Deck Caveats

Raising the deck height of a block, along with the cam bores, is great for maximizing displacement, but this minor tweak in engine architecture creates potential pitfalls that must be avoided for a successful stroker build. The most obvious factor to consider is underhood installation. Because a taller deck height moves the cylinder heads farther outward, it's important to make sure that the motor clears the shock towers or any other section of the engine bay. Tall-deck blocks often require custom headers, as the blocks raise the location of the exhaust ports in relation to the rest of a car's chassis. Likewise, bolting an intake manifold to a tall-deck block requires sandwiching an adapter plate between the cylinder heads and the intake. The exception is intake manifolds designed specifically for tall-deck applications that utilize longer intake runners. Raising the camshaft tunnel necessitates using a longer timing chain, along with a taller rear seal cover. Fortunately, all of these components are readily available directly from the block manufacturer or other aftermarket companies.

Factory GM Blocks

Block	PN	Material	Deck Height	Bore	Max Bore	Max Stroke	Main Cap
LS1/LS6	12561166	Aluminum	9.240	3.900	3.910	4.000-4.125	Iron
LS2	12568950	Aluminum	9.240	4.000	4.010	4.000-4.125	Iron
LS3/6.0L	12584727	Aluminum	9.240	4.065	4.075	4.000-4.125	Iron
LS4	12571048	Aluminum	9.240	3.780	3.790	4.000-4.125	Iron
LS7	19213580	Aluminum	9.240	4.125	4.135	4.000-4.125	Billet steel
LS9	12621983	Aluminum	9.240	4.065	4.075	4.000-4.125	Billet steel
LSA	12623968	Aluminum	9.240	4.065	4.075	4.000-4.125	Billet steel
Vortec 6.0L	12572808	Iron	9.240	4.000	4.030	4.000-4.125	Iron
Vortec 4.8/5.3L	12551315	Iron	9.240	3.780	3.900	4.000-4.125	Iron

Aftermarket LS Blocks

Block	PN	Material	Deck Height	Bore	Max Bore	Stroke Max	Main Cap
C5R	12480030	Aluminum	9.240	4.117	4.160	4.000-4.125	Billet steel
Dart	N/A	Billet aluminum	Custom	Custom	Custom	Custom	Billet steel
ERL	P2HMCHLSIO	Aluminum	10.200	4.200	4.200	4.500	Billet steel
LSX	19213964	Iron	9.260	3.880	4.250	4.250	Billet steel
LSX	19244059	Iron	9.720	3.880	4.250	4.500	Billet steel
LSX376	12444055	Iron	9.240	4.065	4.250	4.250	Billet steel
LSX454	19244057	Iron	9.240	4.185	4.250	4.250	Billet steel
RHS	54900	Aluminum	9.750	4.165	4.165	4.600	Billet steel
RHS	54901	Aluminum	9.750	4.125	4.165	4.600	Billet steel
RHS	54902	Aluminum	9.240	4.165	4.165	4.125	Billet steel
RHS	54903	Aluminum	9.240	4.125	4.165	4.125	Billet steel
RHS	54900U	Aluminum	9.750	4.160	4.165	4.600	Billet steel
RHS	54901U	Aluminum	9.750	4.120	4.165	4.600	Billet steel
RHS	54902U	Aluminum	9.240	4.160	4.165	4.125	Billet steel
RHS	54903U	Aluminum	9.240	4.120	4.165	4.125	Billet steel
RHS	54904	Aluminum	9.760	4.100	4.165	4.600	Billet steel
RHS	54905	Aluminum	9.250	4.100	4.165	4.125	Billet steel
Warhawk	086505	Aluminum	9.240	3.990	4.155	4.125	Billet steel
Warhawk	086525	Aluminum	9.800	4.115	4.155	4.500	Billet steel

potentially re-using a block for future rebuilds, the pistons should be left a few thousandths of an inch below the deck surface. This leaves adequate material for subsequent decking procedures.

For many years, the Sunnen HBS-2100 has been the industry standard fixture for decking blocks.

The decking process begins with placing the main bearing bulkheads of a block on a bar of square-tube steel. Before any cutting begins, a dial gauge is run across the surface of the deck in numerous spots to make sure it's completely flat. Positioning the cutting head into place requires a delicate touch and lots of experience. It is lowered until it just barely touches the deck surface, and then the machine goes to work.

Align-Boring and Honing

The basic principles of align-boring and honing are similar to those of standard boring and honing, but for main caps instead of cylinder walls. There is a big difference. Overboring a cylinder is a common rebuild procedure, but because the crank rides on a set of bearings, only blocks that have been severely abused or have spun bearings require align-boring. The process entails removing material from the mating surface of the main caps, torquing them down to spec with the crankshaft removed, boring out the main saddles to within a few thousandths of an inch of the proper inside diameter spec, and honing them the rest of the way. This ensures that the main bearing bores are consistent from cap to cap and eliminates crank binding.

Align-boring is accomplished with a Sunnen boring fixture that attaches to a Sunnen CH-100 honing machine. They are the industry standard for align-boring and honing. The fixture can be configured to match the bellhousing bolt pattern of just about any motor, and the boring bar slides inside a pair of sleeves that sit inside the front and rear mains to ensure straightness. The bar spins at a set rate, and the machinist manually applies

The first step in honing involves shimming the stones for the final bore size. For the ultimate in precision, a machinist can choose among different grit stones, depending on the finish desired.

During the honing process, it's standard practice these days to bolt a torque plate to the deck surface to simulate the stress the cylinder heads and bolts exert on the block. Based on bore size and cylinder length, the machinist can set the rotational rate and the dwell rate of the honing shaft. It's hinged on a series of universal joints to position it straight within the bore. During the honing process, the machinist allows the block to cool every 10 to 15 minutes to prevent it from distorting.

During the decking process, the rotational speed of the cutter and the rate at which the cutter moves across the deck from front to back are manually adjustable. After each swipe, a dial gauge is used to track progress, and the entire process takes about an hour.

CHAPTER 4

Bore vs. Stroke

From the factory, all Gen III/IV motors feature over-square dimensions where the diameters of their bores are larger than the lengths of their strokes. Conversely, an under-square engine has a bigger stroke than bore. There are pros and cons to both arrangements, but GM's decision to utilize over-square cylinder architecture in each of its LS variants is quite revealing. If two engines have equal displacement, but one is over-square and the other is under-square, chances are the over-square motor produces more horsepower. This is because a larger bore helps de-shroud the intake valves and improves airflow. Likewise, a larger bore provides extra clearance between the cylinder wall and intake valve, which allows fitting a larger intake valve into the cylinder head for improved high-lift airflow.

Improvements in flow, however, are just part of the equation. Since under-square motors rely on a longer stroke, the extra distance the pistons must travel between TDC and BDC results in an increase in friction and a decrease in horsepower. Once mean piston speed exceeds 4,000 fps, frictional power losses skyrocket. Consequently, it's not surprising that the most competitive forms of high-end racing overwhelmingly favor over-square engine designs.

To achieve NASCAR's 358-ci displacement limit, the Chevy R07 Sprint Cup motor combines a massive 4.185-inch bore with a short 3.250-inch stroke. Likewise, 500-ci NHRA Pro Stock engines use a 4.700-inch bore and 3.600-inch stroke. Perhaps the most extreme over-square motors of all are in Formula One, in which engines turn a jaw-dropping 18,000 rpm. To keep piston speeds as reasonable as possible, the 2.4L V-8s used in F1 match a 3.779-inch bore with a 1.629-inch stroke, which equates to a 2.32:1 bore/stroke ratio. In addition to decreasing friction, a shorter-stroke crankshaft decreases connecting rod angularity for reduced side loading of the pistons in the bores, and it has smaller counterweights that create less windage in the oil pan. Furthermore, packing maximum cubic inches into a standard- or low-deck block allows shortening the pushrods, in turn reducing valvetrain flex and improving high-RPM stability.

The benefits of an over-square motor seem rather obvious, so why would anyone ever build an under-square motor in the first place? Some enthusiasts contend that a small-bore/long-stroke engine generates more torque than an over-square combination. The theory is that a longer stroke provides greater leverage on the crankshaft's rod journals, thereby boosting torque. However, several of the most distinguished race engine builders in the country have conducted extensive testing on under-square engine combinations that thoroughly disproves this claim. As the air/fuel mixture is ignited and begins pushing down on the top of a piston, mechanical leverage exerted on the crankshaft is greatest when the connecting rod is at a 90-degree angle to the crank throw. In relation to the crankshaft, this point occurs when the piston is about 80 degrees ATDC. The problem is that peak cylinder pressure is achieved approximately 30 degrees ATDC, when the connecting rod is still at an acute angle in relation to the crank throw. This is well before the piston and rod reach the point where they can apply maximum mechanical leverage on the crankshaft. Furthermore, by the time the rod is perpendicular to the crank throw, cylinder pressure has already dropped dramatically.

Even so, there is still a time and place for under-square motors. Although they don't necessarily produce more torque than an over-square motor, they often reach peak torque at a lower RPM. Further, that torque is usually carried over a broader RPM range for improved area under the curve. That being the case, under-square motors are well suited for heavy vehicles or towing applications where low-RPM torque and a flexible powerband are a priority.

Granted that an over-square motor offers several advantages over an under-square engine, the pitfall to avoid is sacrificing cubic inches just for the sake of hitting a certain target bore-to-stroke ratio. Let's say you're building an LS motor that's limited to a small 3.900-inch bore. Increasing the stroke from the stock 3.622 inches to 4.000 inches would bump displacement from 346 ci to 382 ci. Although this would create under-square 3.900- x 4.000-inch bore-and-stroke dimensions that may appear less than favorable on paper, it's still a far superior setup compared to retaining the stock 3.622-inch stroke. The truth of the matter is that the extra 36 ci afforded by a longer 4.000-inch stroke will more than offset any theoretical disadvantages of a slightly under-square combination.

The debate is more pertinent if you already have a target displacement figure in mind—such as building a motor for a sanctioned racing class that limits maximum cubic inches—and there are multiple bore-and-stroke configurations at your disposal that can be used to hit that target. So, although an over-square motor is more efficient and yields more power than an under-square combo, potential gains in cubic inches should never be sacrificed just for the sake of having over-square bore-and-stroke dimensions.

ENGINE BLOCKS

The main caps in most production LS motors aren't held in place with dowel pins, so they tend to shift over time. Even so, used blocks that haven't endured much abuse typically only require align-honing, and many machinists also like to align-hone new blocks.

pressure to determine how quickly the caps are bored. The depth of the cutter is set by measuring off the block side of the mains, and the caps are bored in multiple stages until they're .0025 inch from the final main bore diameter. The process usually leaves strips of shrapnel along the edges of the caps that must be carefully chamfered off with the cutter. The more contact a bearing has with the mains, the more heat it can dissipate into the block, so a smooth, even surface is very important. The operator adjusts the tension of the stones with a thumbwheel, and he can increase pressure in small increments to slowly attain the desired final diameter. The process typically requires 1 to 1½ hours, and if done correctly, the parting line between the cap and block will hardly be noticeable.

Re-sleeving the GM LS Block

Both GM and the aftermarket have released blocks whose bores have continually grown in diameters over the years. Even so, there are still instances when re-sleeving a factory aluminum block is appropriate. With extensive experience in NHRA Top Fuel, Outlaw, and Pro Import drag racing, Darton is the undisputed leader in sleeving technology. All of the aforementioned racing classes share cars that produce thousands of horsepower, and Darton brings that same durability into the LS market. All Darton sleeves are built from ductile iron, which offers 130,000 psi of tensile strength. The result is a sleeve that's more than three times stronger than a factory GM iron liner.

The company offers both dry and wet sleeves, and both have their advantages and drawbacks. To install dry sleeves, the factory iron liners are removed, and the aluminum portion of the cylinder walls is left intact. The Darton sleeves are then pressed into position, and they are held to the remaining parent material of the block with an interference fit. The sleeve can be bored to 4.125 inches, but that reduces wall thickness to about .060 inch. Furthermore, the installation procedure leaves very little of the parent material remaining to support the sleeve. On the other hand, installing Darton's wet sleeves—which the company calls its Modular Integrated Deck system—is far more involved. Unlike the dry sleeve system that relies on the factory aluminum cylinder walls for support, a wet sleeve system eliminates the cylinder walls entirely; the walls are removed. The sleeves are, instead, pressed into the very bottom of the block near the crankcase. The tops of the sleeves have flanges that mate with the deck of the block, and they also lock together with adjacent sleeves for additional support.

Because wet sleeves don't rely on the factory cylinder walls for support, they're much thicker at .287 inch at a 4.125-inch bore. According to Darton, this makes the wet sleeves substantially stronger than its dry sleeves. In the event that a single sleeve is damaged, it can be replaced individually. Although many enthusiasts question the durability of a re-sleeved factory aluminum block, Darton's MID sleeves are the same ones used in ERL's Super Deck II LS2 blocks, and they have proven to be reliable in race applications exceeding 2,000 hp. Another benefit is that Darton's latest MID LS2/LS7 sleeves can accommodate a 4.200-inch bore. A set of wet sleeves costs $1,400, and the machine work necessary to install them will set you back another $1,000. That's on top of the price of block, so the process isn't cheap. Dry sleeves cost roughly $500 less.

CHAPTER 5

CRANKSHAFTS

Back in the stone age of building stroker motors, which was only about 15 years ago, hot rodders had to settle for miniscule displacement gains through primitive means, such as offset grinding production crankshafts. Fortunately, that's no longer the case. Due to the rise of affordable aftermarket stroker crankshafts in the past decade, cubic inches are cheaper than ever, and installing a long-arm crank is the easiest way to increase displacement. As our hobby frolics in a golden age of horsepower, no single engine component, save for the cylinder head, has advanced the cause as much as the modern crankshaft.

Simply increasing the stroke of a standard 3.900-inch-bore LS1 from 3.622 inches to 4.000 inches adds 36 ci to the displacement tally. So unless your sanctioning body forbids it, you're probably in the market for a new stroker crank if you're building a motor. However, the choices are many, and not all cranks are created equally, which raises many questions. Should you settle for a cast steel piece, or step up to a forging? What's the difference between 5140, 4130, and 4340 steel alloys? Does billet live up to its mystique? And, most importantly, what's the right crankshaft for your application? Fortunately, this chapter helps sort everything out.

Stroking for Displacement

In essence, stroking an engine for additional displacement involves taking advantage of extra space inside the cylinders and crankcase. Because this moves the pistons farther up and down the bores, there is a prac-

Small increases in stroke yield large increases in displacement, which is why a long-arm crankshaft is at the heart of every big-inch engine combo. The overwhelming volume of affordable stroker crankshafts on the market is what has forced the rest of the aftermarket to develop blocks and cylinder heads that can keep pace.

tical limit to how much stroke can be increased before clearance issues arise. As the stroke of a crankshaft is increased, the distance between the crank centerline and connecting rod journals increases. This pushes the crankshaft counterweights farther outward, reducing the clearance between the counterweights and the oil pan rails. Additionally, longer strokes increase the angularity of the connecting rods as they swing from side to side in the block, causing them to come closer to the bottom of the cylinder sleeves and the crankcase. Another area to look out for is rod-to-camshaft clearance, as longer strokes push the connecting rods closer to the camshaft as the pistons near TDC.

Fortunately, none of these issues are insurmountable. Low-profile counterweights, small base circle camshafts, and judicious grinding of the block are usually enough to provide adequate clearance for all moving components. Even so, it's important to remember that the longer the stroke of a crankshaft, the more it pushes the limits of the available space inside a block. Generally, with careful parts selection, a production GM block can safely accommodate a 4.000-inch crank. However, some engine builders choose to take it one step further with a 4.100- or 4.125-inch stroke. Both can be made to fit, but using too short of a connecting rod can certainly pull the piston too far down the cylinder wall. In such an application, using custom pistons designed to reduce piston rock at BDC is highly recommended.

Factory Crankshafts

Most stock LS crankshafts are cast from nodular iron and have proven to be very durable in high-horsepower applications. They boast rolled fillets on the rod journals for improved strength and variable-radius undercuts on the counterweights for increased surface area. Many hot rodders have pushed stock cast cranks to 500 hp and 7,000 rpm without failure. Unlike Gen I small-block engines that were manufactured with a variety of main journal diameters, multiple rear main seal designs, and both internal and external balancing, LS engines have a crankshaft design that is far more universal. That means there's a great deal of interchangeability, which simplifies the process of building a stroker motor. The majority of factory LS crankshafts utilize a 3.622-inch stroke; the only exceptions are the 4.000-inch units found on the LS7 and the 3.267-inch cranks used in 4.8L truck motors. All Gen III/IV crankshafts share 2.559-inch-diameter main journals and 2.100-inch rod journals. The LS7, LS9, and LSA are the only LS small-blocks equipped with forged crankshafts from the factory.

For the most part, the 3.622-inch crankshafts used in the 5.3L, 5.7L, 6.0L, and 6.2L Gen III/IV engines are all the same. A few noteworthy differences are the thicker flywheel/flexplate flanges that were used in many Vortec truck motors and the 58-tooth (instead of the previous 24-tooth) reluctor wheels that GM began phasing in with the introduction of the Gen IV small-block in 2005.

Also, all LS-series crankshafts built prior to 2009 have a universal six-bolt flywheel/flexplate pattern. From 2009 onward, the LSA uses an eight-bolt pattern, which it shares with the GMPP LSX454 crank, while the LS9 crank comes with a nine-bolt pattern.

None of these changes impacts performance at all. The factory computer uses the reluctor wheel to detect the position of the crankshaft, so it's important to make sure that the wheel and computer are compatible. The aftermarket offers cranks with both styles of reluctor

The 4.000-inch LS7 crankshaft is the longest crank ever used in any Chevy small-block of any generation. It's forged from 4140 steel and features a crank snout that's nearly 1 inch longer than that of a standard Gen III/IV crank; it's made longer to accommodate the dry sump oil pump. With the introduction of the Gen IV LS2 in 2005, GM began replacing 24-tooth reluctor wheels with 58-tooth units. (© GM Corp.)

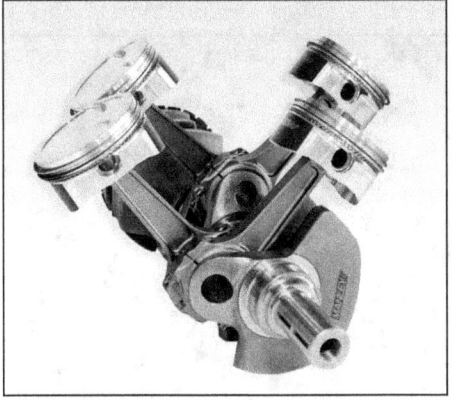

A longer stroke pulls the piston farther down the bore at BDC, decreasing the clearance between the counterweights and the piston skirts. Making sure there are no interference issues is a balancing act among counterweight height, piston skirt design, and connecting rod length.

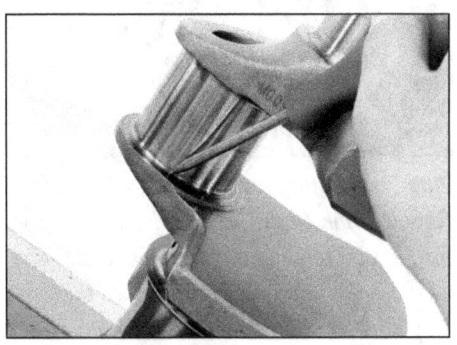

An area of the crank notorious for failure is where the rod journal meets the counterweight. Some contend that the forging process exacerbates this condition, because it is the area where the grain flow is stretched and contorted.

Aftermarket cranks typically employ a fillet radius at the edge of the journal to relieve the area of stress risers and improve durability. This is accomplished by forcing a roller into the edge to compact the metal and create a smooth transition. A sharp, grooved edge is typical with factory cranks, but the stock LS design is an exception to the rule. In addition to a fillet radius, stock LS cranks have a variable radius undercut on the counterweights to increase bearing surface area.

wheel, and the wheels can also be removed and swapped out, if necessary.

Because all LS crankshafts have the same main and rod journal diameters, they fit into any LS block. This allows bolting a 4.000-inch LS7 crank into a 5.3L, 5.7L, 6.0L, or 6.2L block for a nice bump in displacement. Unfortunately, these cranks can be difficult to balance, as they were designed to be used with super-lightweight titanium connecting rods found in the LS7. Likewise, a 3.622-inch crank can also be fitted in a 4.8L Vortec motor for a gain of 32 ci, but such a swap is very uncommon in practice, because a 325-ci motor is still relatively small in the wake of stroked small-blocks. Due to the affordability of aftermarket crankshafts, they're a much more popular alternative for stroking an engine. They're offered in a variety of stroke lengths ranging from 3.622 to 4.600 inches.

Just as important as the extra displacement that long-arm crankshafts offer are the dividends in strength they provide. Not only does the typical stroker motor make more power than a production engine, but it also turns more RPM. As RPM increases, the bending and twisting loads transmitted through the crank jump dramatically. Stock nodular iron crankshafts were never intended to survive under these conditions, so aftermarket forgings are highly recommended for engines that produce more than 500 hp and routinely turn 7,000 rpm or more. Premium forged steel aftermarket cranks can easily handle 1,000-plus hp, and considering how easy it is to make serious power with an LS small-block, their popularity is hardly surprising.

Cast vs. Forged vs. Billet

Two of the most important factors that determine the strength of a crankshaft are the material it's made from and how that material is processed. Casting and forging are the two most common manufacturing methods, and each has its benefits and drawbacks. Cast cranks start life as liquid iron or steel, which is poured into a mold. This allows the raw casting to closely resemble its final shape, which reduces the amount of final machining required. Because the equipment necessary to produce cast cranks is relatively inexpensive, it's obvious why they're the predominant choice of the OEMs, including GM. Aftermarket cast steel cranks offer significant improvements in strength, and they can be had for as little as $500.

In contrast, the forging process requires heavy-duty presses and more extensive final machining operations. Forging involves heating a cylindrical slug of metal to a molten state, then pounding it into shape with 200-ton presses and dies. It is this compressing action that creates an inherently stronger end product over a casting. In a casting, the grain structure is very loosely held together. In a forging, the force of the press compresses the grain together, so it becomes one uniform grain flow. As the space between the molecules is compressed, they are forced to bond together, which dramatically improves strength. In fact, forged small-block cranks routinely handle in excess of 1,000 hp.

Compared to a cast crank, the drawback of a forging is cost. The heavy-duty hydraulic presses used in the forging process cost at least $100,000, so aftermarket manufacturers must sell vast

Like the LS7's crank, the crankshafts in the LS9 and LSA are built from forged steel. Because the crankshaft must cope with the rigors of driving a supercharger, it has a keyway integrated into the crank snout to prevent the harmonic balancer from spinning out of place. (© GM Corp.)

When comparing a cast crank (left) to a forged crank (right), it's obvious why the forged unit fetches a higher price tag. The cast crank's rough surface shows that very little finishing machine work is required, as the casting process yields a shape that closely resembles the end product. The forged crank's smoother and more refined appearance reveals the extensive machining operations required after the crank leaves the forging die.

Distinguishing a cast crank from a forged unit at the swap meet or on eBay is easy. Cast cranks have a distinct parting line, a vestige from where the casting cores were separated during the manufacturing process.

quantities of cranks before they even recover their equipment costs. This leads to a costlier product, typically about $900.

Billet cranks are closely related to forged cranks. Like a forging, a billet crank starts out as a large cylindrical ingot of steel. However, while a forged crank is compressed during the forging process, the steel ingot used in a billet crank is already forged, albeit not quite as compressed as in a forged crank. The key difference between the two is how the ingots are shaped into cranks.

The metal bar used to make a forged 4.000-inch Gen III/IV crank measures about 4.75 inches in diameter, and the crank's total width ends up being 6.75 inches when the forging process is complete. The metal bar used in a billet crank of the same stroke is much larger at roughly 8 inches, and it weighs 350 pounds, compared to the 150-pound metal bar used to make a forged crank.

Instead of twisting and pounding the metal in different directions as done in forging, a CNC mill whittles away the metal of a billet crank into its final shape, so the grain structure runs parallel throughout the entire length of the crank. Due to the increase in materials and labor over a forged crank, billet cranks are the most expensive of them all. Custom one-offs carry price tags in the neighborhood of $3,000.

A price tag that steep makes a billet crank impractical for the average street/strip motor. If money is no object, however, billet cranks represent the pinnacle in strength. By nature, a forging is not as strong as billet, because the forging process stretches and shears the grain structure. A forging starts out as a round bar of metal and gets twisted and turned to make the rod throws. What used to be centerline of the bar is now offset, and the grains get stretched, traumatized, and weakened, although some sections of it are substantially stronger than those in a casting. With billet, there are no stress riser areas, because the grain structure runs parallel to the length of the entire crank. Forgings are stronger than billet in bolts and axles, because the metal isn't stretched and sheared, but not in crankshafts. The most demanding forms of racing—including NHRA Top Fuel, NASCAR Sprint Cup, and Formula One—all rely on billet cranks.

Strength

Before delving into the specifics of metallurgy, I'll mention that there are strength characteristics universal to all castings and forgings that are worth nothing. In a lab, metal is often tested for strength by pulling a 1-inch round bar apart until it breaks. Tensile strength relates to the amount of force required to start to stretch the bar. Yield strength describes the force needed to continue to

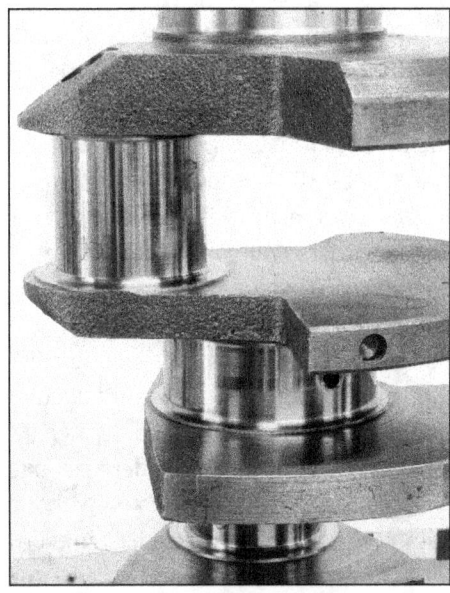

Crank overlap is simply the portions of the rod and main journals that overlap each other. Stroker cranks move the rod journal farther away from the main journal, thereby reducing overlap. Reducing the diameter of either the rod journal or the main journal decreases parasitic friction but compromises strength.

Billet cranks, like this 4.000-inch unit from Bryant Racing, offer the ultimate in strength. However, a custom billet crank costs $2,000 to $3,000, and a forged unit works just as well for most street motors at a fraction of the price.

In order to balance this 4.500-inch Callies crank, several slugs of heavy metal had to be added to the counterweights. The long stroke necessitates reducing the height of the counterweights to ensure adequate piston skirt clearance, and heavy metal must be added back in to compensate for the loss in mass.

Not that long ago, entry-level forged crankshafts were built from 5140 and 4130 alloys. These days, lower manufacturing costs have enabled aftermarket companies, such as Compstar, Eagle, and Scat, to offer premium 4340 crankshafts for roughly the same price as cranks made of lesser grades of metal. Consequently, 5140 and 4130 forgings are not common these days.

pull the bar apart. The difference between tensile strength and yield strength between castings and forgings is significant. With a casting, the cross section of the bar only needs to be reduced by 6 percent before it breaks, but with a forging, the cross section can be reduced by 20 percent before the bar breaks.

Furthermore, designing a durable crank is an exercise in striking a balance between hardness and ductility. Increased hardness can lead to a stronger crank, but it still has to have some give in it so it can bend without cracking, a property that is referred to as ductility. A good way to explain ductility is by comparing glass to rubber. Glass is very hard, but it cracks easily, so it's not ductile. Rubber bends easily, so it is very ductile, but not hard. Like a fishing pole, a crank should, ideally, give a bit under load, but it should snap back into shape without being permanently deformed. Cranks do, in fact, flex under load, and in a motor with an aluminum block, they can bend as much as .200 inch.

Where premium forged cranks shine is in their ability to be extremely hard while still maintaining ductility. The ideal crank is one that can be very hard and maintain its shape to spread bearing loads evenly throughout the crank while still having enough ductility to prevent cracking. Generally, as a crank's hardness increases, so does its tensile strength. Having higher carbon content in steel increases hardness, but it sacrifices ductility in the process. That's why too much carbon content in a crank isn't always a good thing. Cast iron is the least ductile material used to build cranks, and the next step up the ladder is 5140 alloy, followed by 4130 and 4340. As you go up scale, you can increase hardness without sacrificing ductility.

Metallurgy

In an alloy consisting primarily of iron, the small quantities of metal added to that iron are what determine the differences in strength between various grades of steel. A set of standards established by the American Iron and Steel Institute (AISI) determines the content of metal grades, in addition to their nomenclature. Generally, increasing the carbon content in proportion to iron improves strength. The most basic cranks are cast iron, which typically have a tensile strength of about 70,000 to 80,000 psi. Slightly increasing the carbon content of iron produces nodular iron, resulting in a tensile strength of roughly 95,000 psi. Both materials are used extensively by the OEMs, but they won't handle the demands of aftermarket stroker crank applications. Commonly used in entry-level aftermarket crankshafts, cast steel has greater carbon content than nodular iron and a tensile strength of about 105,000 psi.

Factory forged cranks are usually made from steel alloys, such as 1010, 1045, and 1053. Although their tensile strengths are similar to that of a cast steel crank, their elongation rating is more than three times greater. This translates to a far less brittle material. In these types of alloys, chrome and nickel are what make them stronger. There are other materials involved, but they're used to make sure everything mixes together properly and don't impact strength. Nonetheless, factory forgings are a far cry from the ultimate durability of an aftermarket steel crank. Factory forged steel

Nitriding penetrates .010 to .012 inch into the crank, improving surface hardness and fatigue life on critical areas, such as the bearing surfaces. Although the most common heat-treating process used in aftermarket cranks, nitriding produces a relatively thin surface compared to induction hardening, which is favored by the OEMs.

Balancing is performed on machines, such as the Sunnen DCB-750 digital balancer, which is the industry standard. Essentially a glorified tire balancer, the machine holds the crank in place on two stands, and then it spins the crank and bobweights up to 750 rpm. The stands on each side detect how much imbalance exits, and the machine calculates how much weight must be removed or added to correct it.

cranks have high carbon content, but they often lack the chrome and nickel content of the premium alloys used in aftermarket cranks. Forged from 4140 steel, the cranks used in the LS7, LS9, and LSA are an exception to the norm.

The most basic aftermarket-grade steel is 5140, which boasts a tensile strength of about 115,000 psi. This material used to be—and to some extent still is—an excellent choice for racers on a budget, but it is less common than it was in years past, due to the increasing affordability of premium alloy cranks. These include 4130 and 4340 forgings, which have tensile strength ratings of approximately 125,000 and 145,000 psi, respectively. Engine builders and crankshaft manufacturers universally accept 4340 as the ideal alloy for strength and durability. Because aftermarket LS 4340 cranks start at $900 for most engine platforms, the lesser grades of steel are dwindling in popularity. In fact, almost all aftermarket forged LS crankshafts are made from 4340 steel.

Overlap

Just as the term implies, journal overlap is simply how much of a crank's main and rod journal diameters overlap. If you were to stand a crank up vertically, it can easily be seen, as the portions of the main and rod journals overlap each other. As stroke is increased, moving the rod journals farther away from the main journals reduces overlap and compromises strength and durability. To compensate for this, when GM increased the stroke from 3.480 inches to 3.750 inches in the Gen I 400-ci small-block Chevy, it also increased the size of the mains from 2.45 inches to 2.65 inches to maintain adequate journal overlap.

However, with improved modern alloys, crank overlap isn't as important as it used to be. For instance, GM was able to maintain the same main and rod journal diameters throughout the Gen III/IV family when it increased the stroke to 4.000 inches in the LS7. A common practice in high-end race motors is to run smaller rod and main journals to reduce the surface area of the bearings. This, in turn, reduces friction and can increase power, but it also reduces overlap. It also requires either turning down the crank journals or

Drill charts from crank manufacturers specify how much weight a given drill size and drill depth will remove. Because the crank acts as a lever, the farther away from the centerline weight is removed or added, the greater effect it has on balance. Typically, balancing takes 1 to 1½ hours to perform.

After the spin cycle, the crank is rotated by hand, and an encoder on the balancer very accurately measures crankshaft position to help a machinist pinpoint the exact spot where the counterweight must be modified. A digital readout on the balancer tells the operator the exact location where weight must be added or removed and the amount of the weight. Balancing to "x" number of ounces simply means how much imbalance, in ounces, exists 1 inch from the crank centerline.

With today's lightweight rods and pistons, weight is removed from the counterweights the majority of the time when balancing a rotating assembly. If an unusually large amount of weight must be removed, the counterweights can either be Swiss-cheesed with a bunch of holes or be turned down in a lathe.

ordering a custom billet crank, and both options are very expensive. Unless you're racing in a class where 5 hp can determine the winner of a race, sticking with factory LS main and rod journal diameters makes the most sense.

Twist vs. Non-Twist Forging

Forged cranks are pressed into place on a die, but there are two different techniques used to accomplish this. The simplest method is to forge one of the crank throws at a time in a flat forging die. The crank is then twisted, and the die forges the next throw. Conversely, in a non-twist forging, all four throws are forged simultaneously, which requires a more complex die. Non-twist forgings are said to reduce internal crankshaft stresses during the manufacturing process, but whether or not that's true is up for debate. If all variables are controlled properly during the forging process, there's little, if any, difference between twist and non-twist forgings. Most aftermarket cranks these days are non-twist forgings anyway, so there's no sense in arguing either way.

Heat-Treating the Crankshaft

In addition to materials and casting or forging techniques, heat-treating can greatly impact the strength of a crankshaft. Nitriding is the most prevalent method of heat-treating used in aftermarket cranks; it is where ionized nitrogen is vacuum-deposited onto the crank surface in an oven. By penetrating .010 to .012 inch into the metal surface and changing the microstructure of the steel, surface hardness is doubled from 30 to 60 on the Rockwell scale, and fatigue life is increased by 25 percent. Although the process does strengthen the crank a bit, improving the impact and wear resistance is the real benefit of nitriding, and this reduces the potential for cracking. That's very important, because impact and wear are the most common causes of crank failure.

The older method of heat-treating is induction-hardening, in which the journals are heated using a magnetic field and then plunged into water. This results in deeper penetration into the metal surface (.050 to .060 inch), but it is more localized than with nitriding, which treats the entire crank at once. Induction-hardening can be performed with cheaper equipment, so it's usually the method of choice for the OEMs. However, if the rate of cooling isn't carefully controlled, it can create stress risers and soft spots. For this reason, most aftermarket crankshafts are heat-treated through the nitriding process.

Knife-Edging the Crankshaft Counterweights

For decades, hot rodders have maintained that knife-edging a crank's counterweights reduces windage, and, therefore, increases horsepower. However, this is more of an old wive's tale than reality. The theory is that because oil is viscous and has resistance, a crank that's more narrowly profiled slices through it more easily. However, with windage trays and today's low-profile oil pans, like the ones used in LS small-blocks, windage isn't much of an issue. In reality, knife-edging was developed more for ease of balancing than power and won't increase horsepower much at all on a street motor. Oil hits a knife edge and gets thrown all over the place when it should ideally land on the nose and flow off to the side, like snow on a snow plow blade. A bull-nose rounded leading edge is the most efficient, like the bow of a ship, and it is the design more commonly used in modern crankshafts.

Balancing the Crankshaft

In every performance engine build, the crankshaft must be balanced to match the rest of the rotating assembly. Otherwise, a motor can literally rattle itself to death. By nature, a 90-degree V-8 isn't the smoothest-running engine configuration, so balancing a performance rotating assembly requires some extra precision.

When balancing a rotating assembly, the goal is to make the reciprocating mass equal to the rotating mass. This yields a smoothly running motor free of unwanted vibrations that reduce bearing life. With today's lightweight aftermarket pistons and rods, weight is removed from the counterweights the majority of the time. Only in applications where extremely heavy-duty nitrous or blower

It's a common misconception that bobweights simply duplicate the weight of a pair of pistons and rods. Bobweights are actually equal in mass to 100 percent of the rotating weight (big rod ends and rod bearings) and 50 percent of the reciprocating weight (pistons, pins, locks, and small rod ends). In a 90-degree V-8, each piston has a companion piston it travels with to TDC at the same time. So, to equalize rotating and reciprocating weight, only half the total reciprocating weight is taken into account when balancing. After carefully measuring both the rotating and reciprocating weights, bobweights are selected that match that formula when balancing a crankshaft.

CRANKSHAFTS

Many manufacturers drill holes through the rod and main journals to reduce weight. The amount of weight that's reduced isn't as important as the location the weight is removed from. Drilling the main journals removes mass from the centerline of the crank, but it doesn't do much at all for performance. Conversely, removing weight from the rod journals and counterweights reduces rotating mass, which is far more effective. That said, lightweight cranks do little to improve the performance of the average street/strip motor.

parts are used, or where space constraints reduce the size of the counterweights, is weight added.

When balancing a rotating assembly for a street motor, the goal is to equalize the rotating mass and the reciprocating mass. However, in race motors, it's not uncommon to overbalance the crank. A balancer generally spins a crank 500 to 750 rpm, and for obvious safety reasons, you can't replicate the actual RPM the crank experiences in a running engine. However, if you spin a motor at very high RPM, say 7,000 to 8,000 rpm, parts can stretch and move around. Aluminum rods might stretch as much as .030 inch. This stretch increases load on the crank and bends it, making the pistons and rods behave as if they're heavier than they really are, due to dynamic inertial effects.

To the crank, the pistons feel heavier, so if you have a rotating assembly that calls for a bobweight of 1,800 grams, a motor may run more smoothly if you overbalance the crank by 2 percent. This compensates for the inertial loads the crank endures at high RPM by balancing the rotating assembly to a bobweight of 1,836 grams instead of 1,800 grams. Although the balancer indicates that the crank isn't balanced, the bearings actually look better when you tear the motor down.

On a 6,500-rpm street motor, there's no need to overbalance. It's more for race engines that run 7,000 to 8,000 rpm all day. When in doubt, it's advisable to consult with your machinist to see if overbalancing is necessary.

Crankshaft Weight

Many hot rodders are under the impression that reducing crankshaft mass equates to an increase in horsepower. Although that can hold true in some instances, not all lightweight cranks are created equal, and few street/strip engines can actually benefit from them. The theory is that a lightweight crank has less rotating mass and is, therefore, easier to accelerate, which increases horsepower. However, the overall weight of a crankshaft is less important than how and where that weight is allocated throughout the crank.

Simple physics dictate that the farther weight is from the centerline of the crankshaft, the more difficult it is to turn. Consequently, removing weight from the centerline of a crank does nothing for performance. On the other hand, there are gains to be had by removing weight from the crank throws and counterweights, thereby reducing rotating mass, as long as it doesn't compromise the strength of the crank.

The effect is similar to running a lightweight flywheel. On a street car, you may notice slightly improved acceleration, but lightweight cranks aren't really intended for street cars, or drag cars, for that matter. In circle track and road race applications, where a motor is moving up and down the powerband over and over again and maximum acceleration on corner exits is important, a lightweight crank makes more sense. Of course, lighter cranks also decelerate more quickly, which in circle track application can unload the suspension too quickly when entering a corner.

Reduced rotating mass also relieves main bearing loads and puts less stress on the block. However, in drag applications, a lightweight crank probably won't determine the winner of the race, and the extra money it would cost to buy one is better spent on cylinder heads. Moreover, if a lightweight crank isn't matched with a lightweight rotating assembly, it could require adding heavy metal to the counterweights for proper balancing. So without careful planning, it's possible to spend lots of money on a lightweight crank, only to have to put weight back into it during the balancing process.

Dampeners

Four-stroke internal-combustion engines operate by converting the reciprocating motion of the pistons and connecting rods into rotating motion. This

In engine combos exceeding 600 hp, an aftermarket balancer is a wise investment. The ATI Super Damper is a favorite of many engine builders, and it is SFI-approved for competition use.

HOW TO BUILD BIG-INCH GM LS-SERIES ENGINES

CHAPTER 5

Sourcing Your Rotating Assembly

Most people who undertake the challenge of building a stroker motor aren't blessed with unlimited budgets, so looking for the best deals on parts is a necessity. When it comes to the rotating assembly, this often leads to tracking down the crankshaft, connecting rods, and pistons from different sources. Although there's nothing wrong with this approach, caution must be exercised to avoid potential parts incompatibility issues. For instance, most aftermarket crankshafts are advertised with a minimum recommended rod length. The reason is because a shorter connecting rod pulls the piston farther down the bore at BDC than a longer rod, which means that the piston can come into contact with the crankshaft counterweights. Furthermore, anytime the stroke or rod length is changed, the wrist pin must be moved higher up or lower down in the piston. Otherwise, the piston can be pushed beyond the deck of the block at TDC, or sit too far below the deck.

To help ensure all components in the rotating assembly are compatible, most crankshaft manufacturers–such as Eagle, Scat, Lunati, and Callies–offer complete stroker kits. These bundles typically include the crankshaft, rods, pistons, wrist pins, rings, and main and rod bearings. Some companies even offer balancing as an option. Stroker kits not only eliminate the parts incompatibility issues, they're also less expensive than purchasing each component individually. Gen III/IV rotating assemblies with forged crankshafts start at around $2,300.

process naturally sends vibrational pulses into the crankshaft every time each cylinder fires. At a certain RPM, these pulses start to resonate and can literally destroy the crankshaft. To prevent this from happening, all production engines come equipped with harmonic balancers attached to the crankshaft snout to dampen these vibrations. Stock balancers work just fine at stock horsepower levels, but as output and RPM increase, a more rugged unit is always a good idea. Interestingly, street motors are more susceptible to uncontrolled resonant harmonics, because they spend more time at a sustained RPM. By comparison, drag and road race engines that are constantly moving up and down the RPM range are less vulnerable.

Stock GM harmonic balancers are of an elastomeric design that sandwiches vulcanized rubber between a pair of rings. Car and truck LS variants use different balancers, but these units have proven to be extremely durable and effective up to 600 hp. There really is no definitive point at which an aftermarket harmonic balancer is necessary, but they do offer a greater degree of dampening ability in high-horsepower applications. Some aftermarket units are filled with viscous fluids, and others are similar in principle to GM's elastomeric design. Because the centrifugal force a dampener must endure increases significantly as engine speed rises, there is a risk that a stock balancer can self-destruct at high RPM. For safety concerns, many sanctioning bodies require SFI-approved aftermarket balancers in certain racing classes.

Manufacturer Choices

With the basics of crankshaft design covered, it's time to take a closer look at the specific cranks offered by the aftermarket. Although it's impossible to list every LS crankshaft on the market, here's a breakdown of the most popular stroker cranks. Whether it's due to durability, overall value, or reputation, many LS enthusiasts rely on these cranks for stroker builds.

Callies Crankshafts

For more than two decades, Callies crankshafts have been synonymous with bulletproof performance. Today, the company offers premium domestic cranks under its Callies brand and more affordably priced off-shore cranks under its Compstar banner. For Gen III/IV applications, Callies' entry-level Dragonslayer cranks are offered in 3.625- and 4.000-inch strokes. Made of forged 4340 steel, these feature drilled main and rod journals, nitrided wear surfaces, and have roundness and taper tolerances held within .0003 inch. While Callies doesn't publish an official maximum horsepower rating for its Dragonslayer crankshafts, they have proven reliable in 1,800-hp drag cars.

Moving up the ladder, Callies Magnum and Magnum XL cranks offer many of the same features of the Dragonslayer lineup, but in a lightweight package. They're available in strokes up to 4.600 inches and have a unique counterweight design that spreads balance forces evenly throughout the entire length of the crank for improved bearing life. For LS7 and LS9 engines, Magnum cranks are available with longer snouts to maintain compatibility with the factory dry sump oil drive system. A 4.000-inch Magnum crank weighs 47 pounds, and Magnum XL cranks can weigh as little as 36 pounds. For the ultimate in strength and customizability, Callies also offers Ultra Billet cranks. Made from Timken steel, they can be tailored to just about any configuration imaginable.

Designed for sportsman racers, Compstar cranks are forged overseas and imported to the United States, where Callies performs the finishing machine work in-house. Forged from 4340 steel, Compstar cranks feature profiled counterweights, drilled rod journals, and nitrided wear surfaces. They're available in strokes up to 4.250 inches and in both 2.100- and 2.000-inch rod journal diameters. Compstar's Sportsman label can be a bit misleading, as these cranks routinely handle in excess of 900 hp.

Eagle

Ever since overseas crankshafts started hitting the hot rodding scene in the late 1990s, Eagle has established itself as one of the market leaders. Much of that has to do with the quality and diversity of products the company offers. As is common in the industry, Eagle sources its forgings from overseas, and then performs the final machine work at its Mississippi facility. For the LS-series small-block, Eagle's catalog is packed with 4340 steel non-twist forgings in 3.622-, 4.000-, 4.100-, 4.125-, 4.250-, and 4.375-inch stroke lengths. Rated at an impressive 1,500 hp, Eagle cranks are shot-peened and nitrided, and they also boast micro-polished wear surfaces. To simplify the stroking process, Eagle bundles together its cranks and rods with pistons and bearings from leading manufacturers to offer turnkey rotating assemblies.

Lunati

Lunati's LS-series crankshafts are 100 percent made in the United States. The company's Pro Series crankshafts are some of the highest quality forgings on the market, and they come in 3.622-, 4.000-, 4.125-, 4.185-, 4.250-, 4.500-, and 4.600-inch sizes. They're constructed from 4340 aircraft-grade steel to ensure optimal levels of cleanliness and purity. Journal roundness is kept within .0001 inch, and Lunati cranks feature lightening holes drilled into the rod journals. Other highlights include contoured counterweights and polished-and-induction-hardened bearing surfaces. According to Lunati, the Pro Series cranks easily endure 1,500 hp of punishment.

Manley

Although best known for high-quality valvetrain components, Manley also offers a line of crankshafts for Gen III/IV small-blocks. These 4340 steel forgings come in two stroke lengths, 4.000 and 4.100 inches. All Manley cranks are shoot-peened and stress-relieved with profiled counterweights and polished-and-drilled journals. They're available in lightweight and super-lightweight designs, which weigh 50 and 46 pounds, respectively. Manley cranks are slightly less expensive than competing designs, making them a great value.

Scat

During the development phase of the LS-series small-block, GM turned to Scat to manufacture the cranks and rods in its prototype engines. Scat was one of the first companies to release aftermarket LS crankshafts. Today, Scat offers high-quality forged 4340 steel crankshafts in 4.000-, 4.125-, and 4.250-inch strokes. Scat's entry-level standard-weight cranks boast profiled counterweights, straight-shot oiling holes, large-radius journal fillets, lightening holes, and nitrided bearing surfaces. The mid-level Pro Comp cranks feature aero-wing counterweights for reduced mass and windage. The top-of-the-line Superlight cranks add pendulum undercuts on the inner face of the counterweights to further reduce mass without sacrificing strength. For most street/strip applications, Scat's standard-weight cranks provide the best value and can handle more than 1,000 hp. The company can also custom-build billet cranks in any configuration imaginable, but be prepared to spend more than $3,000.

Crankshaft end play should be set at .005 to .008 inch because too much fore-and-aft crank movement can prematurely wear out the bearings. Since the thrust bearing is located on the number-3 main cap, end play is measured with the center cap torqued down.

CHAPTER 6

Connecting Rods

Few components in an engine are as underappreciated as the connecting rods. While they're not much to look at, connecting rods attach the pistons to the crankshaft, and they are, therefore, burdened with the responsibility of converting the reciprocating motion of the pistons into rotating motion at the crankshaft. As such, the connecting rods are some of the most highly stressed components in an engine, and the loads placed upon them increase dramatically as cylinder pressure, RPM, and horsepower increase. In extreme racing applications, the loads on a rod can exceed 12,000 pounds as the piston is pulled back down the bore from TDC. Potential rod failure isn't something to take lightly, because a rod that cracks in half can catapult past the block deck and destroy a piston, taking the cylinder head along with it. In other words, it pays to make sure that the connecting rods you select for your stroker project are up to the task of handling the abuse you plan on throwing at them.

As with crankshafts, the past 15 years have produced an influx of affordable aftermarket connecting rods. Consequently, enthusiasts have more choices than ever, and it's no longer cost-prohibitive to step to some aftermarket forgings. Quality aftermarket rods are now so affordable, in fact, that tried-and-true practices, such as shot-peening and reconditioning stock connecting rods, are a thing of the past. Rugged 5140 forged steel aftermarket rods can be had for under $300, and $600 buys a set of H-beams that will handle up to 1,400 hp. Connecting rods come in a variety of shapes and sizes, and they are made from several different materials, so it pays to study before laying down cash on a set of rods for your stroker project.

Stock Rods

Factory Gen III/IV connecting rods incorporate a very durable design that has proven to be reliable up to 500 hp. They're built from powdered metal, a process that involves packing powdered steel into a mold, heating it, and then forging it into the shape of a rod. A parting line is then machined onto the big end of the rod before cracking off the cap. The result is a cap that fits perfectly into the grooves of the rod when bolted

Except for the LS7 and LS9, all stock LS motors rolled out of the factory with powdered metal rods. Although they're capable of standing up to 500 hp, the stock rod bolts become marginal at 6,500 rpm. The cost of new rod bolts, resizing the big end, and press-fitting the rod back onto the piston is just as much as an entry-level forged I-beam rod, so stock connecting rods are destined for the scrap heap most of the time.

CONNECTING RODS

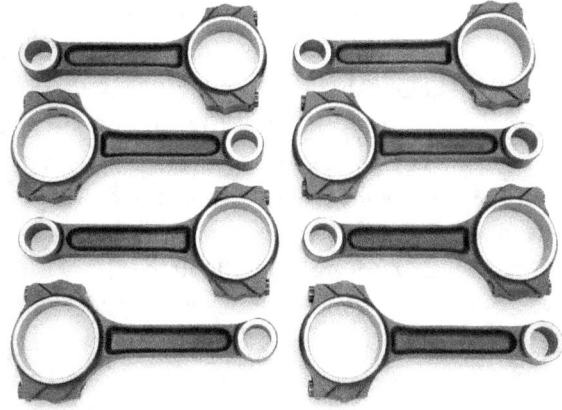

GM didn't cut any corners when developing the LS7, and it fitted the engine with titanium connecting rods. At just 434 grams each, their low mass is essential for reducing rotating weight at the LS7's 7,000-rpm peak engine speed. (© GM Corp.)

down. Stock LS rods are actually stronger than the coveted "pink" rods used in select Gen I small-blocks.

GM manufactured LS connecting rods in three different lengths. Rod length is measured from the center of the big-end bore to the center of the small-end bore. The vast majority of Gen III/IV small-blocks—including 5.3L, 5.7L, 6.0L, and 6.2L car and truck motors—utilize 6.098-inch rods. Of these, most feature press-fit piston wrist pins. The exceptions are the rods used in 6.0L Vortec truck motors, which have floating pins and a slightly thicker beam. With the launch of the Gen IV small-block in 2005, GM began phasing in rods with bushed small-ends in order to support full-floating wrist pins. Otherwise, all 6.098-inch factory LS rods are very similar.

To minimize production costs, GM also manufactures a longer 6.275-inch rod for 4.8L Vortec truck motors. Because these smaller engines are equipped with a shorter 3.267-inch stroke, a longer rod allows GM to use the same piston casting for the 4.8L as for the 5.3L. One of the latest iterations of factory GM rods is also the most extreme. To keep reciprocating mass to a minimum, GM developed a brand-new 6.067-inch titanium connecting rod for the LS7. These ultra-lightweight rods tip the scale at just 464 grams, about 30 percent lighter than stock powdered-metal rods, which is part of the reason why the LS7 revs freely to 7,000 rpm. At more than $400 for each rod, however, the LS7 forgings are extremely expensive for anyone considering bolting them to a stroker motor.

Because stock connecting rods are adequate to the 500-hp mark, they are a viable option for a budget-oriented stroker build. However, the factory rod bolts become marginal once engine speeds approach 6,500 rpm. This is because every time the piston is pulled back down the bore after it reaches TDC, tremendous loads are placed upon the rod bolts. In fact, rod bolts are subjected to the greatest amount of stress in the entire engine. Consequently, in any performance application where the stock rods are re-used, the bolts must be replaced with quality replacements from a company, such as ARP. Doing so requires machining the inside housing diameter of the big end of the rods, because new fasteners may change their shape.

The biggest drawback to re-using stock connecting rods is labor costs for

For most hot rodders, aftermarket forged steel rods offer the best balance of strength and cost. As with crankshafts, 4340 steel has become the standard for aftermarket rod forgings. Due to the minor difference in price between 4340 steel and weaker alloys, such as 5140 and 4130, these lesser materials are rarely used anymore. These 4340 H-beam rods from Scat feature a lightening hole right above the big end housing to reduce mass.

Due to the increase in power and cylinder pressure that results from strapping a supercharger onto the LS9, GM had to raise the rod bar once again. Compared to the LS7 rods, the LS9 rods are also built from titanium, but their beams are larger near the big end. Unlike earlier LS rods, the LS9 units attach to the pistons with floating wrist pins that are secured by lock rings. Dowels help locate the rod caps, which is a feature usually exclusive to aftermarket rods. An interesting side note is that the LS9 rods are built by Austria-based Pankl, a leading supplier of Formula One engine components. (© GM Corp.)

CHAPTER 6

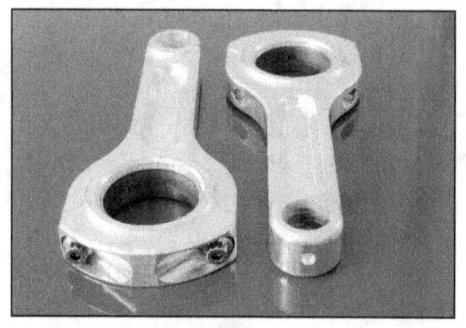

The only benefit aluminum rods have over steel rods is a weight reduction of 25 percent. Although that's rather significant, it comes at the price of substantially reduced tensile strength and fatigue life. Not surprisingly, they're rarely used in street motors and are best suited for drag race engines.

resizing; they can come close to the price of new aftermarket forgings. Re-sizing a set of eight connecting rods costs about $80. Most stock LS rods must be press-fit onto the pistons, which racks up another $80 in labor. Throw in the $100 that quality rod bolts will set you back, and the total cost to recondition a stock rod is almost enough to buy a set of forged I-beam aftermarket rods.

Forging Materials

Thanks to the efficiency and low cost with which aftermarket connecting rods can be manufactured in today's market, cast rods are virtually nonexistent. As with crankshafts, forged steel alloys are most common, and extremely exotic and expensive materials, such as titanium and aluminum, are also available. There are tradeoffs in strength, weight, and cost with each, so it's important to know the difference between each material in order to select a rod that's both durable and affordable.

The three most popular grades of steel used to manufacture aftermarket connecting rods—in ascending order of strength—are 5140, 4130, and 4340 alloys. Just as with crankshafts, higher-grade alloys offer advantages in tensile strength and ductility. This is due to their higher concentration of carbon, nickel, and chrome content. Typically, entry-level aftermarket rods are forged from 5140 or 4130 steel, and pricier high-end rods are built from a premium 4340 alloy. After the forging process, aftermarket rods are heat-treated, shot-peened, and stress-relieved to further enhance durability. They're also fitted with rod bolts or cap screws that offer up to 280,000 psi of tensile strength.

For mild street applications up to 600 hp, 5140 and 4130 steel rods are sufficient, but 4340 rods are advisable at anything beyond that point. With the increasing affordability of 4340 steel, however, 5140 and 4130 alloys are becoming less prevalent, even in entry-level rods. Interestingly, the number of entry-level connecting rods in the $300 range on the LS market is extremely limited compared to their higher-end alternatives, with Scat and Eagle being the primary players this arena. This is probably due to the fact that the factory Gen III/IV rods are very strong, and most performance LS stroker builds can easily approach or exceed the 600-hp mark where premium rods are a necessity. Not surprisingly, Scat and Eagle sell more of their premium-grade rods than their entry-level rods.

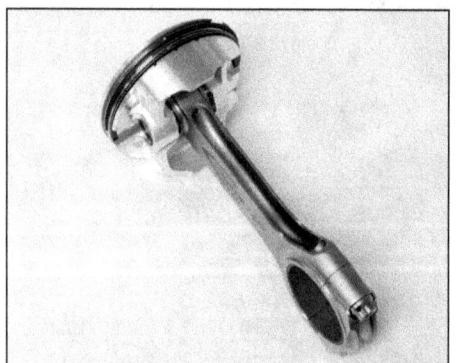

Unlike stock-style rods that are held together with bolts and separate nuts, most aftermarket rods employ cap screws that thread directly into the rods themselves. This means that no part of the rod protrudes into the shoulder, which improves rod bolt clearance around the camshaft. Aftermarket cap screws and bolts are available in tensile strength ratings ranging from 190,000 to 280,000 psi.

The majority of aftermarket rods are H-beams (bottom), which have led many people to assume that they are stronger than comparable I-beams (top). However, this isn't always the case, as companies, such as Oliver, offer some of the most durable rods around and use an I-beam design exclusively. Lunati offers these premium 6.125-inch I-beams, which are just as strong as its H-beams and 60 grams lighter.

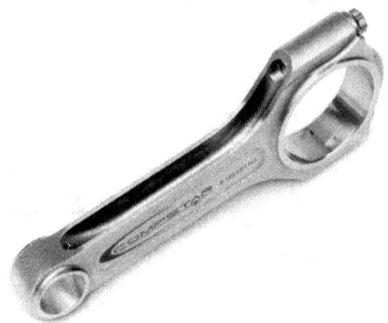

Blurring the line between H- and I-beam rods, Compstar now offers hybrid H/I-beam rods that incorporate elements of both designs. They feature triangulated big and small ends that increase beam thickness by 25 percent with only a 6-percent weight penalty. Compstar recommends using its H/I-beam rods in applications exceeding 1,000 hp.

Rotating vs. Reciprocating Weight

The crankshaft, connecting rods, and pistons are collectively referred to as either the rotating assembly or the reciprocating assembly. Both terms are correct, because the pistons and rods move up and down the bores—or reciprocate—and the crankshaft rotates inside the mains. As pointed out in Chapter 5, the benefits of reducing the rotating weight of a crankshaft are questionable on a street motor. That's because it's only effective if that mass is removed from locations that are an appreciable distance from the crankshaft centerline. On the other hand, efforts to reduce reciprocating mass are far more effective, because the pistons and rods are accelerated and decelerated in rapid succession as they traverse from TDC to BDC and back up to TDC. This constant changing of directions places tremendous tensile loads on the pistons and rods, so removing just a small amount of weight from the reciprocating parts can dramatically improve component longevity.

Some engine builders say that removing 1 ounce, or 28 grams, of weight from the rods and pistons is more beneficial than removing 1 pound of rotating weight from the crankshaft.

It's best to prioritize weight reduction of the pistons over using lighter connecting rods. If lightweight rods are combined with relatively heavy pistons, the inertia of the pistons will impart significant stress on the rods. A much better combination would be matching heavier rods with lighter pistons. For instance, if the choice is between running a 500-gram rod with a 550-gram piston, or a 550-gram rod with a 500-gram piston, the latter option puts less stress on the rods, even though both piston/rod combos weigh 1,050 grams.

Two of the more exotic materials used to manufacture connecting rods are aluminum and titanium. Available from aftermarket companies, such as GRP and Howards Cams & Racing Components, and popular in racing applications where low mass takes precedence over ultimate strength and long-term durability, aluminum rods can be forged or cut from blocks of billet. Because they weigh 25 percent less than a steel forging, aluminum rods reduce reciprocating mass, and, therefore, improve power output. However, they only offer half the tensile strength of steel, and they have a much shorter fatigue life. That means that as aluminum rods accumulate mileage and are subjected to repeated heat cycles, they tend to stretch, harden, and weaken over time. Additionally, aluminum rods must be made bulkier than their steel counterparts to compensate for their lower tensile strength. Consequently, they are unsuitable for street motors, and they must frequently be checked for stretching in race motors. According to some rod manufacturers, the fatigue life of an aluminum rod is 90 percent lower than that of a steel rod. For these reasons, aluminum rods are most frequently used in high-dollar drag race engines that are rebuilt multiple times per season.

Striking a balance between steel and aluminum is titanium, which offers the highest strength-to-weight ratio of all materials used to build connecting rods. The most commonly used material for automotive applications is 6AL-4V titanium, an alloy that contains 6 percent aluminum and 4 percent vanadium for improved machinability. Although titanium's tensile strength is 15 percent lower than that of steel, it's 30 percent lighter. As a result, titanium rods are often used in applications that operate at extremely high RPM, such as 9,500-rpm NASCAR Sprint Cup motors, 18,000-rpm Formula One engines, and even 7,000-rpm LS7s. Offered by aftermarket companies, such as Crower and Cunningham, the biggest drawback of titanium rods is price. A set of eight titanium rods usually costs twice as much as a set of comparable steel rods. Furthermore, despite their extra weight, steel rods are more than up to the task of enduring sustained engine speeds above 8,000 rpm.

Although the term "billet" doesn't refer to any specific material and can more accurately be described as a manufacturing process, billet is worth discussing to determine where it falls in the

Carrillo is known for making some of the most durable H-beam rods on the market, but the company also offers A-beam rods. They look similar to I-beam rods, but with more beam material around the big end. The company recommends using them in moderate-load applications.

CHAPTER 6

hierarchy of connecting rods. A billet rod starts out as a single ingot of forged steel, aluminum, or titanium and is machined into the final shape of the rod. The primary advantage of this manufacturing technique is customizability. Because they don't rely on very expensive forging dies and presses to pound them into shape, billet rods can be manufactured in custom lengths much more easily. With a forging, building a custom-length rod requires building a new set of dies, which is cost-prohibitive. Billet steel rods are machined from a purer, more highly refined alloy than most forgings. Additionally, they feature a longitudinal grain flow with excellent molecular bonding properties for enhanced strength. Although billet steel rods aren't as strong around the big end as forged steel rods, due to the absence of a circular grain flow, they're much more resistant to the formation of surface cracks. Overall, billet steel rods are stronger than forgings, but also cost twice as much.

Like all fasteners, rod bolts distort as they are tightened. Unlike most fasteners, if a single rod bolt fails, it can destroy an entire engine. Consequently, simply torquing down a rod bolt to spec won't suffice, because the friction of the bolt rubbing against the rod cap will make torque measurements inaccurate. A far more precise method of making sure the rod bolt is properly torqued is to measure bolt stretch. Bolt manufacturers, such as ARP, publish target stretch figures with all of their rod bolts. Attaching a stretch gauge to the bolt and slowly tightening the bolt until the target stretch is achieved ensures optimal bolt performance.

Rod Shape

The shape of a connecting rod is just as important as the material it's made from. Like most factory rods, Gen III/IV small-block units utilize an I-beam design; aftermarket rods are shaped into both I-beams and H-beams. Making a blanket statement as to which design is stronger wouldn't be accurate, as each offers distinct advantages. Most rod manufacturers agree that I-beams are lighter and stronger in compression, because they distribute stress more evenly throughout the rod. Conversely, H-beam rods are heavier and can withstand greater tensile loads, due to their bulkier design. In theory, these attributes would indicate that I-beams are better suited for forced-induction and nitrous applications, and that H-beams are more durable in high-RPM race motors. In practice, however, this isn't the case.

Most companies that sell connecting rods manufactured overseas market their I-beams as entry-level offerings and their H-beams as premium offerings rated at higher horsepower limits. As a result, many hot rodders have concluded that H-beam rods are a stronger overall design. However, this isn't always the case, as manufacturers, such as Manley and Lunati, have recently introduced heavy-duty I-beam rods that are rated at a higher horsepower level than their own H-beam rods.

For instance, Manley rates its standard-weight 4340 steel H-beam rods at 800 hp and 8,000 rpm and its standard-weight Pro Series I-beam rods at 850 hp and 8,500 rpm. Furthermore, companies, such as Oliver, have been manufacturing some of the highest-quality and most durable connecting rods for decades. They're used in the most demanding racing applications, including everything from circle track cars to monster trucks to

Many production engines, including early LS small-blocks, use wrist pins that are press-fit onto the small end of the rods. The problem with this arrangement is that if the pin ever seizes up in the piston, it will impede the rod's ability to pivot and snap it in half. Most aftermarket rods have a bushed small-end bore that can accommodate a full-floating pin. The bushing acts as a bearing, allowing the rod to float around the wrist pin on a thin film of oil. Floating pins must be secured inside the pistons with lock rings.

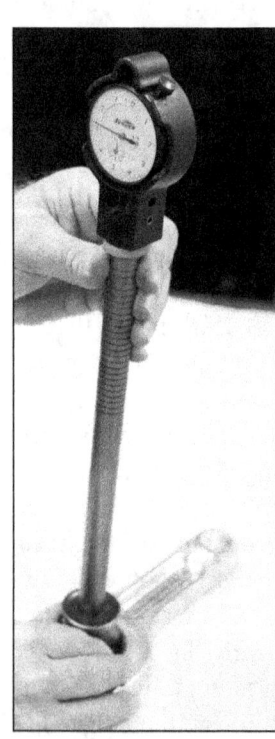

When measuring rod bearing clearance, the caps must first be torqued down in a vise. Next, the dial bore indicator must be positioned on the vertical surfaces of the big end housing. The reason for this is because the bearings have a slight horizontal taper.

HOW TO BUILD BIG-INCH GM LS-SERIES ENGINES

sprint cars. Interestingly, Oliver utilizes an I-beam design exclusively in all of its rods. Consequently, both I-beam and H-beam rods can be designed to handle serious abuse, and generalizing as to which is stronger is futile.

Although "I-beam" and "H-beam" refer to the general design of a rod, that doesn't mean that all H-beams and I-beams are shaped the same. Some offer more clearance than others. Due to the tight clearance between the rods and camshaft in stroker motors, most aftermarket connecting rods have profiled shoulders to buy some extra space. Likewise, the rod bolts can also compromise clearance. As a piston approaches TDC, the top of the rod bolt nears the cam, and as a piston approaches BDC, the bottom of the rod bolt nears the crankcase and oil pan. To combat this problem, aftermarket rods are often fitted with low-profile bolts. Some companies take it one step further by using cap screws in lieu of bolts, which thread directly into the big end of the rod instead of relying on a separate nut.

Regardless of the particular style of fastener that is used, aftermarket rods come equipped with heavy-duty bolts or cap screws. ARP offers 8740 chromoly fasteners rated at 220,000 psi of tensile strength, and some rod manufacturers offer their own proprietary fasteners rated at up to 280,000 psi. Considering that they're the most highly stressed fastener in an entire engine, quality rod bolts are cheap insurance.

Rod Length

In stroker builds utilizing a standard-deck block, 6.100-, 6.125-, 6.200-, and 6.250-inch rods are most common. Longer 6.460- and 6.560-inch rods are used more frequently in tall-deck motors with longer strokes. Like those in the Gen I small-block, LS crankshafts incorporate 2.100-inch rod journals. This means that Gen I and Gen III/IV connecting rods are interchangeable, because they share the same big-end housing diameter. One important difference is that Gen I rods have a smaller .927-inch small-end bore than the .945-inch bore on rods used in stock LS motors. Consequently, using Gen I rods in a Gen III/IV motor requires matching them with pistons that have a smaller .927-inch small-end diameter. Although most aftermarket LS rods are built with the smaller Gen I small-end, some are offered in a .945-inch housing bore to make them compatible with pistons that use stock-size LS wrist pins.

One of the most controversial topics in engine building is the supposed benefits of maximizing connecting rod length. Most people tend to overgeneralize this issue, and legions of hot rodders firmly believe that using a longer connecting rod yields dividends in horsepower over a shorter rod. An entire chapter can be written on this topic alone, but suffice it to say that the benefits of using a longer connecting rod over a shorter rod are two-fold.

Proponents contend that a longer connecting rod increases high-RPM horsepower, because it forces the piston to move more slowly away from TDC during the power stroke. In theory, this allows for a greater buildup of cylinder pressure and increases power. Longer rods also reduce the angle of the connecting rods in relation to the pistons. This relieves side loading and friction from the piston skirts, which is said to improve both durability and horsepower. Unfortunately, very few engine builders and hot rodders have gone through the painstaking efforts necessary to test this theory. Interestingly, those who have—including GM engineers and the Pro Stock engine builders at Reher-Morrison—aren't convinced that longer connecting rods provide any performance benefits at all.

A more accurate way to compare connecting rod length between different engine combinations is by looking at their rod-to-stroke ratios. For example, most LS small-blocks that have a 3.622-inch stroke use a 6.098-inch connecting rod, and this equates to a rod-to-stroke ratio of 1.68:1. From a mathematical standpoint, a couple thousandths of an inch of rod length doesn't impact the ratio much at all. In an exhaustive series of dyno tests that Reher-Morrison performed on NASCAR engines for GM, the shop varied the rod-to-stroke ratio from 1.48 to 1.85:1. In the test, mean piston speeds were in the 4,500- to

Although maximizing rod length is a topic of much debate, many of the top engine builders in the country assert that it isn't something to lose sleep over. Extensive dyno testing by NHRA Pro Stock teams has proven that a higher rod-to-stroke ratio makes no difference in power output. Any ratio of 1.55:1 and 1.85:1 works well in most street engines.

After going through the effort of setting the rod bearing clearance, it's easy to overlook checking the rod side clearance. The distance between the sides of the rods should be checked with a feeler gauge and measure .010 to .012 inch. To a certain degree, this controls how much oil drains back into the crankcase.

CHAPTER 6

Compressive vs. Tensile Loads

As engines burn fuel and turn RPM, they subject the rotating assembly to both compressive and tensile loads. As the term implies, whenever an object is squeezed, the load is compressive. In a four-stroke engine, when the air/fuel mixture ignites during the power stroke and pushes the piston down the bore, both the piston and rod are compressed. Likewise, loads are also compressive after the piston reaches BDC, and it is then pushed back up the bore. In contrast, tensile loads try to stretch an object apart. Tensile loads are most severe as an engine transitions between the exhaust and intake strokes, and rods take the brunt of the abuse. Right before the piston is pulled back down the bore following the compression stroke, the force of compression and combustion cushion the tensile loads. However, as an engine transitions between the exhaust and intake strokes, there is no combustion pressure to offset the upward inertia of the pistons. During this period, tremendous stress is placed upon the rod, rod cap, and rod bolts as tensile loads try to stretch them part.

Considering that the amount of compressive loads on a rotating assembly actually exceeds the amount of tensile load, this might not seem like a big deal. Nothing could be further from the truth, however, as objects are far weaker when stretched than they are when compressed. This applies to cookie dough and bridge supports, as well as connecting rods. The real kicker is that tensile loads increase exponentially with RPM. So at 6,000 rpm, the tensile loads placed on the connecting rods are four times greater than at 3,000 rpm. Hence, it's just one more reason why building a big-cube engine that needn't turn high RPM is a more reliable combination in the long run.

4,800-fps range, and painstaking measures were taken to minimize variables. The result was zero difference in average power and no difference in the shape of the horsepower curves. According to Reher-Morrison, one could have laid the curves over each other without being able to distinguish the difference between the different rod-to-stroke ratios on paper.

Although the effects of varying rod-to-stroke ratios might not always be evident on the dyno, there are some pitfalls of going above and below a certain point. At anything below a 1.55:1 ratio, rod angularity is extreme enough that it increases the side loading of the piston by a noticeable margin, increases piston rock, and increases skirt load. Although this doesn't necessarily change the actual power an engine makes, it does accelerate wear. Conversely, above a 1.80:1- or 1.85:1 ratio, there's so little piston movement at TDC that it hurts the ability of the pistons to draw in air on the intake stroke. Compensating for this requires advancing the cam, or decreasing the cross-sectional area of the cylinder head ports or intake manifold to increase air velocity. When it comes to rod length, the biggest mistake a hot rodder can make is compromising an entire engine combination by trying to achieve a target rod-to-stroke ratio. Consequently, according to Reher-Morrison, from a performance standpoint, connecting rods are nothing more than pieces of metal that connect the pistons to the crankshaft. It's as simple as that.

Manufacturer Choices

Trying to distinguish one manufacturer's connecting rods from another based on looks alone can be difficult. To help you sift through the dozens of aftermarket rods available, here are some of the most well-known LS rods on the market for both street and strip applications. With such a broad selection of quality aftermarket rods now available, reconditioning stock rods is a thing of the past.

Callies

As with its premium crankshafts, Callies' Ultra connecting rods are 100 percent American made. Forged from a proprietary 4340 Timken steel alloy, the units are premium rods with a premium price of roughly $1,300 per set. That investment buys hardware replete with innovative design features capable of withstanding more than 1,000 hp. The Ultra rods have gussets around the cap screws to help fortify the big end of the rod. Profiled shoulders improve clearance in long-stroke engines, and the cap screws are rated at 260,000 psi. Additionally, the Ultra rods' I-beam design reduces mass over a comparable H-beam. Covering a wide range of stroke lengths and block deck heights, they're available in 6.100- to 6.560-inch lengths.

Compstar

Although Compstar was conceived as Callies' Sportsman line in 2004, the company puts tremendous effort into ensuring top-notch quality in its entry-level products. Forged overseas to keep costs down, Compstar rods start at $400, making them an excellent value. All Compstar rods are forged from 4340 steel, and they are offered in I-beam, H-beam, and H/I-beam configurations. Common features throughout the Compstar line include premium ARP 2000 rod bolts, chamfered and honed pin bushings, and stress-relieved surfaces. According to Compstar, its rods clear 4.000-inch-stroke cranks and cams with up to .660-inch lift without any modifications.

Compstar's most affordable rods are its I-beams, which can support 650 hp and cost less than $400 per set. They feature a fortified shoulder, a large parting line footprint, added material around the pin collar, a twin-rib cap, and ARP L19 cap screws. For engines that require a stronger rod, Compstar's H-beam rods come in lengths ranging from 6.100 to 6.560 inches. Officially, they have no published horsepower rating, but engine builders routinely push them past 850 hp without a problem. For forced-induction and nitrous motors producing more than 1,000 hp, Compstar offers a unique H/I-beam hybrid rod design in a 6.125-inch configuration. The added strength comes from a 25-percent-thicker beam and triangulated big-end and pin bores.

Eagle

As with its crankshafts, Eagle offers a diverse lineup of connecting rods to suit virtually all power levels and engine combinations. The entry-level SIR I-beam rods are forged from 5140 steel, and they can handle up to 700 hp. They come in 6.125-, 6.200-, and 6.250-inch sizes. At $300 for a set, they pack some serious value. For not much more money, Eagle's H-beam rods can handle much more horsepower. Equipped with standard rod bolts, Eagle H-beams are rated at 750 hp. Upgrading to ARP 2000 bolts increases that figure to 1,100, and stepping up to a set of ARP L19 bolts increases the horsepower rating to 1,400. Eagle's premium H-beams cost just $550, which explains why overseas rods have become so popular in recent years. As far as strength per dollar is concerned, Eagle rods are hard to beat.

Lunati

Lunati's connecting rods for LS-series small-blocks come in three different trim levels. Its entry-level H-beams are forged overseas from 4340 steel, and they are rated at 700 to 800 hp. The rods are finished in-house, and then they're heat-treated, shot-peened, and stress-relieved. They're offered in just one size, 6.125 inches, and sell for $630. For just $30 more, Lunati's Superlight H-beam rods have many of the same features as its standard-weight H-beams, but they are 75 grams lighter (680 vs. 605). The reduced reciprocating weight they offer makes them well suited for circle track and land-speed engines in which prolonged high-RPM operation is the norm. At the top of the Lunati totem pole are its Pro Series connecting rods. These I-beams are made in America from aerospace-grade 4340 steel. At $1,300, they're a bit on the pricey side, but the benefit is that they can handle well in excess of 1,000 hp. In fact, Lunati says that they'll handle just about anything you can throw at them. Available in 6.125- and 6.300-inch lengths, the Pro Series rods are an excellent choice for extreme power adder applications.

Manley

Throwing a monkey wrench into the I-beam-versus-H-beam debate, Manley positions its I-beams at the very bottom and top of its connecting rod lineup. Manley's Sportsmaster I-beam rods are forged overseas from 4340 steel and measure 6.100 inches in length. The rods are shot-peened, stress-relieved, and heat-treated. Additionally, the Sportsmaster rods are profiled around the main cap area to remove stress risers and reduce mass to just under 600 grams. They're rated at 550 hp and cost $650 per set.

Manley's mid-level 4340 H-beam rods are also forged overseas. They measure 6.125 inches and are available with ARP 8740 or ARP 2000 bolts, for power ratings of 725 and 775, respectively. Interestingly, they're priced cheaper than the Sportsmasters at $600.

At the top of the heap are Manley's Pro Series 4340 I-beam rods, which are manufactured in the United States. Priced at $1,500 a set, these 6.125-inch rods can handle more than 1,000 hp. In addition to brute strength, the Pro Series rods are very light at just 609 grams.

Scat

Like many aftermarket companies, Scat forges its rods overseas, and then it performs final machine work in the United States. To ensure quality control and exacting tolerances, Scat rods are machined with modern diamond tooling, and they are heat-treated using temperature-controlled cooling.

Scat's entry-level Pro Comp I-beam rods feature 4340 steel construction and are offered in 6.100- and 6.125-inch lengths. They're lightweight at roughly 600 grams, and they are available with ARP rod bolts or cap screws. Rated at 550 to 650 hp, they're best suited for mild naturally aspirated engine combinations, and they are budget priced at $325 per set.

Scat's premium Gen III/IV rod offering is its Pro Sport 4340 H-beams. Available in 6.100- and 6.125-inch lengths, Scat's H-beam rods are rated at 800-plus hp, making them ideal for forced-induction and nitrous motors. ARP 8740 cap screws come standard, and ARP 2000 fasteners are optional. With prices starting at $450, the Scat H-beams offer excellent durability for the money.

CHAPTER 7

PISTONS

The internal-combustion process is downright brutal, and the pistons are quite literally on the front lines of the battlefield. The nature of converting reciprocating energy into rotating force means that the four-stroke process tries to eject the pistons out of the block deck and blow them out through the oil pan in brutal succession. At 6,000 rpm, this melee goes down 100 times each second. Furthermore, advances in cylinder head and valvetrain technology allow modern engines to turn more RPM and pack more cylinder pressure than ever. To top it all off, forced induction and nitrous often intensify the beat-down, and the quality of pump gas has degraded in recent years with higher ethanol content and lower octane ratings. Given these formidable circumstances, it's truly amazing that piston failure is so rare these days.

Although something nicknamed "slugs" suggests that pistons are nothing more than archaic hunks of forged aluminum, the technology involved in their development is astonishing. There's far more to piston design than merely pounding an aluminum ingot into a cylindrical shape and calling it a day. Some of the design elements of a piston that hot rodders typically obsess over are insignificant, while other factors that most people aren't even aware of can be the difference between being a hero and blowing up. With the easy horsepower and high-RPM potential of the Gen III/IV small-block, selecting the right pistons is an important step in successfully designing any engine combination.

Factory Pistons

Like the stock crank and rods used in most LS engines, the factory pistons are adequate up to roughly 500 hp. They're cast from hypereutectic aluminum, meaning that they incorporate a high-silicon content of about 11 percent. Compared to a traditional cast-aluminum piston, hypereutectic pistons are stronger, more resistant to detonation, and have half the thermal expansion. This allows for tighter piston-to-wall clearance, as well as reduced blow-by and piston slap. The downside is that the higher silicon content makes them more brittle, and hypereutectic pistons are not nearly as strong as aftermarket forgings.

The LS9 is the only factory Gen III/IV engine that came equipped with forged pistons from the factory. Nevertheless, because larger-diameter pistons must be used anytime a block is overbored, the virtues and drawbacks of stock pistons are somewhat irrelevant in a stroker motor.

Alloys

For stroker builds where pinching every last penny is essential, companies, such as Keith Black, offer quality hypereutectic pistons for as little as $300. They're built from a stronger alloy than factory pistons and are subjected to a T6 heat-treating process that makes them 30

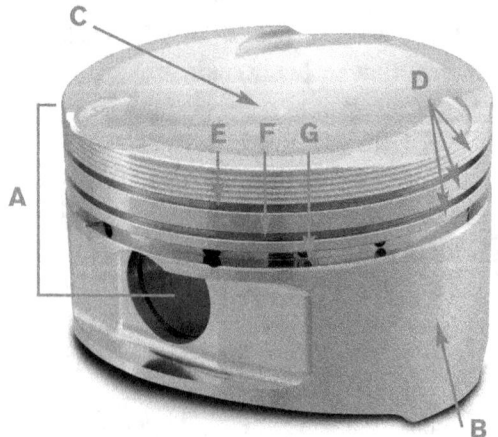

The critical areas of a piston include its compression height (A), skirt (B), crown (C), ring land (D), top ring groove (E), second ring groove (F), and oil ring groove (G).

percent stronger. Available in many popular bore sizes, these pistons work just fine in most naturally aspirated stroker buildups. That said, it makes little sense to invest in a forged crank and rods, only to top them off with a set of cast pistons. A more effective means of budgeting is to match a cast crank with forged pistons because the pistons are naturally exposed to more extreme abuse.

For the ultimate in durability, however, forged pistons are substantially stronger than their hypereutectic counterparts. At $600 to $800, forged pistons are at least twice as expensive as hypereutectic pieces, but they're well worth the premium in a high-performance stroker motor.

During the manufacturing process, they start out as hunks of aluminum that are compacted in a mold by a press. This eliminates porosity and forces the molecules of aluminum together, creating a denser and stronger material. Afterward, they're precisely machined into shape. A key benefit of the forging process is that it yields an extremely robust piston that's actually lighter than a casting. Because the overall structure of a forged piston is stronger, this allows removing material from the piston skirts to reduce mass.

Two of the most common alloys used in piston forgings are 2618 and 4032 aluminum, and many companies manufacture pistons from both materials. The main differences between the two are found in their material composition and thermal and fatigue characteristics. Pistons made from 4032 alloy have a silicon content of approximately 12 percent, and 2618 pistons have less than .2 percent. This means that the 2618 alloy expands approximately 15 percent more than the 4032 alloy when exposed to elevated temperatures. Some people prefer 4032 alloy for street-driven vehicles because the pistons require less cold clearance and reduce startup noise. Mechanically, both are very similar, with 2618 having higher strength at all temperatures.

When selecting the proper material for a piston, manufacturers factor in its strength at both the room temperature and operating temperature. According to its composition, 2618 outperforms 4032 by a large margin, as it's significantly stronger at temperatures of 500 degrees F and above. Because many racing engines operate above that temperature range, 2618 has the clear strength advantage for these applications. Consequently, 2618 is used extensively in Formula One and NASCAR, and 4032 is better suited for naturally aspirated street motors that don't see much track time.

Skirts

Piston skirt design is often a compromise between providing piston stability within the bore and reducing friction. In essence, the piston skirts allow the piston to perform its primary and secondary movements. The primary movement of a piston is when it traverses from TDC to BDC and back up to TDC again. Its secondary movement is the effect of the piston rocking in the bore. The rocking effect is caused by frictional and viscous drag, piston center of gravity location, constantly changing side loading, and changes in temperature.

To control skirt wear, reduce parasitic power losses, and improve ring seal, piston manufacturers must accurately predict the secondary motion of the pistons.

Despite the fact that it's equipped with a factory supercharger, the LSA comes equipped with hypereutectic pistons. This is made possible by efficient intercooling and advanced engine management software that can retard timing instantaneously, if necessary. Since 2003, GM has applied a polymer coating to LS piston skirts. This minimizes scuffing and tightens up piston-to-wall clearance for reduced piston slap on cold starts. (© GM Corp.)

Companies, such as Speed-Pro and Keith Black, offer economical hypereutectic pistons in a large variety of bore diameters. At about $300 for a set of eight, they're stronger than stock castings and work well in naturally aspirated street motors.

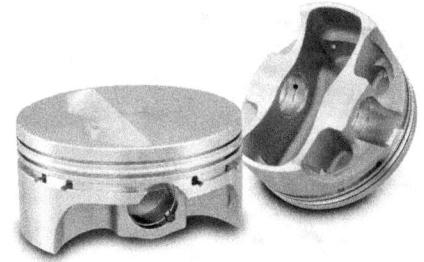

The two most commonly used alloys in aftermarket forged pistons are 2618 and 4032. Although 2618 is stronger at all temperatures, 4032 has a greater silicon content, which reduces its thermal expansion. This allows for a tighter fit inside the bore and reduced blow-by. These SRP 4032 pistons are a great choice for a naturally aspirated street motor that only sees occasional track use.

CHAPTER 7

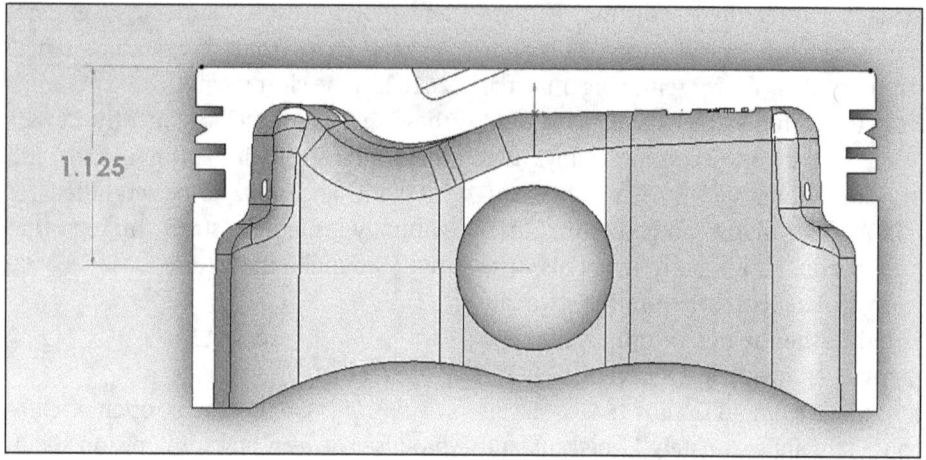

Compression height is defined as the distance between the wrist pin centerline and the top of the piston. This is arguably the most important dimension in the design of a piston, as it significantly impacts strength and durability. (Photo courtesy of JE Pistons)

Frictional losses associated with the piston skirt are substantially influenced by its width, length, and by how much of its surface area contacts the cylinder bore. As the contact area is decreased, viscous drag from the oil tends to fall, along with frictional forces. However, as the load-bearing area and viscosity decrease, so does the oil film thickness. If the film thickness approaches a critical point, it results in boundary lubrication and an increase in friction. Consequently, the contact area and the access of oil to that area need to be optimized. The two methods of reducing the contact area include reducing skirt length and changing the surface shape of the skirt. Reducing skirt length decreases friction, but it increases the secondary motion effects that impact ring seal. Changing the shape of the skirt is more effective, as the contact patch and secondary motion can be reduced.

Gas Porting

Aftermarket pistons continue to improve by the day, and gas porting is one of the latest innovations now offered by most manufacturers. However, gas-ported pistons are not always a good idea for street cars. Gas ports are small holes that feed cylinder pressure into the top ring groove. Their purpose is to allow pressure from behind the top ring to increase the sealing effect of the rings. Without gas ports, the top ring seals itself primarily from the pressure acting upon its top face.

Gas ports are usually needed in engines with high cylinder pressure or in conjunction with very narrow top rings. They can be vertical or lateral in design, each with its own benefits. Vertical gas ports are most popular in drag race applications where maximum pressure behind the top ring is desired; lateral gas ports provide slightly less pressure on the ring and are more desirable in endurance applications. Both styles of gas ports significantly reduce ring life and are not recommended for street use. In addition to gas ports, some piston manufacturers also offer gas distribution grooves. These small grooves intersect the entire upper half of the top ring groove and help evenly distribute pressure around the circumference of the top ring.

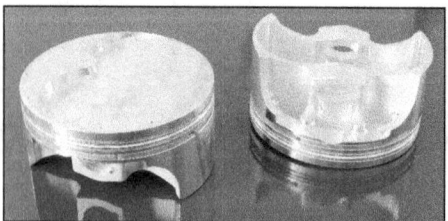

Piston skirt design is a balancing act between trying to minimize friction by reducing the surface area and trying to maintain enough surface area to stabilize the piston in the bore. Designed to survive in a 9,500-rpm drag motor, these custom Wiseco pistons feature scalloped skirts for reduced friction and mass.

In street motors that turn moderate RPM, wrist pin stiffness is often more important than low mass. For race applications where both stiffness and low mass are important, Precision Products offers these titanium pins that weigh a scant 84 grams. They're also coated in Casidiam for improved lubrication.

Lengthening either the stroke or the connecting rod requires moving the wrist pin higher in the piston. Otherwise, the piston gets pushed past the block deck at TDC. There is a limit to how much stroke and rod length will fit inside any given deck height because the compression height of the piston should never be reduced below 1.000 inch.

Wrist Pins

The job of keeping the connecting rods attached to the pistons falls on the wrist pins. They don't look like much, which makes it easy to overlook the important role they play in the overall piston equation. Although pistons transfer energy to the connecting rods, the wrist pins serve as the only link through which this transfer takes place.

The wrist pins see the loading that each piston puts upon its respective crankshaft big-end journal, which amounts to a combination of inertial forces and combustion pressure. The pin is loaded by both the rod and the piston in a complex combination of forces varying both in magnitude and direction. The loading on the pin promotes bending along its axis and also ovalization, and the combination of them can lead to frictional binding and twist. Consequently, pin stiffness is extremely important. Pin stiffness not only impacts the pin's ability to function as a journal, it also influences the stiffness of the entire piston-and-pin assembly. Increased pin stiffness can actually translate into a more stable ring platform, resulting in improved oil control and reduced blow-by.

Premium aftermarket pistons feature full-floating pins that can rotate and slide inside the wrist pin bore. On the other hand, the pins used in many stock LS pistons are interference fit in the small end. This requires heating of the small end each time the pin needs to be removed, which isn't very practical for a race engine that is frequently rebuilt. Additionally, press-fit pins are subjected to both load-bearing and bending forces. Conversely, with a floating pin, the fatigue cycles are more evenly spread around the outer surface fibers of the pin. If the pin is allowed to rotate, its velocity relative to the individual bearing surfaces will be lower. Rotation also has the effect of moving the oil around within the pin bores, reducing the possibility of dry spot formation.

Compression Height

Defined as the distance from the centerline of the wrist pin to the top of the piston crown, the compression height of a piston must be changed whenever the connecting rod length, crankshaft stroke, and the deck height of the block are changed. The reason for this is simple. As crankshaft stroke or rod length is increased, the wrist pin bore of the piston must be repositioned closer to the piston crown. Otherwise, the top of the piston will protrude through the top of the block at TDC. Likewise, whenever stroke or rod length is decreased, the wrist pin bore of the piston must be lowered to prevent the piston crown from sitting below the top of the block at TDC. To make things easier for engine builders, piston manufacturers usually publish the compression heights of their pistons, along with the stroke and rod lengths that they're compatible with. Calculating the piston compression height is as easy as subtracting the length of half of the stroke and the length of the rods from the block deck height:

$$\text{Compression Height} = \text{Deck Height} - (\text{Rod Length} + 1/2 \text{ Stroke})$$

Using this formula, a 402 stroker motor that uses a standard-deck 9.240-inch LS block, a 4.000-inch stroke, and 6.125-inch connecting rods would need pistons with a compression height of:

$$9.240 - (6.125 + 2) = 1.115 \text{ inches}$$

Decreasing compression height also decreases weight, alleviating stress on the rods at high RPM. For example, a JE forged LS piston with a 1.340-inch compression height weighs 434 grams, while a piston from the same family with a 1.050-inch compression height weighs 390 grams. Multiply that 44 grams of weight savings by eight pistons, and the reduction in reciprocating mass of 352 grams is significant. This is one advantage of using a longer connecting rod that can't be refuted. That said, reducing compression height too much compromises piston strength, so there is a practical limit to how much this critical dimension can be reduced.

Because the area of the piston above the wrist pin must accommodate all three piston rings, reducing compression height forces them closer together. As a result, the wrist pin bore actually

The crown of a flat-top piston isn't always flat. With long-duration camshafts and big valves, it's often necessary for piston manufacturers to cut valve reliefs into the top of the piston.

The D-shaped recess of an inverted-dome (left) piston features a flat quench pad that helps create turbulence inside the combustion chamber and homogenizes the air/fuel mixture. With a concave-dish (right) piston, this perk is entirely eliminated. (Photo courtesy of JE Pistons)

CHAPTER 7

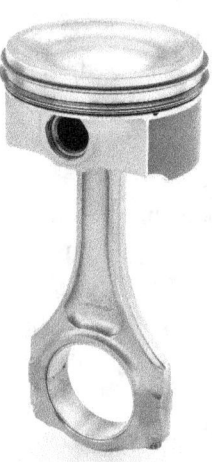

The increased cylinder pressure and turbulence created by forced induction negates the benefits of an inverted dome piston. Consequently, it's not surprising that GM opted for a concave dish design in the LS9. (© GM Corp.)

intersects the oil ring groove, which necessitates reinforcing it with a separate support rail. Such an arrangement has proven to be durable in both street and race motors, but the bigger problem at hand is that having too short of a compression height pushes the top ring closer to the piston crown. The closer the top ring is to the top of the piston, the more combustion heat it absorbs. Not only is that heat hard on the wrist pins, but it can also distort the top ring and compromise its sealing ability.

Flip through the catalog of any piston manufacturer, and it's extremely rare to find any off-the-shelf piston offered with less than a 1.000-inch compression height. That figure is generally accepted as the bare minimum. Thanks to advances in modern alloys and forging techniques, as long as a piston has at least a 1.000-inch compression height, it has the ability to provide acceptable oil control and cylinder seal. Even if you don't subscribe to the long-rod theory, the popularity of engine combinations that utilize long connecting rods has forced the aftermarket to maximize piston strength with a minimum of compression height.

Dishes and Domes

For the most part, the shape of the piston crown is determined by an engine's target compression ratio. Flat-top pistons are most prevalent, as the desired compression ratio can usually be achieved by manipulating head gasket thickness or combustion chamber volume. This isn't always possible, however, in which case the piston crowns can be dished or domed. When it comes to dished pistons, which are sometimes called inverted dome pistons, the terminology can be confusing. This generic phrase refers to a piston where a portion of the crown is recessed into a "D" shape and sits below the deck height at TDC. Dished pistons reduce the static compression ratio, so they're most commonly used in forced-induction applications. Likewise, increasing the size of the bore and stroke bumps up the compression ratio, so larger motors often require a dish to maintain a pump-gas-friendly compression ratio.

Some pistons feature a simple circular dish, as opposed to a D-shaped recess, which is referred to as a concave dish. The advantage of an inverted dome piston is that its D-shaped recess closely follows the contours of the combustion chambers in the cylinder heads. The contour of the crown helps create turbulence in the air/fuel mixture during the compression stroke. This improves mixture homogenization, making a motor more resistant to detonation. With a concave dish piston, this effect is greatly reduced.

However, concave dish pistons are widely used in many high-end race motors, including in NASCAR Sprint Cup, where they have posted gains of 3 to 5 hp over inverted dome pistons. The reason for this is because concave dish pistons are used in conjunction with very small combustion chambers.

Inverted domes aren't just for forced-induction engines. Simply increasing the bore and stroke of a motor—while leaving the piston compression height, deck clearance, and piston dish volume the same—can dramatically increase the static compression ratio. With a 4.200-inch bore and a 4.500-inch stroke, these -28-cc pistons still squeeze out 10.8:1 compression in a 500-ci LS2.

Domed pistons protrude past the block deck to increase the compression ratio. With the high static compression that's possible with today's big-bore, long-stroke, small-chamber stroker combos, domed pistons are reserved strictly for race-gas-burning competition engines.

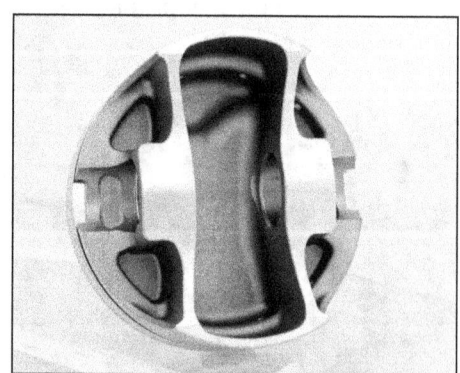

There's more to piston strength than just metallurgy. Pistons designed specifically for power adders feature thicker crowns and wrist pins and more structural stiffening to resist deflection. (Photo courtesy of JE Pistons)

PISTONS

With the infinite number of parts configurations that can be used to build an engine, there isn't an off-the-shelf piston for every combo. Fortunately, almost every piston manufacturer can build custom pistons to your exact specifications at a price that's not that much more expensive than a catalog item. (Photo courtesy of JE Pistons)

In essence, the dished portion of the piston's concave design functions as part of the combustion chamber itself, which positions the spark plug centrally inside the chamber and allows for more even flame travel. The combination of a smaller chamber and bigger dish is more thermally efficient and also reduces the amount of unburned fuel. Additionally, shorter flame paths generate higher combustion temperatures and increase fuel efficiency, which increases energy output and reduces emissions. Even so, concave dish pistons are very uncommon in street motors because their effectiveness is highly dependent upon the shape of the combustion chamber. Also, the thin center sections of a concave dish piston trap additional weight in the piston crowns. The combination of a small chamber and a large dish can also be employed with reverse-dome pistons.

At the other end of the spectrum, domed pistons—in which the piston crown protrudes into the combustion chamber at TDC—are used in engines where maximum compression is desirable. With the current trend favoring engine combinations with lots of cubic inches and small combustion chambers, very high static compression ratios can be achieved with flat-top pistons. For instance, a 408 stroker LS motor that features a 4.030-inch bore, a 4.000-inch stroke, .039-inch head gaskets, 66-cc combustion chambers, and flat-top pistons with -4-cc valve reliefs will yield an 11.7:1 compression ratio. Depending on camshaft selection, that's really pushing the limits of pump gas.

Consequently, the only reason to use a domed piston is in a race-gas application where the compression ratio approaches or exceeds 13.0:1, so they're even less of a necessity in bigger-inch motors. A tall-deck stroker build that uses a 4.200-inch bore, a 4.500-inch stroke, .039-inch head gaskets, 66-cc combustion chambers, and flat-top pistons with -4-cc valve reliefs will have a 13.89:1 compression ratio. A major drawback of domed pistons is that their piston crowns tend to interfere with flame front propagation during the power stroke.

Power Adder Pistons

There are far more naturally aspirated engine builds than forced-induction and nitrous-oxide combinations. Consequently, most off-the-shelf pistons are designed for naturally aspirated engines. Even though forged pistons are remarkably stout, power adder applications call

Piston crown coatings are proven performers. By reflecting heat, they enhance a piston's ability to resist detonation and high temperatures.

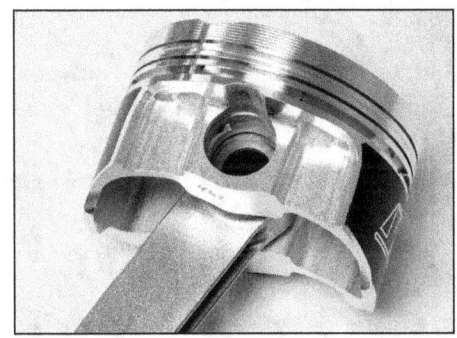

Wiseco pistons are very popular with LS enthusiasts due to their high strength and low weight. These heavy-duty nitrous pistons have a 1.115-inch compression height and weigh 462 grams.

Compression Ratio

Optimizing the static compression ratio of an engine is a critical step in maximizing the performance of any stroker combo. Although there is a point of diminishing returns, increasing the compression ratio generally improves horsepower output, fuel economy, and emissions. Compression ratio simply refers to how much the air/fuel mixture inside the cylinders is squeezed during the combustion process. For example, if the cylinder volume of an engine is 50 ci with the piston at BDC, and 5 ci when the piston is at TDC, it has compression ratio of 10.0:1.

Compared to old-school small-block Chevys with iron heads and carburetors, modern engines operate with much higher static compression ratios. Not long ago, a compression ratio of 9.5:1 was considered extreme for a pump-gas street/strip motor. These days, stock LS1s leave the factory with 10.0:1 compression, and LS7s push the envelope even further with 11.0:1 compression. In stroker LS combos with long-duration camshafts, compression ratios approaching 12.0:1 are common. Improvements in engine management controls and fuel distribution make this possible. Electronic fuel injection greatly enhances cylinder-to-cylinder fuel distribution and homogenization of the air/fuel mixture, while also offering precise control over ignition spark timing. Furthermore, knock sensors provide a safeguard against detonation and can momentarily retard spark timing, if necessary. The extensive use of aluminum cylinder heads in modern engines enables them to dissipate more heat compared to their iron forebears.

Aftermarket manufacturers publish the compression ratios their pistons will achieve, but these figures are merely approximate values that don't take the specific components used in an engine package into consideration. The only accurate way to determine the compression ratio of your parts combo is to calculate it yourself. By far, the easiest way to do so is by using one of the dozens of compression ratio calculators available online. However, it never hurts to learn how to do it the old-fashioned way using simple math, which will also help you understand how the various dimensions inside an engine affect the ratio itself. The first step in calculating compression is determining the piston-swept volume of a cylinder using this formula:

Cylinder Volume = Bore x Bore x Stroke x .7854

For this example, our subject is a 402-ci stroker combination with a 4.000-inch bore, a 4.000-inch stroke, 70-cc combustion chambers, .039-inch-thick head gaskets, and pistons with -4-cc valve reliefs. Using those figures, the 402 has a cylinder volume of:

4.000 x 4.000 x 4.000 x .7854 = 50.27 ci

To keep all measuring units uniform, the combustion chamber volume of the cylinder heads must be converted from cubic centimeters to cubic inches. This is accomplished by multiplying the combustion chamber volume, in cc, by .061:

Chamber Volume ci = Chamber cc x .061
70 x .061 = 4.27 ci

The next step is determining the volume of the head gaskets, which uses the same formula as the cylinder volume calculation, but substitutes gasket thickness in lieu of stroke length. Most head gasket openings are larger than the diameter of the cylinder bore, so the calculation below assumes a gasket bore of 4.060 inches.

Gasket Volume = Bore x Bore x Gasket Thickness x .7854
4.060 x 4.060 x .039 x .7854 = .50 ci

The final dimension that must be computed is the piston deck volume, which is the volume of space between the piston crown and the top of the block deck. If the block is zero decked, this step isn't necessary. However, for illustrative purposes, the formula below assumes a negative deck height of .005 inch. This formula is also just a slight variation of the piston volume formula:

Piston Deck Volume = Bore x Bore x Deck Height x .7854
4.000 x 4.000 x .005 x .7854 = .006 ci

The last figure that's needed is the volume of the valve reliefs or piston dish. Fortunately, piston manufacturers publish these figures in their catalogs. So, the only computing necessary is converting the volume of the valve reliefs from cubic centimeters to cubic inches.

$$4 \text{ cc} \times .061 = .244 \text{ ci}$$

Using all of the above calculations, the overall volume of a single cylinder can be determined:

Cylinder Volume at BDC =
Cylinder + Chamber + Gasket + Piston Deck + Piston Dish

$$50.27 + 4.27 + .50 + .006 + .244 = 55.29 \text{ ci}$$

Subtracting the piston-swept cylinder volume from the cylinder volume at BDC yields the cylinder volume at TDC:

$$55.29 - 50.27 = 5.02$$

Finally, dividing the volume of the cylinder at BDC by the volume of the cylinder at TDC reveals the static compression ratio of this engine:

Compression Ratio = 55.29 / 5.02 = 11.01:1

Granted, the static compression ratio is a helpful tool when planning a stroker build, but it's rather worthless unless you know how much compression you can squeeze into your engine combination before experiencing detonation. This isn't as easy as it appears, because the amount of compression an engine can handle is dependent upon fuel quality and camshaft dynamics. A much more useful figure in determining the maximum compression ratio for a given fuel type is dynamic compression. Unlike static compression ratio, dynamic compression takes camshaft dynamics, stroke, and rod length into account. Because understanding the concept of dynamic compression ratio requires an understanding of valvetrain dynamics, the formulas for how to calculate it is discussed in Chapter 10.

---

for extra-rugged pistons designed specifically for boost and nitrous. The major difference between a naturally aspirated engine and a nitrous or blower motor is cylinder pressure and operating temperatures, so it's important to design a piston accordingly. Higher pressures require pistons with thicker crowns and more structural stiffening. Additionally, the wrist pins must be thicker in diameter, and the rings require more tension, making them thicker and more durable. For moderate doses of boost and nitrous, a 4032 alloy is sufficient, but a 2618 alloy piston is a necessity in heavy-duty power adder combinations.

Custom Pistons

With the endless combinations of bore diameters, stroker cranks, rod lengths, block deck heights, cylinder heads, and power adders that can be integrated into an engine design, there are certain instances when the ideal piston isn't available as an off-the-shelf forging. Fortunately, piston manufacturers are more than happy to build custom pistons for your specific application for not much more money than off-the-shelf pistons.

The process of making a piston is highly automated, with CNC machines whittling raw forgings into the final shape of a piston. As such, a set of custom pistons might only set you back an extra $100, and in some cases, might cost the same as a catalog piston. Furthermore, some piston companies can turn around a set of custom slugs in one or two days. By comparison, custom cranks and rods are astronomically expensive, so it's far easier to design a piston around the rest of the rotating assembly and short-block than doing things the other way around.

Coatings

In recent years, engine builders began testing the virtues of applying coatings to various engine components,

Most aftermarket pistons utilize 1/16-inch first and second ring grooves and a 3/16-inch oil ring groove. This arrangement provides excellent cylinder seal.

including pistons. They're typically used on the piston crown and skirts to protect the aluminum from the rigors of internal combustion. Coating the piston crown with a thermal barrier helps maintain surface hardness and resist surface erosion and pitting due to detonation. The coating also allows the pistons to last longer under high temperatures.

Although the crown coating is beneficial to the piston, engine builders must also consider the effect the coating has on the rest of the engine. Because less heat is being dissipated through the piston and rings with a crown coating, that means the heat is reflected elsewhere in the combustion chamber. This extra heat may adversely affect the combustion chambers, valve faces, and exhaust ports, which may require coating. In contrast, skirt coatings help reduce cold-start scuffing, surface friction, and wear. In some cases, a skirt coating can also be used to decrease piston-to-cylinder-wall clearance safely.

Weight

Reducing reciprocating weight takes stress off the crank and rods, but if saving a few grams of weight requires laying out a big wad of cash, it might not be worth it. Because weight is often directly related to strength, there's a risk of compromising piston strength to reduce mass. According to JE, in an engine that turns 9,500 rpm and produces 1,764 psi of cylinder pressure, a 3,500-gram piston imparts 16 kilo-newtons (kn) of tensile force and 67 kn of compressive force on the small end of the connecting rod. On the big end of the rod, the tensile force is 25 kn, and the compressive force is 58 kn. With all else being equal, increasing piston weight to 400 grams changes loads to 18 kn of tensile force and 65 kn of compressive force on the small end of the rod and 27 kn of tensile force and 56 kn of compressive force on the big end of the rod. So while there is a difference in loading, it's not always worth spending lots of money to reduce piston mass by a few grams.

Manufacturer Choices

Piston technology is evolving by the day. To stay on top of the latest trends, leading manufacturers are actively involved in the most elite forms of racing such as NHRA Pro Stock and NASCAR Sprint Cup. Fortunately for hot rodders, the technology and innovation gathered from on-track competition eventually trickles down into the grassroots market. Thanks to highly automated manufacturing processes, cutting-edge pistons can be had at a very affordable price. Here's a look at some of the most popular LS pistons on the market today.

With the cylinder heads bolted in place, quench area is defined as the space between the top of the piston and the bottom of the area surrounding the combustion chamber. Reducing this gap squeezes the air/fuel mixture very tightly on the compression stroke, causing it to shoot into the chamber and help homogenize the fuel droplets. This improves an engine's detonation resistance and power. The tightest quench clearance recommended by race engine builders is .039 inch.

Diamond

In addition to having a decorated history that dates back more than 40 years, Diamond offers what's possibly the most comprehensive line of off-the-shelf pistons for Gen III/IV small-blocks. Even if you think your application requires a custom piston, chances are Diamond already stocks what you need. Not surprisingly, Diamond is a very popular choice among LS enthusiasts. All Diamond pistons are forged from rugged 2618 aluminum and feature offset wrist pins for quiet operation. Furthermore, Diamond pistons come in a dizzying array of compression heights and bore sizes with valve reliefs for both cathedral- and rectangle-port heads. Available in flat-top, dished, and domed crown designs, Diamond's diverse line of naturally aspirated, nitrous, and forced-induction pistons have a proven track record of quality and durability.

JE

Founded in 1947, JE is one of the most respected names in performance pistons. From NHRA Top Fuel to NASCAR Sprint Cup to the World of Outlaws, JE has always been actively involved in the highest levels of motorsports. Over the years, the company has evolved tremendously, leaving behind its manual cutting machines for a warehouse full of dozens of CNC machines. Like most high-end piston manufacturers, JE can build a set of custom pistons for any application, but it also stocks a full line of off-the-shelf LS-series pistons in flat-top and inverted dome configurations.

Forged exclusively from 2618 aluminum, most of JE's Gen III/IV pistons are designed for standard-deck-height short-blocks utilizing 4.000-inch-stroke cranks and 6.125-inch rods. Available bore sizes range from 3.905 to 4.130 inches, and the majority of JE's pistons have valve reliefs machined for standard 15-degree cathedral-port heads, although the company also offers off-the-shelf pistons compatible with 12-degree LS7 heads.

JE pistons can be had with standard skirts or the company's proprietary Forged Side Relief (FSR) skirts. The standard full-round skirts feature a singular central void with a continuous circular band joining the skirts. FSR skirts have multiple external voids in addition to a central void. The full-round skirts are easier to manufacture, and less expensive. On the other hand, FSR skirts are pricier, but offer reduced mass and friction.

Keith Black

During the heyday of NHRA Top Fuel in the 1970s, just about every competitive team relied on blocks or complete motors from Keith Black Racing Engines. A true pioneer in the realm of high-end drag racing, Keith Black felt that there was a shortage of quality blocks and pistons on the market, so he made his own. The lessons learned on the track while powering legendary racers, such as Don Prudhomme, to victory are evident in the high-quality, yet affordable, pistons in the Keith Black catalog today.

For enthusiasts on a tight budget, Keith Black's Silv-O-Lite cast hypereutectic pistons are an excellent choice in naturally aspirated applications. Technically, the Silv-O-Lites aren't stroker pistons, as they're designed for stock-style rebuilds. That means that they're offered for mild .5- to 1.5-mm overbores in stock 1.330-inch compression heights for 5.3L, 5.7L, and 6.0L LS-series small-blocks. Nonetheless, for hot rodders looking to build a performance III/IV engine with a stock crankshaft, the Silv-O-Lite pistons cost half as much as a comparable forged piston set.

The company also offers forged 2618 pistons under its KB Performance label. They feature fully machined crowns and valve reliefs and drilled oil drain backs. Available in both flat-top and dished configurations, KB Performance LS-series pistons come in diameters ranging from 3.905 to 4.030 inches in the popular 1.115-inch compression height. Consequently, they represent an affordable option for 383-, 402-, and 408-ci stroker builds.

Mahle

A long-time OE supplier, Mahle recently entered the LS market with a comprehensive line of quality pistons. The company offers pistons for just about every bore, stroke, and rod length combination conceivable for cathedral- and rectangle-port heads. Forged from 4032 aluminum, Mahle pistons are offered in both flat-top and inverted dome designs and feature the company's Grafal low-friction skirt coating, Furthermore, all Mahle pistons are hand-deburred prior to shipment, and they require minimal prep work before installation. Further enhancing their value, Mahle includes matching rings with all of its piston sets.

SRP

For Sportsman racers and enthusiasts on a restrictive budget, JE's line of SRP and SRP Professional pistons offers an affordable alternative to JE's top-of-the-line pistons. SRP pistons are forged from a high-silicon 4032 alloy for low thermal expansion, although they do not perform as well at high temperatures as 2618 alloy pistons. All SRP LS-series pistons have a 1.115-inch compression height and large dishes ranging from 25 to 29 cc. This makes them best suited for moderate boost applications. Unlike SRP Gen III/IV pistons that are only compatible with cathedral-port heads, the SRP Professional pistons work with L92-style heads. Other differences include FSR skirts with a low-friction coating and integral accumulator grooves for improved ring seal. SRP Professional pistons are available in 1.115- and 1.315-inch compression heights with either flat-top or inverted dome crowns. Bore sizes range from 4.005 to 4.070 inches.

Wiseco

Buying ingots of forged aluminum from outside suppliers, then machining them into shape, is common practice for piston manufacturers these days. Wiseco, on the other hand, has its own forging facility in-house. This allows Wiseco to custom-design raw forgings around the intended use of the pistons, instead of the other way around. Thanks to this flexibility, Wiseco pistons are characterized by their combination of low mass and high strength. Furthermore, Wiseco's comprehensive catalog of Gen III/IV pistons has made the company one of the most popular brands among LS-series engine builders.

Wiseco's LS off-the-shelf piston catalog is too extensive to list the products one by one in this book. The company offers pistons for 3.905- to 4.200-inch-bore diameters and compression heights accommodating strokes ranging from 3.622 to 4.125 inches. All Wiseco LS-series pistons feature a strutted skirt design that allows for piston-to-wall clearances as tight as .004 inch to minimize slap and wear. The skirts are also coated with ArmorGlide, a moly-based compound that reduces friction. Other highlights include radiused and de-burred valve pockets for optimized airflow and detonation resistance, anti-detonation grooves around the ring lands, and valve reliefs designed to fit both cathedral- and rectangle-port heads. Also, complete ring packs are included with every set of Wiseco pistons.

CHAPTER 8

OILING SYSTEM

Chevy engineers did a lot of things right with the Gen I small-block, but one of the engine's most standout, yet under-appreciated, design features is its oiling system. Although it was originally designed for a tiny 265-ci engine producing just 165 hp, with some very basic modifications, the small-block Chevy oiling system could easily support more than 600 hp. In an era when competing engine makes were plagued by oiling problems, this was quite an accomplishment. Building upon this foundation, the factory oiling systems in LS-series small-blocks are outstanding performers. With nothing more than a modified stock or aftermarket pump, the factory system is reliable past the 800-hp mark. The stock LS oiling system is so good, in fact, that there is very little engine builders can do to actually improve upon it.

Unlike the Gen I small-block, the oil pump on Gen III/IV engines mounts to the front of the block and is driven directly off the crankshaft. The pump housing and drive gear slide over the crankshaft snout, and the pump gear is rotated by the crank keyway. By eliminating the camshaft-driven oil pump driveshaft used in the Gen I small-block, the Gen III/IV arrangement reduces drag placed on the valvetrain, as well as deflection and pumping losses.

The pump draws oil from the pan through a pickup tube, and after it's pressurized, oil is sent down the main gallery on the driver side of the block en route to the oil filter. The oil then travels up the back of the block to the main feed gallery, which runs through the lifter bores. From there, oil trickles down to

Oil lubricates virtually every moving part in an engine. A thin film of oil is the only thing preventing those components from seizing up, so it's critical to maintain proper flow, volume, and pressure. The crankshaft main and rod journals are two of the highest friction areas in an engine. The surface area of the journals, the loads placed upon them during the combustion process, and RPM all dramatically increase friction.

OILING SYSTEM

the main bearings. Just like the Gen I small-block, LS-series engines direct oil to the cylinder heads through holes drilled into the lifters and pushrods. This lubricates and cools the valvesprings and rocker arms, and the oil then drains back into the pan through passages in the cylinder heads and block.

Lubrication Basics

Oil is the only thing preventing the moving parts in an engine from seizing up. Before delving deeper into the specifics of the LS-series oiling system, it's important to investigate the very basic principles of lubrication, which can be divided into three different states. Hydrodynamic lubrication describes the ideal situation where a continuous film of fluid separates two sliding surfaces. During hydrodynamic lubrication, the viscosity of the oil supports the entire load between moving parts and prevents them from touching.

The extreme opposite end of the spectrum is boundary lubrication, which is the last line of defense before metal-to-metal contact occurs. When oil is squeezed out from between moving parts in high-load areas, such as the main journals and bearings, all that's left to prevent excessive wear are the anti-wear additives in the oil.

Mixed film lubrication is a little bit of both, where some oil has been squeezed out, but a thin coat of oil is still present.

Each state of oil is present somewhere in the engine, which makes formulating oil very complicated. Ideally, hydrodynamic lubrication would be achieved under all conditions, but because this isn't possible, it makes the oil much more important.

Pressure vs. Volume

Oil control is a balance between pressure and volume, and although cars come equipped with pressure gauges, there's no way for the average hot rodder to measure the volume of oil that's flowing through an engine. In essence, oil pressure is used as an indirect method of measuring oil volume. As oil is pressurized in the pump, the resistance against the pump outlet creates oil pressure. Elementary physics dictates that pressure must be present in order to move oil through an engine, so in this regard, pressure is a good thing. However, excessive pressure merely increases an engine's pumping losses and adversely affects power output. Because pressure demands increase with RPM, it's generally recommended that an oil pump should be able to supply 10 psi of pressure for every 1,000 rpm. In other words, an engine turning 6,500 rpm needs roughly 65 psi of pressure for proper lubrication.

Even so, as long as sufficient volume is present to fill the clearances between moving components and remove heat from the bearings and journals, oil pressure is somewhat irrelevant. This is important to remember in performance engine builds that typically employ

The Gen I small-block's oil pump mounts on the rear main cap, and it is driven by a shaft that meshes with the camshaft. The LS-series small-block does away with this arrangement; the oil pump is bolted directly to the front of the motor. The pump's gerotor gear fits around the crank snout, and it is driven by the crank keyway. This eliminates the valvetrain stress and deflection associated with the Gen I design.

Since the Gen III/IV oil pump is mounted on the front of the motor, it uses a long pickup tube, supported by the center main cap, that runs rearward to draw oil from the pan sump. Many performance Gen I small-block builds do not incorporate a windage tray. In contrast, Gen III and IV small-blocks boast factory-installed windage trays.

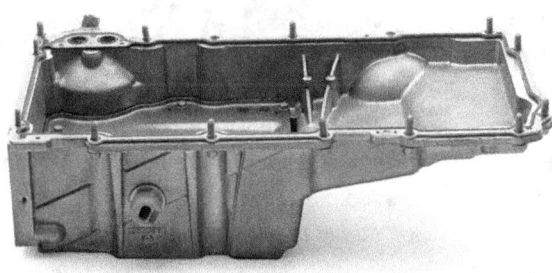

LS-series engines use the oil pan as a structural component of the block to reduce noise and vibrations. Hence, the pans are very rugged in design and built from cast aluminum. The F-body oil pan, originally installed on 1998 to 2002 Camaros and Firebirds, is the most popular with engine swappers, due to its rear sump location and generous ground clearance.

HOW TO BUILD BIG-INCH GM LS-SERIES ENGINES 73

CHAPTER 8

looser bearing clearances than stock engines. As clearances increase, a greater volume of oil is needed to maintain a target oil pressure. High-volume oil pumps help increase pressure to the desired level, but they aren't always necessary. It's quite possible that a stock pump can supply plenty of volume and pressure in a typical stroker buildup. Furthermore, oil pressure is also affected by oil viscosity and temperature. Thicker oils, and colder oil temperatures, increase oil pressure, but not volume. This merely reinforces the point that although having sufficient oil pressure is important, having proper oil volume is an even greater priority.

Oil Pumps

Sticking with the philosophy of not fixing things that aren't broken, there are only three basic types of oil pumps used by GM throughout the entire LS engine lineup. All Gen III/IV small-blocks use identical oil pumps, except for displacement-on-demand engines, which use higher-volume pumps. Consequently, there is no advantage to taking an oil pump off an LS6 and installing it onto an LS1, or using an LS3 pump on a 6.0L truck motor. The one major

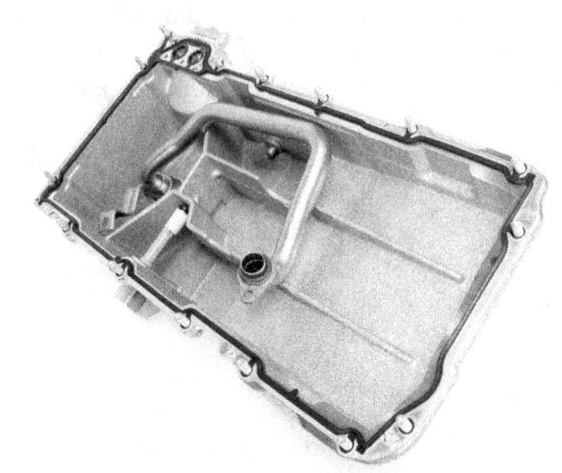

Factory GM oil pans are just as impressive on the inside as they are on the outside. They utilize internal strengthening ribs, which double as oil control baffles to prevent oil from sloshing around under cornering loads. (© GM Corp.)

Companies, such as Moroso, Canton, and Milodon, offer aftermarket oil pans built from sheet metal that fit a variety of vehicle chassis for both street/strip and road racing applications. Since road race machines sit low to the ground, oil pans designed for these cars have T-shaped sumps, which provide the necessary oil capacity without compromising ground clearance.

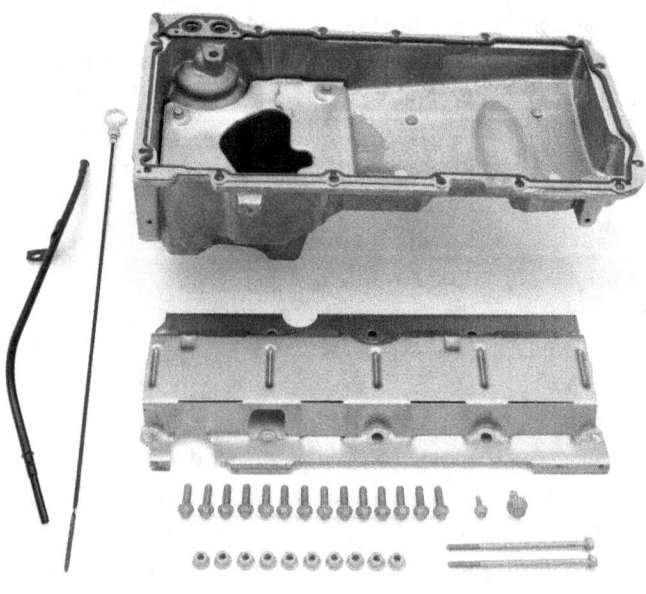

Enthusiasts installing LS small-blocks into older muscle cars are often forced to modify the sump on factory oil pans for frame clearance. GMPP recognized this problem, and now it offers its own aftermarket oil pan designed specifically for engine swaps. It includes a windage tray and features the same robust cast-aluminum construction as the factory pans. (© GM Corp.)

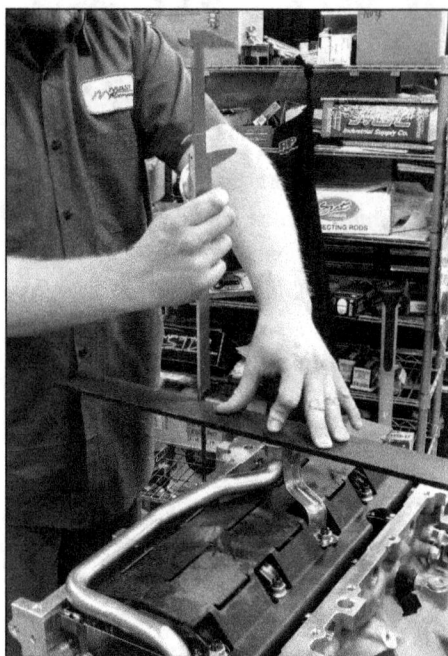

One critical measurement that should never be overlooked is the pump pickup-to-pan clearance. If the oil pump pickup sits too close to the bottom of the pan, it will starve the pump of oil and result in inadequate flow and pressure. Engine builders recommend having .375 to .5 inch of clearance.

OILING SYSTEM

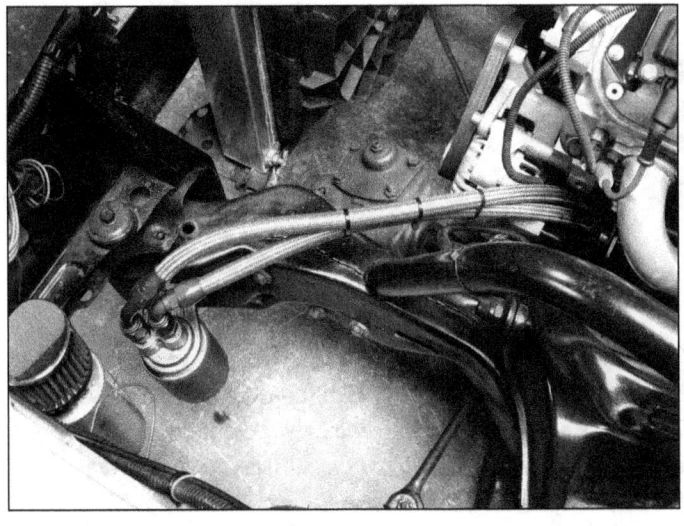

Every chassis presents its own installation challenges, and in some instances, there might not be enough space for the oil filter. In these situations, a remote filter installation kit can be used to mount the filter virtually anywhere in the engine compartment.

deviation within the LS family is the LS7 pump, which is completely different, because it's designed to feed a dry sump system. The LS7 unit is actually two pumps in one, as it moves pressurized oil like a conventional pump, and it also scavenges air and oil out of a dry sump pan. As a result, the LS7 pump isn't compatible with any other LS-series small-block, unless a motor has been converted to the factory dry sump system.

Aftermarket oil pumps are available from Melling and GM Performance Parts. These units are offered in both standard-volume and high-volume configurations. For engines with loose bearing clearances, these aftermarket pumps can increase oil volume by 10 to 33 percent. That said, a standard-volume pump typically supplies enough oil for the average stroker small-block. Companies, such as Lingenfelter Performance Engineering and SLP, also offer pumps, which are slightly modified versions of the aftermarket or stock replacement oil pumps.

Many engine builders opt to port the inlet and outlet passages of the oil pump. This process involves radiusing the inlet and outlet passages of the pump to create a smooth transition point between the block and oil pump pickup. In theory, this is said to improve oil flow volume, but in practice, it has a negligible impact on pump performance.

Stock Pans

The Gen III/IV oil pan is a unique design in that it serves as a structural member of the engine. This enhances block stiffness and helps reduce vibration. Throughout the LS-series production run, GM has used several different types of oil pans, primarily to account for the installation needs of various types of vehicles. Early LS-series small-blocks featured three basic oil pan designs. They included the F-body pan used on fourth-gen Camaros and Firebirds, the "batwing" oil pan used on C5 Corvettes, and the deep sump oil pan used on trucks and SUVs. As with intake manifolds, each of these pans was designed more for fitment within the chassis than achievement of certain performance benchmarks. Still, each of them offers excellent oil control, and as a testament to the seriousness with which GM approaches oil control, each style pan incorporates a windage tray.

Because its sump location allows the best fitment into a wide variety of chassis, the F-body oil pan is the most popular choice for engine swappers. In contrast, the truck pan's extremely deep sump doesn't provide adequate ground clearance in most street machines, so it

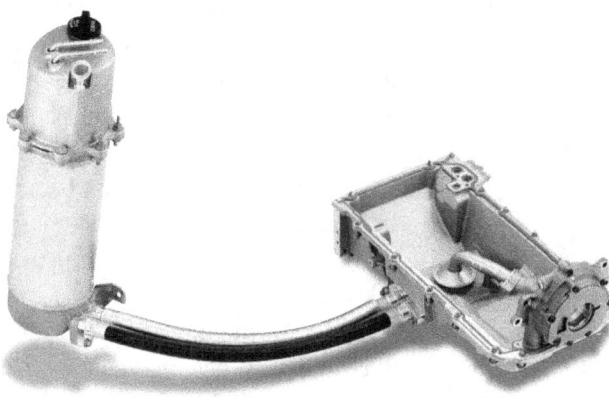

Due to the extreme cornering loads the Corvette Z06 and ZR-1 are capable of producing, the LS7 and LS9 both use the most exotic oiling system ever installed on a GM production car. Their dry sump configuration means that the oil is stored in a separate tank, and the pan merely acts as a drip pan. Oil is pumped out of the storage tank and into the block, where it drips down onto the pan after circulating through the engine. The pump then scavenges the oil and sends it back to the tank, and the process repeats itself. (© GM Corp.)

The LS7's dry sump system sends a frothy mix of oil and air to the storage tank, so baffles and air/oil separators are integrated into the tanks. Without them, the oil would foam up and lose all of its lubrication properties. (© GM Corp.)

CHAPTER 8

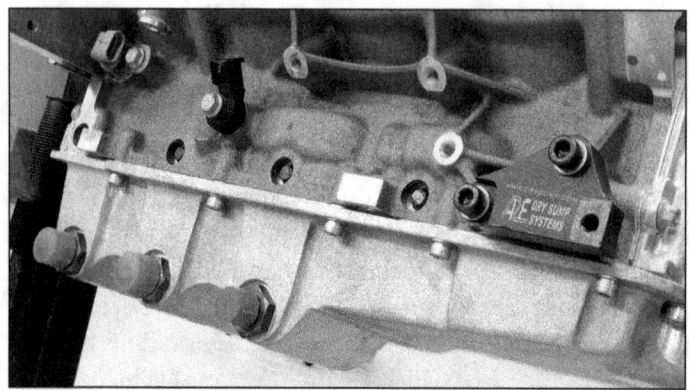

Aftermarket companies, such as ARE Dry Sump Systems, manufacture dry sump oiling systems for road racing applications. Aftermarket systems employ an external oil pump that is driven off the accessory drive belt.

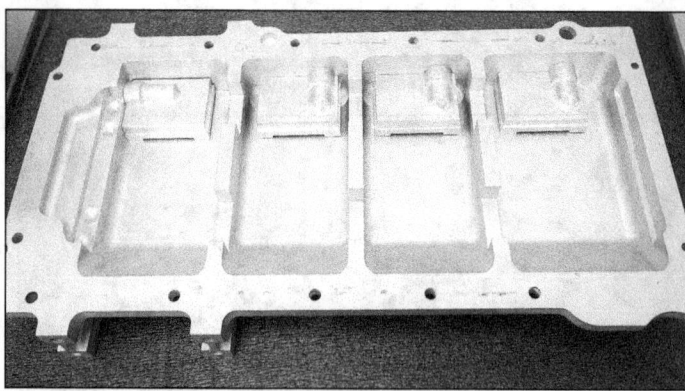

Dry sumps aren't just for road-race vehicles. High-RPM drag racing motors also benefit from them, because they virtually eliminate windage. Katech's four-stage billet pan has four separate oil pickup points.

isn't a very practical option for anything other than a truck. Due to the Corvette's very low ride height, engineers had to get creative by kicking the oil pan sump out to the sides to ensure adequate oil capacity and ground clearance. This also means that the Corvette pan provides excellent oil control under high cornering loads, but its unique shape makes it difficult to install into most chassis.

As GM installed the LS-series small-block into more cars, it produced several variations of its three early oil pan designs. The LS2 Corvette oil pan did away with the C5 pan's batwing design, and it features a long 13.5-inch sump section that makes it difficult to fit into most cars. Likewise, the oil pan used on the Cadillac CTS-V features a sump design deeper than the F-body pan but shallower than the truck pan. Even so, it offers inadequate ground clearance for many engine swap applications. The same applies to the LH8 oil pan used on 5.3L-powered Hummer H3s. It has a long sump section that clears most crossmembers, but its deep 7.5-inch sump makes it difficult to install.

Aftermarket Pans

Because extensive research and development (R&D) efforts went into designing factory GM oil pans to make sure they performed well under both longitudinal and lateral loads, and had rugged cast-aluminum construction, the most compelling reason to use an aftermarket oil pan is for improved chassis fitment. Aftermarket pans are typically constructed from aluminum sheet metal, which gives engineers more flexibility in designing a pan because they don't have to invest in the tooling required to build a cast pan. The number of aftermarket oil pans for the LS platform is staggering, and each is designed to fit in a specific chassis. Although it isn't feasible to list all of the available aftermarket oil pans here, most pans generally offer a similar list of benefits.

Many aftermarket pans are built with the average street cruiser in mind, but companies also offer specialized designs for drag racing and road racing applications. Because drag racing oil pans only need to perform optimally during straight-line acceleration and braking, they tend to have much deeper sump designs. In contrast, road race pans have kicked-out sumps for improved ground clearance. Furthermore, drag racing pans usually have a single trap-door baffle that prevents oil slosh and helps keep the pump pickup submerged during acceleration and braking. Trap doors function by trapping a pocket of oil under normal driving, and then swinging open under high

For street cars that see time at the autocross or on the road course, an accumulator system is a nice alternative to stepping up to a costly dry sump setup. Accumulators store several quarts of oil in an air-charged canister. When oil pressure drops below a preset level, the oil is discharged out of the system and into the block. The oil is then replenished after oil pressure recovers. Accumulators are available from several companies, such as Moroso and Canton.

OILING SYSTEM

Although oil is primarily thought of as a lubricant, it also helps cool the rotating assembly, valvetrain, and bearings. As a result, it's very important to keep an eye on oil temperature. Ideally, the oil temperature should stay within 10 to 15 degrees of the coolant temperature.

Well aware of the importance of managing oil temperature, GM installs factory oil coolers on Gen IV small-blocks, such as the LS3, L99, and LS9. The cooler is essentially a small heat sink integrated into the driver side of the oil pan. (© GM Corp.)

g loads to release a pocket of oil to keep the pickup submerged in oil. Road racing pans take this concept one step further by employing several trap-door baffles for superior oil control under cornering loads.

Dry Sump Systems

Once considered the exclusive territory of full-blown race cars, enthusiasts were in disbelief when GM revealed that the LS7 would feature a dry sump oiling system. Even though dry sump systems have found their way into high-end street cars, they're still rather exotic by nature. As their name implies, dry sump oiling systems don't use a conventional oil pan. Instead, oil is stored in an auxiliary tank mounted elsewhere in the chassis, and the oil pan merely functions as a collection bin that catches oil dripping off the crank, rods, and block. A crank-driven pump scavenges this oil, and then circulates it into the storage tank before making its way back into the block.

Although complicated, this arrangement offers several benefits. For one, having no oil in the pan eliminates windage and frees up horsepower. This reduction in windage is why many drag race engines that turn 8,000-plus rpm utilize dry sump oiling systems. Second, storing the oil in an auxiliary tank takes oil slosh completely out of the equation, ensuring an uninterrupted supply of oil to an engine's critical parts under even the highest of cornering loads. Additionally, the low-profile design of a dry sump pan allows mounting an engine extremely low in the chassis for improved handling. That said, only a very small fraction of LS builds require a dry sump oiling system. If deemed necessary in an autocross or road racing application, the stock LS7 system can be retrofitted into just about any chassis very easily. Furthermore, several aftermarket companies offer dry sump conversion systems.

Oil Coolers

An oil's ability to properly lubricate moving parts is dependent upon its operating temperature. For every 18-degree increase in oil temp, the oxidation rate doubles. That means that although the difference between 200- and 220-degree oil temps might not seem like a big deal, every last degree of temperature increase has a dramatic effect on oil performance. Consequently, it's not surprising that GM installed a factory oil cooler on just about every Gen III/IV small-block ever built. Late-model engines typically operate at higher coolant temperatures than older engines in an effort to reduce emissions output, which explains why factory oil coolers are so common. Although they're not mandatory on stroker small-blocks, which are typically set to operate at lower coolant temperatures, they're cheap insurance and help extend oil longevity and performance. Stock oil coolers are usually integrated into a car's cooling system, so in engine swap applications, it's easiest to install an oil cooler offered by several aftermarket manufacturers, such as TCI and B&M.

Installing an oil temperature gauge is an easy way to keep an eye on how much heat is in the oil. Under steady state cruising, where a constant supply of air is moving through the radiator and oil cooler, oil temps generally mirror coolant temps. In stop-and-go traffic and heavy acceleration, however, oil temperature usually gets much higher than coolant temperature. Without a gauge, trying to figure out oil temp is just a guessing game.

HOW TO BUILD BIG-INCH GM LS-SERIES ENGINES

CHAPTER 9

CYLINDER HEADS

SAM founder, Judson Massingill, lives by a simple adage: Get a head, flow a head, stay ahead. That's because no single component on an engine affects power output more than the cylinder heads, so it pays big time to get educated.

Without question, a durable, big-inch short-block is the foundation of every stroker motor combination. Even so, stout blocks, forged rotating assemblies, and premium machine work don't mean squat without a set of high-flow cylinder heads capable of feeding those hungry bores with a constant supply of air. Sure, it's tempting to splurge on high-dollar aftermarket blocks and rotating assemblies forged from exotic alloys, but matching a marginal short-block with a killer set of heads yields a combo that handily stomps a mega-buck short-block paired with a mediocre set of heads.

Because internal-combustion engines are nothing more than glorified air pumps, the cylinder heads that flow the most air while maintaining excellent air velocity make the most power. Consensus among engine builders is often elusive, but the importance of cylinder heads in the overall horsepower equation is one universal truth that everyone agrees upon.

The problem is that cylinder head theory is a very complex subject, and it's impossible to make it simple. The top cylinder head designers in the world have decades of experience under their belts, because, quite simply, it takes decades of practice to firmly grasp the complex science of cylinder head theory and design. Reading one chapter in a book can't substitute for years upon years of massaging ports and reshaping combustion chambers, but it will most definitely assist in the selection of the best cylinder heads for any given LS stroker combination. Unlike professional engine builders, who must be at the forefront of cylinder head technology to stay in business, typical hot rodders only have to select the proper heads for their engine combination instead of actually designing them, and that's a great luxury to have.

Outstanding cylinder heads are what give the Gen III/IV small-blocks such a huge power advantage over the competition from the factory, and GM is constantly improving upon the design as the LS platform continues to evolve. In fact, GM's current crop of rectangle-port L92 and LS7 castings put its original cathedral-port LS1 and LS6 castings to shame, even though less than a decade separates when each respective design was first introduced to the market. Factor in the dozens of aftermarket cylinder head

Simple physics dictate that as bore diameter and stroke length increase, an engine's airflow requirements also increase. With the recent influx of aftermarket blocks that are continually pushing the envelope of displacement, cylinder head manufacturers have been forced to keep pace. With the latest LS race heads flowing in excess of 450 cfm, even the biggest of engines rarely run out of breath.

CYLINDER HEADS

offerings that are now available, and the power potential for stroker motors of all applications and sizes—from 383 to 500-plus ci and everything in between—is truly staggering.

Appetite for Air

Four-stroke internal-combustion engines utilize pressure differential to fill their cylinders with air and fuel. As a piston moves down the bore during the intake stroke, it creates an environment where air pressure inside the cylinder is less than the air pressure outside the motor. It's this difference between ambient pressure and cylinder pressure that pushes air past the throttle body, through the intake manifold and heads, and then into the cylinder. Expanding upon this fundamental concept offers two important revelations. First, as displacement and the volume inside each cylinder increases, so does an engine's appetite for air. Second, as an engine's operating RPM range increases, its airflow requirements also increase. Consequently, because stroker motors throw both additional cubic inches and higher RPM into the mix, the airflow demands necessary to properly feed them are staggering.

Cylinder head airflow is measured in cubic feet per minute, or cfm, and the natural inclination for many enthusiasts is to bolt the heads with the highest flow figures onto their short-block. Unfortunately, that can often lead to disastrous results in a street motor. Cylinder heads that post the highest advertised flow numbers can have oversized intake ports that sacrifice low- and mid-lift airflow for greater peak cfm at higher valve lift. That's fine for all-out race motors that spend most of their time at 6,000-plus rpm, but it results in a mismatched combination with poor throttle response and compromised low- and mid-range torque in a typical street/strip application.

The obvious question, then, is how to precisely determine the airflow requirements for any given engine combination. Again, there is no simple answer. Taking a scientific approach requires determining an engine's intended use (drag, endurance, etc.), volumetric efficiency, RPM at peak horsepower, the valve area needed to achieve target airflow, optimum air speeds throughout the induction system, volume of the overall induction system, and an engine's resonant tuning characteristics. Once those variables have been established, they can be plugged into a series of complex mathematical equations to precisely determine the airflow needs of a particular engine combo.

Quite honestly, that's more information than the typical hot rodder cares to process, but it's valuable information to have. Through thousands of hours of flowbench and dyno testing, cylinder head manufacturers have done most of the homework for you. Most offer heads in a plethora of port volumes and chamber sizes compatible with virtually every engine combination conceivable.

The problem is that with the infinite number of ways in which an engine can be configured, there are no simple rules

The theory that polishing a port wall improves airflow is nothing more than a myth. In fact, some roughness is desirable to help create a boundary layer of stagnant air that sticks along the port wall. This reduces the coefficient of friction for air passing over the boundary layer and improves flow. Likewise, the boundary layer reduces the effective cross section of the port, improving velocity. Having ridges perpendicular to the port can also creates turbulence to help keep fuel in suspension without hurting airflow, which is a big perk in carbureted motors. Hand finishing the port walls with 80-grit cartridge rolls nets a surface finish that's close to ideal.

Airflow is measured on the flowbench by mocking a set of valves in the heads and then measuring flow at various lift points. Street heads tend to back up or go turbulent above .600-inch lift, so it's imperative to optimize airflow and low- and mid-lift. With race heads, on the other hand, all that matters is high-lift airflow.

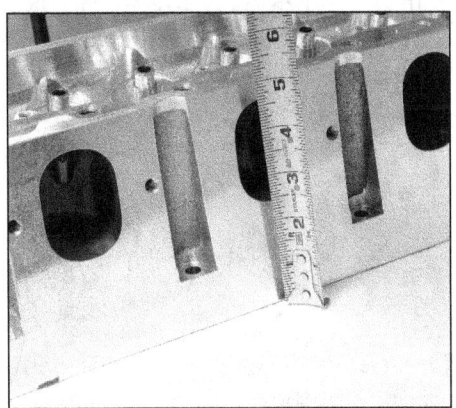

Raising the intake port provides a straight path from the intake port entrance to the intake valve, thereby improving airflow. This effect is enhanced with flat valve angles. The challenge for head designers is raising the intake port as much as possible without making the valvespring pockets too thin.

HOW TO BUILD BIG-INCH GM LS-SERIES ENGINES

of thumb to follow. For instance, it's easy, yet often inaccurate, to make generalizations regarding optimum port volume in relation to displacement. Although a 205-cc cylinder head may work fine for the majority of 346- to 396-ci small-blocks, a 7,500-plus-rpm drag race motor with a solid roller cam can certainly benefit from larger 215-cc ports. Conversely, although a massive 454-ci stroker might have the sheer size necessary to warrant a set of monstrous 245-cc heads, if it's destined to power a heavy muscle car with tall gears and a modest 6,000-rpm peak power target, it will perform much better with smaller 230-cc ports. For the average enthusiast, a very unscientific, yet extremely effective, method of selecting the ideal cylinder heads for an engine is to consult cylinder head manufacturers, experienced engine builders, and fellow hot rodders who have built and tested similar combinations to the one you're putting together. That, plus the information outlined in this chapter, will help point you in the right direction.

Port Volume

The volume of the intake ports is one of the most common points of reference used to determine the airflow and horsepower potential of a cylinder head. Because an intake port features a series of complex contours and curves, the best method of measuring its volume is to turn a head on its side, with the intake valve in place and the intake port facing upward, and then fill it up with water using a graduated cylinder. Although comparing port volumes can be a useful tool when trying to determine the ideally sized cylinder head for an engine combination, it does have its limitations. Relocating the intake port entrance has a tendency to lengthen or shorten the port, which can dramatically increase or decrease port volume without impacting a cylinder head's airflow potential. That's because port volume actually has a negligible effect on how well an intake port can move air.

In practice, the most accurate gauge of an intake port's performance potential is the size of its cross-sectional area. Enlarging a port's cross section can dramatically increase airflow while just marginally increasing port volume. For instance, porting a set of stock LS1 head castings can often increase peak airflow figures from 240 to 320 cfm, but the process might only increase port volume from 200 to 225 cc. Conversely, lengthening a port while maintaining the same cross-sectional area is unlikely to impact airflow much at all. Larger-displacement motors, or smaller motors operating at high RPM, generally benefit from larger ports with larger cross sections, and small-displacement motors that turn modest RPM are better off with smaller cross-section ports.

In essence, comparing the intake port volumes of two cylinder heads is only valid if they share similar port architecture. For example, an 18-degree Gen I small-block Chevy head has a significantly larger port volume for any given cross-sectional area than a 23-degree head. Therefore, making a direct comparison between the two is futile, and the same applies to different Gen III/IV castings.

Compared to their cathedral-port forebears, the rectangle-port L92 and LS7 castings used on the latest Gen IV small-blocks feature vastly different overall port architecture. The raised intake port locations on the L92 and LS7 heads effectively lengthen the ports, resulting in a dramatic increase in port volume. Whereas the intake ports on factory cathedral-port LS1 castings measure 200 cc, the L92's rectangle-port heads feature a 260-cc intake port volume. A difference of 60 cc suggests that the L92 castings were designed to feed a motor nearly 100 ci larger than the 346-ci LS1. However, the truth of the matter is that GM's Gen IV rectangle-port heads are bolted to

The short-turn radius of the intake port is the area where the port floor drops off right before the valve. Raising the intake port takes a load off the short-turn radius, allowing head designers to create a more gradual transition for improved airflow.

The upper ridge that gives cathedral-port heads their unique shape was actually a design compromise. The location of the pushrods limited how wide GM engineers could make the ports, so they had to create a ridge at the top to achieve their desired port volume. This tall-and-skinny port shape resulted in very low port entrance height, which severely compromised flow above .650-inch lift.

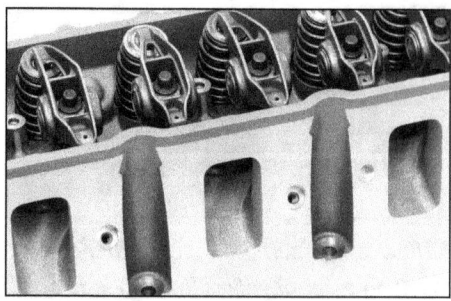

Taking cues from the C5R race heads, GM was able to increase the port volume and cross-sectional area of the LS7 heads by moving the intake pushrod over to the side. That allowed for a more conventionally shaped rectangular intake port.

CYLINDER HEADS

motors (L92, LS3, and L99) that are only 30 ci larger.

Likewise, GM also uses these 260-cc heads on the LY6, which is just 18 ci larger than an LS1. This merely reinforces the point that port volume figures can only be used as a point of reference when comparing heads with similar port architecture. In the wake of Gen III/IV small-blocks, that means port volume should only be used to compare cathedral-port heads to cathedral-port heads and rectangle-port heads to rectangle-port heads.

Flow vs. Velocity

In a high-winding race motor, the only thing that matters is maximizing peak cfm at high valve lifts. On the other hand, designing a cylinder head for a street/strip engine is a much trickier proposition. In these dual-role applications, high-RPM horsepower is still important for the occasional jaunt down the dragstrip, yet low- and mid-RPM performance is arguably the most important design consideration, because that's where street/strip motors spend most of their time. Furthermore, because race engines don't need to last tens of thousands of miles, they employ extremely aggressive camshaft profiles to optimize airflow above .600-inch valve lift. That approach significantly reduces valvetrain durability, so street engines must make do with camshafts featuring much more conservative peak valve lift figures.

Consequently, building a street/strip motor that offers a flexible powerband requires designing a cylinder head with respectable peak cfm, in addition to outstanding port velocity and airflow below .600-inch valve lift. Due to the fact that impressive peak airflow figures often come at the expense of port velocity, and vice versa, balancing these two opposing forces is the biggest challenge facing any cylinder head designer.

Make no mistake that peak airflow through an intake port is extremely important. In a street motor, however, it's just not as important as air velocity. Some head designers contend that air speed is 10 times more important than raw flow numbers. Reducing air velocity by 10 percent can sacrifice 40 percent of the wave and ram energy that dynamically fills the cylinders. Additionally, blind fixation on peak-cfm figures can actually lead to situations in which an engine has cylinder heads that flow more air than it can actually use.

For instance, if a set of 375-cfm cylinder heads is bolted on a short-block that can only use 325 cfm, the engine will not only fail to achieve the power potential of that 375 cfm, but it will also fail to reach the power potential of the 325 cfm that it really needs. That's because the port design necessary to achieve 375 cfm of airflow sacrificed critical air speed in the induction system. The end result is a low air-speed induction system that can't properly fill the cylinder by means of dynamic inertia, and, as a result, the engine will never reach its full power potential.

Furthermore, oversized ports needlessly make an engine combination lazy and soft at low RPM while providing no appreciable benefit at higher RPM. Having extra airflow isn't always bad, but it can't come at the expense of air speed, and the ports must be sized properly. Matching the airflow needs of an engine with properly sized cylinder heads is the key to taking full advantage of every last CFM of air.

In a street engine, a good rule of thumb is to choose the smallest head that flows enough air to meet its horsepower target and properly feed the cylinder at the desired RPM range. In other words, the goal of a head is to move as much air

Compared to the LS-series small-block's original cathedral ports, the rectangle ports used on LS7- and L92-style heads are much shorter and wider. As a result, GM was able to raise the intake port entrance for dramatic improvements in high-lift airflow.

Moving the intake pushrods over to the side to make room for the rectangular port design required GM to design offset intake rocker arms to maintain proper valvetrain geometry. The C5R heads address this problem with shaft-mount rocker arms, but for high-volume production engines, that simply isn't an option. Instead, LS3/L92 engines incorporate offset intake rockers.

In performance applications, a 45-degree valve seat is the most common angle, as it offers a nice balance of airflow and durability. In a typical three-angle valve job, a 45-degree primary cut is matched with a 30-degree top cut and a 60-degree bottom cut. Serdi-style tools allow machining all three angles at the same time.

HOW TO BUILD BIG-INCH GM LS-SERIES ENGINES

as possible through as small a port as possible. A simple way to look at it is if cross-sectional area of a port is increased and flow increases, then velocity hasn't been compromised. On the other hand, if a port is opened up and flow doesn't increase, then velocity has been compromised. It's a delicate balancing act, and air velocity is not uniform throughout a port. There are average velocities and localized velocities, and air moves faster toward the center of the port where friction from port walls doesn't affect it as much. The trick is minimizing the differences between localized velocities.

Many of the secrets to finding good low- and mid-lift flow are in the combustion chamber design, valve job profile, and the actual shape of the valve itself. Back-cut valves are a must, and time must be invested in trying different angles, as well as different widths of those angles. Additionally, the actual width of a 45-degree seat needs to be considered, and the short-turn radius height and shape also play a smaller role. It's a give and take; really strong peak numbers can sacrifice a lot of low- and mid-lift flow, and really strong low- and mid-lift numbers may knock more off the peak than you may be willing to accept.

The goal of the top cylinder head manufacturers is the same: to optimize low- and mid-lift flow while still retaining solid and respectable peak numbers. Part of this reasoning is the fact that a lazy port with big peak numbers may ultimately be handicapped by the intake manifold choice anyway, leaving you with weak low- and mid-lift performance and only mediocre peak flow where you were expecting that combination to shine. Ultimately, when selecting a set of heads for your stroker combination, it's better to err on the side of caution by opting for ports that are too small rather than too large. Although that approach doesn't always yield impressive peak flow figures, it almost guarantees excellent throttle response, drivability, and low- and mid-range grunt.

Valve Angle

The valve angle of a cylinder head is often the topic of discussion in bench racing circles, so it makes sense to explain what it is and how it affects overall airflow dynamics. If the valve stems were placed perpendicular to the deck surface of the block, they would be positioned at a 0-degree angle. Due to underhood installation constraints, this is very difficult to achieve. Consequently, in an OHV engine with an inline valvetrain, like the LS-series small-block, the valves are angled toward the outside of the cylinder bore. In other words, as the valves open, they move closer to the exhaust manifold side of the block.

The inherent drawback of this layout is that air entering the cylinder from the valve seat area of the head tends to shroud up against the bore, which hinders airflow. To combat this, cylinder head designers are always trying to flatten out the valve angle as close to vertical, in relation to the deck surface, as possible. This allows the incoming air charge to move freely down the bore instead of crashing into the cylinder wall. Furthermore, lower valve angles free up additional space, which allows for the fitment of larger-diameter valves. Other benefits include smaller, more efficient combustion chambers; decreased chamber burn time; reduced pumping losses; and a lower propensity for detonation or pre-ignition.

It should come as no surprise, then, that GM engineers opted for a very flat 15-degree valve angle when designing the Gen III cylinder heads. To put that figure into perspective, keep in mind that the Gen I small-block utilized a 23-degree valve angle, and when it comes to Mouse motors, cylinder heads with a 15-degree valve angle are considered full-race hardware.

Naturally, many hot rodders equate a flatter valve angle to a superior port design, but that's not always the case. Valve angle is merely one of dozens of variables that distinguish an excellent cylinder head from a mediocre cylinder head, and the reason why a flatter valve angle isn't always better is actually very simple. Any time the valve angle is reduced, it must coincide with a raised intake port entrance. Flattening the valve

A properly designed combustion chamber is essentially an extension of the valve job. Using this approach, combustion chambers in modern cylinder heads tend to resemble a figure-8. The more efficient a chamber, the less timing advance an engine needs, which reduces pump losses.

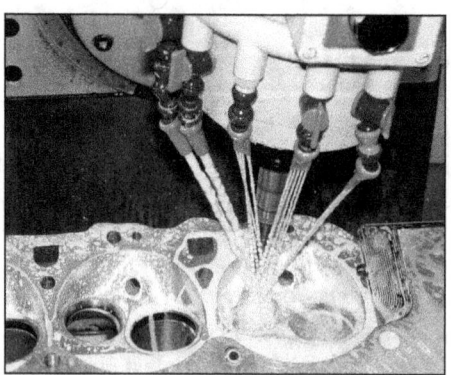

Many aftermarket manufacturers now offer heads with CNC-machined combustion chambers. In the not-so-distant past, engine builders had to hand blend the chambers, which dramatically increased labor and costs.

angle without raising the intake port entrance increases the angle that the incoming intake air charge must negotiate at the short-turn radius.

For example, the Achilles' heel of stock cathedral-port LS castings is their relatively low ports. That, combined with their flat 15-degree valve angle, means that airflow drops off dramatically after .600-inch valve lift. GM wisely addressed this shortcoming with its rectangle-port L92 cylinder heads. Raising the ports allowed engineers to take full advantage of the heads' low valve angle and dramatically improve airflow. Although the L92 heads share the same 15-degree valve angle as their cathedral-port forebears, their raised intake ports flow 320 cfm, compared to the LS1 heads' 240 cfm. The moral of the story is that although valve angle is an important design element to any cylinder head, it's foolish to judge the merit of a head based on valve angle alone.

Angle of Attack

The relationship between the incoming air and the back of the intake valve is sometimes referred to as the angle of attack. Due to its added height, a raised-runner head simply has a better angle of attack, or vantage point, for a straighter shot to the back of the valve. The added height also reduces the angle that the incoming charge must negotiate at the short-turn radius. As a result, the geometry of a raised-runner port is superior to that of a similar non-raised runner design, because it allows additional airflow and a higher terminal velocity before it stalls or backs up. The lower the port gets, the more the air speed increases at the short-turn radius, and the more critical its shape becomes.

Lower ports force head designers to lower the air speed in order to get the air to negotiate the short turn, which wastes energy. Ideally, the short-turn radius needs to be shaped to have the highest air speed throughout the RPM range without disrupting the boundary layer, which is a layer of stagnant air surrounding the port that reduces the coefficient of friction of the air passing over it.

In essence, the short-turn radius controls the shape of the power curve. Standing it up to increase air velocity increases low-end torque and sacrifices top-end power. Laying it back to reduce air speed compromises low-end torque and increase top-end power. Not only do raised intake ports offer more latitude in shaping the short-turn radius, they also yield smaller, fast-burn combustion chambers and offer a better overall induction system path and design. Additionally, raised runners keep the air/fuel mixture in suspension far better, because there's less frictional loss and fuel fallout. An air/fuel mixture entering the combustion chamber from a straight, high-port induction path is more homogeneous and burns faster, producing more power with better brake-specific fuel consumption numbers.

Many of the benefits of any raised-runner design are often overlooked. Due to the higher port inlet locations of a raised-runner head, the intake manifold runner length is naturally increased, as the space between the left and right port banks also increases and allows the manifold designer more room for a smoother-turn radius from the plenum to the intake manifold runners in a single-plane-style intake. Also, in addition to having runner shape advantages, a raised-runner intake manifold has a much better approach angle from the manifold exit to the runner entrance of the cylinder head. This is somewhat irrelevant for fuel-injected motors, but a definite advantage for the growing number of enthusiasts building carbureted Gen III/IV small-blocks.

The extremely flat 12-degree valve angle of the LS7 heads yields very shallow combustion chambers for quick and efficient burning of the air/fuel mixture. Shallow chambers help maintain a more homogenized air/fuel mixture. (© GM Corp.)

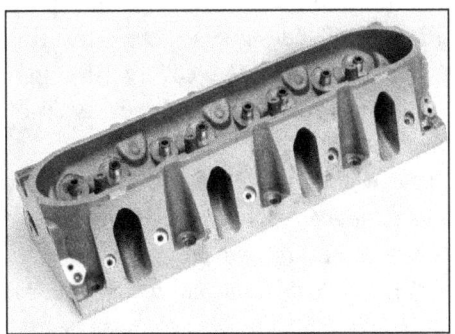

Although they're considered yesterday's news by some, factory GM cathedral-port heads still perform exceptionally well. These stock LS6 castings were ported by SAM to flow more than 350 cfm, and they helped power a 1999 Camaro shop car to mid-9-second ETs.

An inherently weak spot on factory GM cathedral-port castings is the valvespring pocket. Removing too much material from the port ceiling can break through the casting and into the spring pocket. Aftermarket heads have extra metal in the spring pocket area to avoid this problem.

Valve Seat Angle

After air has traveled through the intake manifold, down the intake port, and around the short-turn radius, its final stop before entering the cylinder is the intake valve. The valve opens and closes against a seat machined into the head, and the angle of the valve seat plays an important role in overall airflow dynamics. Higher seat angles give up some flow at low lift, but once lift increases and the valve curtain area opens up, a greater angle is better for performance. With cams that have less than .400-inch lift, a lower angle might be better, but with any moderate amount of cam lift at all, a higher angle always enhances airflow.

A 45-degree valve seat angle is very common, and any angle greater than that makes more power. However, there are some tradeoffs. As the seat angle increases, durability decreases. That's why lower angles are common in many production motors where durability is more of a concern, and just about all diesel engines have 30-degree seats. Typically, 50- to 55-degree seats sacrifice 10 to 15 percent of flow from .200- to .400-inch lift. However, in race applications it's foolish to sacrifice high-lift flow for low- and mid-lift flow, because that's not where power is produced. Some of the top engine builders in the country, such as in NHRA Pro Stock and NASCAR Sprint Cup, don't even turn the flowbench on until .300- to .400-inch lift.

Also, the improved high-lift flow of bigger angles allows opening up the venturi, because at that point the venturi becomes the restriction. A ton of energy is lost when air exits from the port into the cylinder, so a bigger venturi helps maintain that energy. Designing a port is all about area relationships, and you always want to maintain the valve area as the restriction, not the port. In other words, you don't want a weak port with 50- to 55-degree seats. A weak port with a valve seat area that flows well creates lots of turbulence, which hurts flow. The more skilled the head designer, the less that is lost by going with a higher angle seat.

Combustion Chambers

With all the hoopla over port architecture and valve angles, an area of cylinder head design that gets overlooked quite frequently is the combustion chambers. Doing so leaves a lot of horsepower on the table, as the shape of the combustion chambers profoundly impacts airflow. In fact, many head porters agree that combustion chamber design is more important than port design itself, and any time a valve job is performed, the chambers must be reshaped to take full advantage of the increase in airflow. The reason for this is because as air transitions from the tight confines of the intake port into a comparatively large cylinder, it experiences a tremendous loss in energy and velocity.

The purpose of a well-designed combustion chamber is to keep air velocity even around the entire circumference of the valve and decelerate the intake air charge at a controlled rate to minimize this inevitable loss in velocity and pressure. Head designers refer to this dynamic as pressure recovery. Although different heads require different types of chambers, and there is no single shape that's best for all heads, the goal is for the combustion chamber to be an extension of the valve seat area all the way into the cylinder. Following this principle, with wedge heads, a well-designed chamber has a tendency to be shaped like a heart or a figure-8.

A properly shaped combustion chamber is a balance of pressure recovery, wet flow, and flame travel, as these three factors can separate a good cylinder head from a great cylinder head. A chamber that is laid back too far causes a total loss of pressure recovery, flow control, and poor fuel dispersion inside the cylinder. Additionally, the combustion chambers can be highly sensitive to minor changes in shape. Something as simple as milling the heads to increase compression can cause a complete loss of pressure recovery and substantially reduce airflow. Additionally, peak volumetric efficiency is reduced when the pressure recovery is undermined by a chamber that has been laid back too far.

Fortunately, managing the three key factors in combustion chamber design is far easier with flatter valve angles, which explains why Gen III/IV castings have such outstanding chambers from the factory. With very low valve angles, the chamber can come right off the valve seat like a venturi. In contrast, higher valve angles require a deep concave chamber to

Just how good are the factory L92/LS3 heads? By adding nothing more than a 225-at-.050 cam, Gen IV enthusiasts are picking up an additional 65 hp. Some hot rodders feel that the 260-cc intake runners on these heads are far too large to use on small-displacement stroker engines, but that simply isn't the case. It's worth noting that GM uses the L92 castings on the LY6 small-block, which measures just 364 ci. Furthermore, the LY6 produces 382 ft-lbs of torque and is installed on 3/4-ton trucks, illustrating that the cross-sectional area of the L92 castings is well suited for smaller engines, despite the large port volume of the heads. (© GM Corp.)

assist with pressure recovery. Deep concave chambers often have poor wet flow characteristics and reduced pressure recovery, due to valve shrouding.

More than any other factor, the shape of the chamber determines how efficiently a motor burns the air/fuel mixture. Efficient chambers disperse the air/fuel mixture very evenly throughout the cylinder, resulting in even combustion and brisk flame front propagation. As a result, cylinder heads with efficient combustion chambers require less ignition advance, which reduces pumping losses and increases horsepower output. A typical Gen III/IV small-block with ported factory heads or aftermarket castings needs just 26 to 28 degrees of total timing. On the other hand, an iron-headed big-block with massive 118-cc combustion chambers might require as much as 50 degrees of advance.

Factory Cathedral-Port Heads

When the LS1 was introduced in 1997, perhaps the most shocking departure from the Gen I small-block Chevy was its unique cathedral-shaped intake ports. Not only were they much taller and narrower than the rectangular ports Chevy enthusiasts had grown accustomed to, they also featured a triangular ridge at the very top of the port. Many people assumed some sort of voodoo science inspired the intriguing port shape, but in reality, the design was a product of GM engineers tying to hit their target port volume within a limited amount of space.

By nature, the passages inside an OHV cylinder head are crowded close together, as the ports, pushrod holes, and coolant passages must snake their way through the head without intersecting each other. The section of the head where the pushrod tubes run adjacent to the intake ports is referred to as the pushrod pinch area. When designing the LS1 heads, GM engineers realized that the pushrod pinch area constricted the cross-sectional area of the intake ports too much, and the only way they could hit their target port volume was by creating a unique cathedral-shaped design.

History lessons aside, stock GM cathedral-port heads offer exceptional airflow, combustion efficiency, and horsepower potential. In stock trim, 200-cc LS1 castings flow 240 cfm. That's plenty of airflow to support more than 450 hp, and it's right on par with a set of aftermarket 23-degree Gen I heads. Despite the recent influx of aftermarket castings that have hit the LS scene, porting factory cylinder heads is still an excellent choice for hot rodders on a tight budget. With the potential to easily exceed 300 cfm in the hands of a skilled porter, factory cathedral-port cylinder heads move plenty of air to feed a stout 400-plus-ci stroker combination.

LS1 Heads

Although factory cathedral-port LS1 heads have been superseded by GM's newer rectangle-port heads, they're still extremely popular for stroker engine builds for several reasons. Far more Gen III/IV small-blocks have left the factory with cathedral-port heads than rectangle-port heads, making them plentiful and inexpensive. Additionally, the large 2.165/1.590-inch valves fitted to GM's rectangle-port L92 heads require a minimum bore size of 4.000 inches. So, if you're building a small-bore LS engine combo, the L92 castings simply aren't an option. Fortunately, that's not a big deal, because stock LS1 heads can move some serious air. With quality porting, a nice valve job, and larger 2.055/1.570-inch valves, it's not uncommon for these heads to flow more than 320 cfm. Several companies, such as Total Engine Airflow and Patriot Performance, offer porting services that boost stock LS1 castings past the 300-cfm mark for $1,000 to $1,500 in fully assembled trim.

Throughout the LS1's eight-year production run, its cylinder head castings saw several minor revisions. Heads manufactured in 1997 and 1998 had provisions for perimeter-bolt valve covers, and heads produced from 1999 to 2004 were cast for center-bolt valve covers. Some LS1 heads were sand cast, and others were die cast, but there is little to no difference in performance between the various casting numbers. All LS1 heads feature 200-cc intake ports, 70-cc exhaust ports, 67-cc combustion chambers, 2.000-inch intake valves, and 1.550-inch exhaust valves.

LS6 Heads

Manufactured from 2001 to 2004, the LS6 heads—identifiable by their "243" casting number—are essentially an improved variant of the LS1 cylinder heads. The biggest improvement of the LS6 castings is that they feature a raised port floor, which yields a more gradual approach angle at the short-turn radius. Furthermore, the LS6's intake ports have

Many aftermarket blocks are offered with a six-bolts-per-cylinder bolt pattern, but they are still compatible with standard four-bolt heads, as long as the upper and lower bolts aren't used. An option is to weld tabs onto the heads, so that they can be bolted to the extra holes on the block.

an enlarged mid section and raised roof to even out localized air velocity fluctuations. On the exhaust side, the port is .125 inch higher than the port on the LS1 heads, and it is D-shaped instead of oval-shaped. These tweaks help boost intake airflow to 260 cfm. Additionally, LS6 heads have slightly larger 210-cc intake ports, 75-cc exhaust ports, and 64-cc combustion chambers. Compared to the LS1 cylinder heads, where the LS6 castings really shine is at high valve lift. In ported trim, the LS6 heads can flow in excess of 350 cfm, making them highly desirable for stroker motor buildups.

GM also equipped the LS2 and LS4 with the 243 casting. Other than having valves that are slightly heavier than the ones used on the LS6, the 243 castings off the LS2 and LS4 are virtually identical to the LS6 heads. A slight variation of the 243 casting is the "799" casting that came equipped on the high-output L33 and LH6 5.3L Vortec truck motors. These heads are essentially a carbon copy of the 243 castings, and they are highly coveted by hot rodders.

AFR cylinder heads are famous for their high-velocity ports that keep on chugging up top. The heads yield extremely broad and street-friendly powerbands that can more than hold their own at the track. The company's new V2 series heads are revised versions of its original LS castings; the new heads boast improved low- and mid-lift flow, as well as an extra 7 to 10 cfm of peak airflow.

LQ4/LQ9 Heads

As the story goes, once Cadillac engineers caught wind of the LS6 engine development program, they knew they had to integrate some of the same technology into Cadillac's flagship SUV, the Escalade. The results were the LQ4 and LQ9 small-blocks, which are basically 6.0L iron LS motors topped with LS6 heads. The only difference is that the LQ4/LQ9 heads have larger 71-cc combustion chambers that yield a lower compression ratio. Consequently, the LQ4/LQ9 cylinder heads flow every bit as well as the vaunted LS6 design.

Thanks to their large combustion chambers, which allow for lower static compression ratios, the aluminum LQ4/LQ9 castings have carved out a niche in forced-induction circles, where it's common practice to install a set of LQ4/LQ9 castings on an LS1 short-block to reduce the compression ratio to about 9.5:1. That makes them perfect for hot rodders looking to add a turbocharger or a supercharger to a factory short-block. The black sheep of the 6.0L lot are the early iron "873" LQ4 castings manufac-

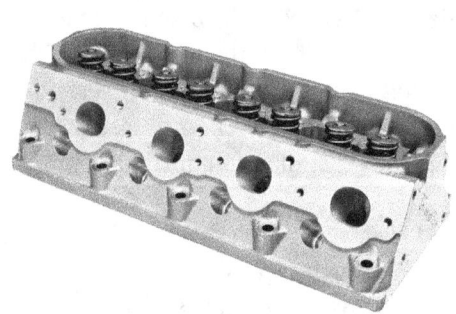

Although the growing popularity of five-axis CNC machines has made CNC-ported cylinder heads much more affordable, head casting technology has improved dramatically to enable the production of competitive heads. Trick Flow offers 225-cc heads that flow 305 cfm, and they are much cheaper than the typical CNC head.

tured from 1999 to 2000. Although they flow just as well as their aluminum counterparts, their iron construction makes them 40 to 50 pounds heavier and much more difficult to port.

4.8L/5.3L Truck Heads

To create the 4.8L and 5.3L Vortec truck engines while retaining the basic Gen III architecture, GM engineers reduced the LS1's 3.900-inch bore to 3.780 inches. This effectively reduced displacement to create the 5.3L; by decreasing the LS1's 3.622-inch stroke to 3.267 inches, the engineers created the smallest of the Gen IIIs, the 4.8L.

Because reducing an engine's bore and stroke also decreases the compression ratio, GM fitted the small-displacement Vortec motors with smaller 61-cc combustion chambers. Along with the reduced bore size, these motors were fitted with smaller 1.890/1.550-inch valves. Other than these tweaks, the 4.8L/5.3L cylinder heads are virtually identical to the 5.7L LS1 castings.

The smaller valves do, in fact, reduce airflow to roughly 220 cfm, but with massaged ports and larger seats and valves, the Vortec heads flow just as well as the LS1 heads. Hitting 320 cfm with these castings is no problem, and thanks to their smaller combustion chambers, they're very popular in naturally aspirated engine buildups, due to the increase in compression ratio that they offer. Using a set of 5.3L heads in lieu of LS1 heads typically boosts static compression by .75 point. That means hot rodders can hit their target compression ratio without having to remove as much material from the deck surface. The 4.8L/5.3L were produced in several casting variations, but there's no real performance difference among them, and the most common casting numbers are "862" and "706." So, despite the fact that they originally served duty in a lowly truck application, these castings are excellent performers.

Factory Rectangle-Port Heads

As great as they may be straight from the factory, the production cathedral-port LS cylinder heads still left plenty of room for improvement. Their biggest design flaw was a relatively low intake port entrance in relation to their flat 15-degree valve angle. This created a very sharp corner at the short-turn radius, causing the intake port flow to go turbulent at roughly .600-inch valve lift. GM addressed this issue to a certain degree with the LS6 castings by reshaping the port floor for a more gradual transition at the short-run radius, but high-lift flow still left something to be desired. Enter the factory rectangle-port cylinder heads used on the LS7, LS3, L92, and L99, which represent a profound departure from their cathedral-port counterparts.

The progenitor to the production rectangle-port castings was actually conceived to power the factory-backed C5R Corvette road racing program in the American Le Mans Series. The team won multiple championships, largely attributable to the potent powerplants under their hoods. When creating the C5R cylinder heads, engineers completely revised the intake port architecture by raising the floors and roofs and implementing an even flatter 11-degree valve angle. This gave the incoming air charge a much straighter path to the back of the intake valve for a substantial improvement in high-lift airflow.

The cathedral port's tall and narrow shape offers a limited cross-sectional area. This bottleneck ultimately limits how much air can flow through the port. In contrast, the rectangle ports used on the C5R heads offer far greater cross-sectional area, port volume, and flow potential. Although the standard cathedral-port design is still used in the majority of production Gen III/IV small-blocks, GM is phasing in its latest rectangle-port castings in a growing number of applications.

LS7 Heads

Regardless of engine make, GM's LS7 cylinder heads are the greatest factory small-block castings ever built. Conceived to catapult the Corvette Z06 to the top of the supercar stage in 2006, the 427-ci LS7 small-block produced 505 hp and spun effortlessly to 7,000 rpm. Feeding that much displacement and RPM forced engineers to design a set of cylinder heads that borrowed heavily from GM's C5R racing program.

On the original cathedral-port LS1 castings, maximum port volume and cross-sectional area was limited by the pushrod pinch area. Packing a symmetrical port layout between each pair of valves only compounded matters. To

Right out of the box, the factory LS7 heads flow 360 cfm, making them an exceptional value for stroker small-block buildups. With some quality hand porting, these heads are capable of delivering up to 400 cfm of airflow. That's better than many big-block heads on the market. (© GM Corp.)

Port Wall Finish

Cylinder head designers never talk about polishing a port. That's because the theory that polishing a port wall improves airflow is nothing more than a myth. A smoother port wall finish isn't always better than a rough finish, and polishing a port or making it pretty with a cartridge roll doesn't improve airflow at all. In fact, some roughness is desirable to help create a boundary layer of stagnant air that sticks along the port wall. This reduces the coefficient of friction for air passing over the boundary layer and improves flow. Also, the boundary layer reduces the effective cross section of the port, improving velocity. Another benefit of having ridges perpendicular to the port is that it creates enough turbulence to help keep fuel in suspension without hurting airflow. It's not that big of a deal with EFI, but it's much more of an issue with carbureted motors.

Hand finishing the port walls with 80-grit cartridge rolls will net a surface finish that's close to ideal. Raw CNC finishes can sometimes be too rough, but some high-end CNC machines produce incredibly smooth finishes. As far as the finish on the exhaust port is concerned, for the most part, it's irrelevant, because exhaust gasses are pushed out of the port by the piston. The bottom line is that you can lose flow by having too smooth of a port wall finish, and it's better to be too rough than too smooth.

CHAPTER 9

The stock LS9 cylinder heads share the same port and chamber design as the L92/LS3 units, but they are cast from a more durable A356-T6 material to handle the rigors of forced induction. One of the most noticeable differences is the LS9's reinforced rocker stud bosses. (© GM Corp.)

work around this issue, GM simply moved the pushrod passages over to the side to create more space for the intake ports, which allowed engineers to create more traditionally shaped rectangle ports. This also enabled raising the intake port entrance to make the most of the LS7's 12-degree valve angle.

Cutting down on production costs is always a design consideration at the OE level, so in order to retain the same valve spacing as in other Gen III/IV small-blocks, GM implemented offset intake rocker arms in the LS7. Consequently, the final spec sheet for the LS7 heads resembles an all-out race head: CNC-machined 260-cc intake ports, 86-cc exhaust ports, 70-cc combustion chambers, 2.20/1.61-inch valves, and 360 cfm of airflow. Further porting can push flow figures to the hallowed 400-cfm mark.

CNC Porting

The term "CNC porting" gets thrown around a lot, but what exactly does the process entail? Entry-level CNC machines can be used for extremely simple tasks, such as cutting out a header flange or engraving a valve cover. With advanced five-axis CNC mills and state-of-the-art coordinate measuring machines, however, a cylinder head designer has the ability to clone ports at the push of a button. In the hands of a skilled operator, a five-axis CNC machine can replicate intricately contoured ports and combustion chambers far more quickly and precisely than ever imaginable by hand. It's like a Xerox machine, but for cylinder heads instead of paper.

Biological creatures are simply no match for the port-to-port consistency and time savings CNC machines offer. When hand porting a cylinder head, it can easily take two weeks to design one intake port, one exhaust port, and one combustion chamber. What makes things eight times more difficult is trying to replicate the same port and chamber design for the remaining seven cylinders to achieve acceptable consistency in flow from port to port. Using snap gauges and molds to try to minimize port-to-port variation can add 10 to 15 hours of labor per head. Likewise, the short-turn radius is very difficult to replicate consistently, as slight variations in its shape will dramatically affect airflow. Even the best porters in the world struggle to get the short-turn radius exactly the same every single time. The more complex the shape of a port, the harder it is to match by hand.

This inherent inconsistency is why almost all profession race teams rely heavily on CNC porting. The process involves using state-of-the-art digital probes and lasers to create a three-dimension clone of the ports and chambers and using powerful computer software. A highly trained CNC operator then translates that data into lines of computer code, which the CNC machine interprets to precisely clone identically shaped ports and chambers with alarming accuracy. With symmetrical-port cylinder heads, like those found on the Gen III/IV small-block, that means a head designer only has to port one set of ports and chambers instead of eight.

After a port has been designed and digitized, a five-axis CNC machine can fully port a pair of cylinder heads in half a day; by comparison, hand porting could easily take two weeks. For the average hot rodder, this time savings has been passed down to the consumer in the form of extremely high-quality, yet affordable, parts. The growing popularity, and mass production capability, of five-axis CNC machines is largely responsible for why the $1,200 cylinder heads of today will easily out-flow cylinder heads from just 15 years ago that were three times as expensive.

In addition to time savings, the greatest benefit of CNC porting, from a performance standpoint, is the accuracy in which the machines whittle away ports. Just a few years ago, if a CNC-machined port flowed within 5 to 10 cfm of a prototype port, it was considered a huge success. These days, it's now possible to get a CNC-machined port to flow within 1 cfm of a prototype port. Just because a head is CNC-ported doesn't elevate it to greatness by default, but if programmed by a skilled machinist, the quality and consistency a five-axis CNC machine offers is almost impossible to match by even the best hand porters in the world.

CYLINDER HEADS

Edelbrock's Victor LSR cylinder heads aren't for the faint of heart or budget. These raw castings feature unfinished ports and combustion chambers, so designing them is up to the end user. The reward for all that hard work is immensely powerful ports capable of flowing more than 450 cfm. (Photo courtesy of Edelbrock)

That's pretty darn close to big-block territory, and at a hair under $3,000 for a set of fully assembled LS7 heads from your friendly GMPP distributor, they're an exceptional value.

L92 Heads

At first glance, the factory L92 cylinder heads look like a slightly detuned variant of the vaunted LS7 castings. Like the LS7 units, the L92 castings feature raised rectangular port entrances measuring 260 cc and 70-cc combustion chambers. Differences include the standard Gen III/IV 15-degree valve angle, smaller 2.165/1.590-inch valves, and as-cast ports, as opposed to the CNC-machined ports on the LS7 heads. Because of this, the L92 heads don't flow quite as well as the LS7s, but at 330 cfm, they're not far behind.

The most shocking figure of all is their price. Because the L92 heads were designed to be produced in much greater volume than the LS7 castings, they sell for just $1,000 fully assembled, a price that includes the mandatory offset rocker arms. That makes them the best value by far out of all the factory and aftermarket LS-series cylinder heads on the market.

The design of the L92 heads actually predates the conception of the LS7 heads. When the LS7 engine program began, engineers had a horsepower target of 500, but they weren't sure how many cubic inches the motor would eventually displace. Consequently, the first sets of prototype heads were designed for use on cylinder bores smaller than the massive 4.125-inch bores engineers ultimately settled upon. Once GM decided to move forward down the 4.125-inch-bore path, the small-bore prototype heads were deemed inadequate for delivering their airflow objectives. As a result, they developed a new head with bigger valves and CNC-machined ports.

Fortunately, the small-bore heads didn't go to waste. GM was working on a replacement for the LQ4 and LQ9 in its heavy-duty truck applications, and engineers realized that the small-bore prototype heads from the LS7 engine program would work perfectly in meeting their 400-hp target. So, in an interesting turn of events, cylinder heads that eventually made their way into heavy-duty truck motors are direct descendents of the factory C5R racing program.

Once engineers knew that the L92 heads were destined for large-volume production, they shifted their focus to reducing manufacturing costs. This is why they retained the standard 15-degree valve angle, which helps maintain the same pushrod length as in other Gen III/IV engines. Moreover, the biggest factor in keeping costs down is that, unlike the LS7 heads that are CNC-ported, the L92s are delivered as cast. As no surprise, porting a set of L92s can yield airflow figures of 370 cfm, right on par with the LS7 heads.

With the success of the L92 heads, GM began installing them on engines across the car and truck lines, most notably in the C6 Corvette and fifth-gen Camaro. Engines equipped with these heads include the LS3, L92, L99, and LY6. Additionally, the rectangle-port castings used on the supercharged LS9 and LSA are essentially L92 heads built from a more rugged alloy for forced-induction duty. Perhaps the most appealing aspect of the L92 castings is that they work on bore diameters as small as 4.000 inches, whereas the LS7 heads require a minimum bore size of 4.100 inches.

C5R Heads

The early days of hopping up the LS-series small-block were a rat race between cubic inches and cylinder head development. At first, ported factory LS1 and LS6 castings flowed more than the typical street/strip engine could reasonably use. However, as machinists mastered the art of sleeving factory aluminum blocks, and displacement figures surpassed the 400-ci mark, the stock cylinder heads began limiting ultimate horsepower in all-out race applications.

It wasn't until AFR released the first aftermarket LS-series cylinder heads in 2004 that enthusiasts had a reasonably priced alternative to the factory castings. Before that long-awaited day came to pass, the only other option for big-inch, high-RPM race engines was the GM C5R cylinder heads. Like the LS7 heads that borrowed heavily from the design of the C5R heads, port architecture was dramatically improved. The intake ports were

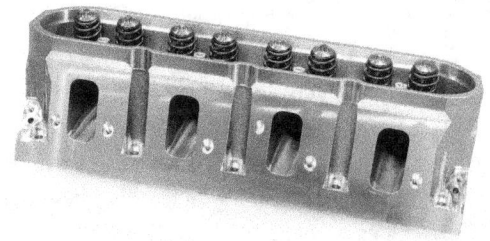

In addition to greater airflow potential, aftermarket cylinder heads boast an all-around superior casting design. Common features include thicker deck surfaces, raised valve cover rails, and beefier port walls.

raised as high as possible without interfering with the valvetrain, and they were widened out substantially to create a rectangular shape. Likewise, the heads were cast from a more durable 355-T7 aluminum.

From GM, the C5R castings are delivered unfinished with no valve seats, valve guides, or valvetrain components. Because professional head designers are often forced to add epoxy to certain areas of the ports to create the ideal shape, the C5R heads feature unfinished ports with tons of material that can be ground away to create the perfectly shaped port. The intake ports measure just 210 cc out of the box, but they can be enlarged by 50 to 60 cc. The same goes for the tiny 30-cc combustion chambers, which are also unfinished.

Although all this extra material gives porters lots of flexibility in designing ports and chambers that are ideally matched to a given race application, the C5R heads require a substantial amount of labor just to make them useable. In essence, with full-race heads like the C5Rs, a head porter is forced to design ports and chambers from scratch, and only race teams with very deep pockets can even afford to use them. Likewise, a set of bare C5R castings costs $3,800, and they also require a custom intake manifold. Even though they're capable of flowing in excess of 400 cfm, the price and labor requirements of the C5R heads puts them out of reach for most enthusiasts, especially since GM and the aftermarket are now offering heads that deliver similar performance at a much lower price. If you stumble upon a set of C5R heads that have already been prepped, then they might be worth the investment. Otherwise, there are much better performance values on the market.

Some aftermarket heads slightly alter the factory valve location. This requires a custom stand bolted between the rocker arm bosses and the rocker arms, which are supplied with the cylinder heads, to maintain proper rocker-tip-to-valvestem geometry. (© GM Corp.)

Most factory and aftermarket rectangle-port heads require a minimum bore diameter of 4.000 inches. Mast Motorsports doesn't think that the big-bore guys should have all the fun, so it also offers its LS3 heads for 3.900-inch-bore engines. These impressive castings flow 353 cfm, despite being limited on valve size. (© GM Corp.)

Aftermarket Heads

Although it took nearly seven years for the first aftermarket Gen III cylinder heads to hit the scene, parts catalogs are now packed full of them. They range from mild 205-cc castings intended for

Angle Milling

Milling the deck surface of a head is usually performed to decrease the size of the combustion chambers in order to increase the compression ratio. The process is performed any time a head is pulled off a running engine to flatten the mating surface and improve head gasket seal.

Engine builders learned long ago that milling the deck surface at an angle–thereby removing more material from the exhaust side of the deck than the intake side–yielded sizable gains in airflow. The reason for this is simple. Angle milling cylinder heads reduces the size of the combustion chambers, raises the intake runners, and helps de-shroud the valves by moving them closer to the center of the combustion chamber. It also allows more material to be removed from the deck surface before hitting the valve seats. However, there is a practical limit to how much a head can be angle milled.

For instance, it's simply not feasible to roll a 15-degree head over to an 11-degree valve angle. Typically, cutting .017 inch off the exhaust side per inch of cylinder head width reduces the valve angle by one degree, and 1.5 to 2 degrees is the absolute max. Optimizing the chambers and seats in addition to angle milling can net a solid 15-cfm increase in a head that flows 300 cfm. The only downside is that the minute change in geometry that results from angle milling may require longer pushrods and some creative installation when fitting the intake manifold and headers.

CYLINDER HEADS

mild, stock-displacement, hydraulic roller cam applications all the way up to full race heads capable of supporting more than 1,000 naturally aspirated horsepower. Obviously, for anyone looking to crack quadruple digits in power, aftermarket cylinder heads are a must. However, because ported factory GM heads can flow just as well as entry-level aftermarket castings, why even bother with aftermarket hardware?

There is a time and a place for both, but aftermarket heads generally offer several advantages. Compared to factory heads, most aftermarket units are cast from a more rugged alloy for enhanced durability. Additionally, aftermarket castings typically utilize thicker deck surfaces for better gasket seal, particularly in power adder applications, along with raised valve cover rails for increase valvetrain clearance. Other common enhancements include reinforced rocker stud bosses and thicker port walls.

All this adds up to a cylinder head that's superior to a factory unit in almost every regard. Furthermore, the cost of porting stock heads and fitting them with quality valvetrain components can run up a tab that's just as expensive as an aftermarket casting.

Perhaps the most important factor to consider is that putting a ported stock cylinder head up against an out-of-the-box aftermarket casting is an apples-to-oranges comparison. Although it's possible for a ported stock casting to match the performance of an aftermarket head, a ported aftermarket head puts a stocker to shame. For instance, although a ported factory LS6 head typically tops out at around 320 cfm, a ported aftermarket cathedral-port casting can easily exceed 350 cfm. Much of this is attributable to the fact that aftermarket heads have thicker port walls, especially in the critical areas around the pushrod tubes and the valvespring pockets. This enables a skilled porter to achieve the cross-sectional area and port volume necessary to push an aftermarket head well beyond the capabilities of a stock casting.

As with factory cylinder heads, aftermarket castings are available in both cathedral- and rectangle-port designs. For the ultimate in performance, rectangle-port heads still have the edge, but it's not nearly as big of a gap in the realm of aftermarket heads.

In the past few years, there has been an influx of cathedral-port heads with massive intake runners designed for big-inch, high-RPM engine combinations capable of supporting 750-plus hp. By taking full advantage of their meaty port walls, these monster cathedral-port heads—from companies such as AFR, Dart, and Trickflow—move upwards of 370 cfm of air. So, although a rectangle-port head may sometimes offer a slight edge in performance, that's not always the case. Interesting, too, are the exotic canted-valve heads that have recently entered the marketplace; they offer monstrous ports approaching 300 cc and more than 420 cfm of airflow.

GMPP offers several versions of its LSX cylinder heads. Common features among them include .625-inch-thick decks, thicker port walls, and a six-bolts-per-cylinder bolt pattern. Port and chamber designs are based on the L92 castings.

Unlike the production LS7 heads that come CNC-ported, GMPP's LSX-LS7 units are delivered as cast. With the benefits of a 12-degree valve angle and raised intake ports, these heads give professional porters lots of flexibility in designing powerful ports.

Throat Diameter of the Intake Port

The section of an intake port directly above the valve seat is known as the valve throat, and establishing the proper throat diameter is a critical step in maximizing airflow. A throat diameter that's too big or too small can seriously impede airflow, but fortunately, getting it right is a straight-forward process.

The general rule of thumb is that the throat diameter should be roughly 90 percent of the valve diameter. On race valve jobs, because the seats are moved farther down near the valve, the guidelines change slightly, depending on the specific valve seat angle. With a 45-degree valve seat, the throat diameter should be .200 inch smaller than the valve, and with a 50-degree seat, it should be .180 inch smaller. Stepping up to a 55-degree seat requires a throat diameter that's .160 inch smaller than the valve.

CHAPTER 9

Needless to say, regardless of brand, it's hard to go wrong with any aftermarket cylinder head these days. Unlike 20 years ago, when enthusiasts had to pick between good heads and junk heads, now the challenge is trying to pick the best heads out of an assortment of heads that offer outstanding performance. And that's a very good problem to have.

AFR

The first company to release all-new aftermarket Gen III cylinder heads in 2004, Air Flow Research offers some of the best street/strip castings available today. Powerful, high-velocity ports that combine respectable peak CFM with outstanding low- and mid-lift performance distinguish AFR heads. On the street, where a broad powerband takes precedence over high-RPM power, that's exactly what you want out of a cylinder head.

It all started with AFR's original 205-cc Mongose LS1 castings, designed for 3.900-inch-bore motors. Despite having ports that are only 5 cc larger than those of a stock LS6 casting, the 205-cc AFRs flow an additional 70 cfm for an advertised total of 298. Common sense says that such a dramatic increase in airflow through a stock-sized intake runner translates to high-velocity ports that promote low-RPM cylinder filling. Flow figures aside, however, AFR's claim to fame is producing cylinder heads that seem to consistently outperform their advertised cfm numbers. With a mild hydraulic roller camshaft with 220 to 230 duration at .050-inch lift, the 205-cc AFRs routinely produce 550 to 600 hp.

AFR recommends its 205-cc cylinder heads for applications ranging from 346 to 396 ci. Although AFR's 205-cc heads are the most competition-proven Gen III/IV heads on the market, the company has recently improved upon them with is new 210-cc V2 castings. These heads offer further-improved low- and mid-lift flow and velocity in addition to an extra 8 to 10 cfm of peak flow.

For larger-displacement, higher-RPM engine combinations, the AFR lineup also includes 215-, 230-, and 245-cc cathedral-port castings. Like the 210-cc V2 cylinder heads, the 230-cc units are an updated version of AFR's original 225-cc castings that utilize a raised intake port entrance for improved efficiency. For the ultimate in cathedral-port performance, AFR's 245-cc heads flow an impressive 360 cfm. These heads have undergone tons of R&D, more so than most competing designs, and these blur the lines between cathedral- and rectangle-port heads, as they flow just as much as a set of factory LS7 castings. As many Gen III/IV engine

Bore diameter, valve size, and valve angle determine whether or not valve-to-cylinder-wall interference will be an issue. To maintain proper clearances, it's very important to pay attention to a cylinder head manufacturer's recommended minimum bore diameter.

Block-to-Head Compatibility

Of the 90 million Gen I Chevy small-blocks produced through the decades, the vast majority were built around a 4.000-inch bore, with variations in displacement primarily achieved through altering the length of the stroke. However, the exact opposite is the case with the LS-series small-block. GM uses a common 3.622-inch stroke in most Gen III/IV small-blocks and elects to alter displacement by changing the bore diameters of the block instead. Consequently, Gen III/IV small-blocks are produced with 3.780-, 3.900-, 4.000-, 4.065-, and 4.125-inch bore diameters. Likewise, aftermarket blocks are offered in a dizzying array of bore configurations, and when machining a block for stroker duty, a hot rodder can specify an infinite number of bore diameters.

Although this variety gives enthusiasts tremendous flexibility when building an engine, careful attention must be paid to the head-to-block compatibility. Larger bore diameters and flatter valve angles offer more space between the cylinder walls and valves. As a result, cylinder head designers take advantage of this additional real estate by fitting heads with larger valves in big-bore applications. To prevent valve-to-cylinder-wall interference, cylinder head manufacturers publish a minimum bore diameter in which their heads can be used. To assist in the head selection process, this information is included elsewhere in this chapter. In the event that the minimum recommended bore size isn't listed for a cylinder head you're considering, it's best to call the manufacturer directly instead of assuming it will work.

CYLINDER HEADS

builders will attest, it's hard to go wrong with a set of AFR cylinder heads.

All Pro

As aftermarket blocks give hot rodders the flexibility to build bigger-displacement motors, it forces cylinder head development to keep pace. All Pro's 12-degree, rectangle-port LS7 cylinder heads prove the point. Featuring 285-cc intake ports, 2.200/1.600-inch valves, a thick .750-inch deck surface, and CNC-machined ports and combustion chambers, the All-Pro heads flow a very respectable 410 cfm. With a flow figure like that, they're ideally suited for big-inch stroker combos in excess of 430 ci. Other highlights include reinforced rocker stud bosses, large 1.625-inch-diameter valvespring pockets, and compatibility with six-bolt aftermarket blocks.

Dart

Few aftermarket companies can boast as rich of a racing heritage as Dart. Company founder Richard Maskin cut his teeth building championship-winning NHRA Pro Stock engines, and the lessons learned on the track have inevitably trickled down into Dart's aftermarket product line.

Dart's Pro 1 Gen III/IV lineup features cathedral-port cylinder heads that retain the factory 15-degree valve angle, and they are offered in 205-, 225-, and 250-cc configurations. The 205-cc castings come equipped with 2.020/1.600-inch intake and exhaust valves and 62-cc combustion chambers, as well as an advertised peak flow number of 290 cfm. Dart's 225-cc castings have a slightly larger 2.050-inch intake valve, and they flow a hair over 300 cfm. To keep costs down, both the 205- and 225-cc cylinder heads have as-cast ports. The heads can be purchased for $1,800 fully assembled, making them two of the most affordable sets of aftermarket heads available. At the top of the Dart LS1 pyramid are the company's 250-cc CNC-ported cylinder heads. Highlights include 2.080/1.600-inch valves, beefier valvespring pockets, and CNC-machined ports, combustion chambers, and bowls. At $2,100 fully assembled, they're also an excellent value.

Edelbrock

With one of the most impressive foundry facilities in the country, Edelbrock uses its unparalleled resources to cast quality cylinder heads for virtually every domestic engine platform in existence. Naturally, the company offers a number of different cylinder head options for the LS-series small-block.

Edelbrock's 203-cc Performer RPM castings were designed in conjunction with Lingenfelter Performance Engineering, and they feature reinforced spring pockets, CNC-ported runners and bowls, 2.020/1.570-inch valves, and 65-cc combustion chambers. Advertised flow ratings spec in at 320 cfm, and they cost $2,600 for a fully assembled set.

Although Edelbrock's Performer RPM heads flow plenty for the vast majority of enthusiasts, the company also offers one of the most serious castings in the entire Gen III/IV market. Designed strictly for competition engines, Edelbrock's Victor LSR cylinder heads offer what is arguably the most flow potential of any LS casting on the market. The heads are cast utilizing a hot isostatic pressure process, in

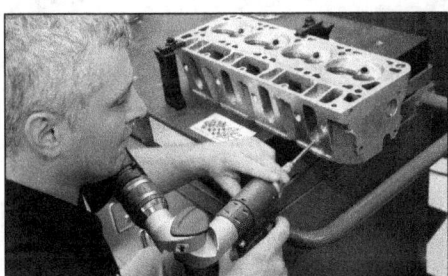

A CNC machine is only as good as the person who programmed it, and the first step in the CNC porting process is to create a prototype port by hand. Next, a space-age coordinate measuring machine, called the FARO arm, creates a virtual computer model of the cylinder head. By simply running a probe across the surface of the ports and chamber, the FARO arm exports data points into your computer.

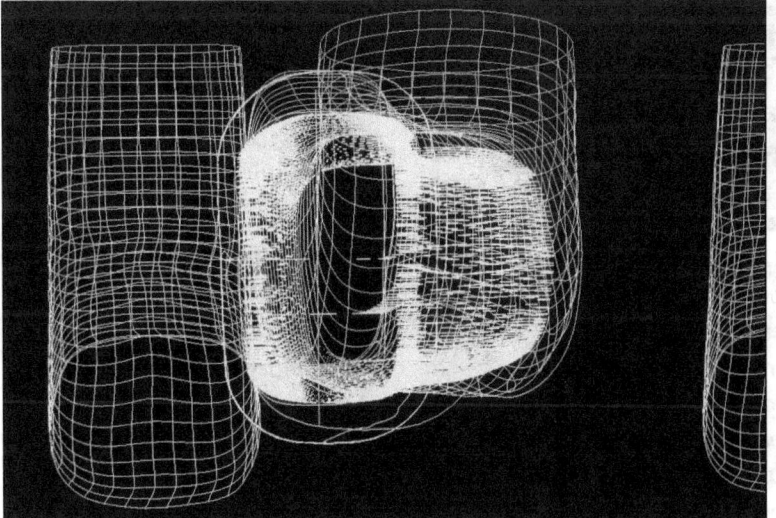

Since the probe inevitably passes over the same spot multiple times, redundant data points can be filtered out after digitization is complete. A huge perk of digitizing the ports is that dimensions that are difficult to calculate manually, such as the average cross-sectional area, can be precisely measured.

As the probe is moved throughout the ports, a 3-D model is created on-screen, which enables the operator to gauge how much progress is being made.

which the heads are placed in a vacuum chamber to remove porosity and contaminants. After that, they are pressurized at 30,000 psi with nitrogen during heat-treating. The end result is an extremely durable head that can handle the most abusive of environments.

However, the key word to remember with these heads is "potential," as the LSRs are pure race castings that arrive unfinished. That means it's up to end users to design their own custom ports and combustion chambers from scratch. Because the heads have extra-thick port walls and space for massive 2.250/1.600-inch valves, some of the first race shops to get their hands on these heads have been able to coax 450-plus cfm out of the LSRs. That's not just big-block Chevy territory; that's Big Chief Rat motor territory. Nonetheless, that kind of potential comes at $2,400 for a pair of raw castings, so the entry price point is reasonable. However, factor in the labor involved with designing and machining custom ports and chambers, and the total development costs for a finished set of LSR heads can easily cost 10 times as much.

So, although it's all in good fun to admire the airflow potential of the Victor LSR heads and appreciate just how far the LS engine platform has advanced, unless you own a five-axis CNC machine and have your own in-house R&D department, forget about bolting these beasts up to anything but a mega-dollar race engine. That said, as more race shops get their hands on the LSR castings and put forth the initial investment in R&D to development port and chamber designs for them, it is quite possible that they may someday be within reach for the deep-pocketed sportsman racer.

GM Performance Parts

During the 50 years that separate the genesis of the Gen I small-block Chevy and the Gen III small-block platform, engineers and racers learned a thing or two about building performance engines. That partially explains why Gen III/IV engine development—both at the OE level and in the aftermarket—has advanced at such a blistering pace. What can't be forgotten, however, is the influence of GM's internal Performance Parts division, which simply didn't exist in 1948. By leveraging the stacks of R&D data compiled while designing production parts with the vast resources of GM, the company's Performance Parts division has been at the forefront of Gen III/IV aftermarket parts development since day one. Just as GMPP's LSX blocks upped the durability and displacement ante, its new lineup of cylinder heads improves upon production castings that are already excellent performers.

Currently, GMPP offers five different LSX rectangle-port cylinder heads, for everything from stock-displacement engines to drag race and circle track applications. All LSX heads are cast from a durable 356-T6 aluminum alloy and feature 5/8-inch-thick decks and beefier port walls. GMPP's entry-level aftermarket

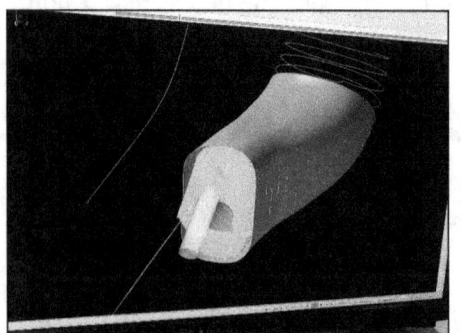

The path the CNC tool travels to create the desired port shape is called the tool path. After creating a 3-D model of the ports and chamber, the projected tool path is put into motion on-screen to check for potential hang-ups. The tool path is then run through a post processor to write the actual program, which is called the G-code. Different CNC machines have different axes and ranges of travel, so post-processing software is specific to each machine.

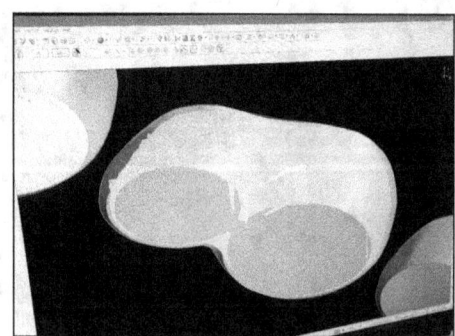

The digitizing process is repeated for the combustion chamber. Because the chambers have very complex contours with tight radiuses, it's often necessary to attach a tiny 3-mm probe onto the FARO arm. The digitized chamber data can also be sent to the piston manufacturer to help create a dome that fits perfectly inside the chamber.

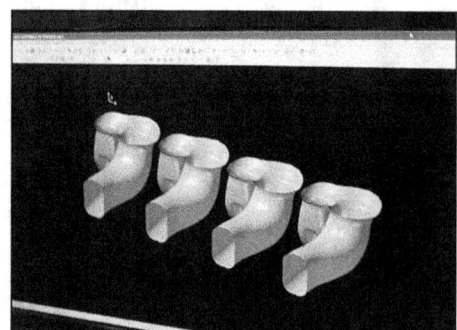

With symmetrical heads, such as GM Gen III/IV castings, the prototype ports and combustion chamber are cloned for the remaining three cylinders. This eliminates the need to design each and every port one at a time, and it ensures that every single port and chamber in the heads are identical, a feat that's nearly impossible when porting by hand. The port on the left is a hand-ported port, and the others have been cloned using computer software based on bore spacing of the block. The software is so precise that it allows modifying a hand-ported surface even further.

CYLINDER HEADS

head, the 250-cc LSX-L92, is essentially an improved version of the stock L92 castings designed for enthusiasts with small 3.900-inch-bore engines. To maintain small-bore compatibility, they're fitted with 2.000/1.550-inch valves.

In comparison, the LSX-LS3 heads retain the stock L92's 260-cc ports and 2.165/1.590-inch valves. The LSX-LS9 heads are the same as the LSX-LS3's, but with the addition of titanium intake valves and sodium-filled exhaust valves. An improved version of the stock LS7 cylinder heads, the LSX-LS7 heads feature a 12-degree valve angle, giant 2.200/1.610-inch valves, 270-cc as-cast ports, and six-bolt-per-cylinder bolt pattern for use on aftermarket blocks.

The upper echelon of GMPP's aftermarket cylinder heads is an evolution of the C5R castings. These monsters come in two configurations—for circle track and drag racing applications—and are appropriately named LSX-CT and LSX-DR. Common features include an 11-degree valve angle, 1.625-inch valvespring pockets, raised valve cover rails, a spread-port exhaust configuration, CNC-machined ports and combustion chambers, and intake ports that have been raised an impressive 10 mm.

The LSX-CT heads utilize epic 302-cc intake ports, 45-cc combustion chambers, and 2.200/1.610-inch valves. They flow more than 420 cfm, and they can support 850 hp. The LSX-DR heads are even meaner, with 313-cc intake ports, 50-cc combustion chambers, 2.280/1.620-inch valves, and 450 cfm of airflow capable of producing 900 hp.

As their cavernous ports and tiny combustion chambers suggest, both the LSX-CT and LSX-DR heads are intended strictly for race motors running race gas. Aside from stunning airflow, what makes these heads even more appealing is that GMPP offers matching intake manifolds for them, which eliminates the need to custom fabricate an expensive sheet-metal unit. The bottom line is that the LSX-CT and LSX-DR castings are extraordinary heads for extraordinary applications.

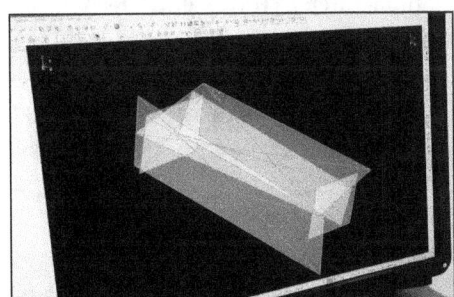

In addition to mapping out the ports and chamber, the FARO arm creates virtual planes based on the angle and position of the deck, intake port, exhaust port, and valve cover rail surfaces. The dowel locations and front and rear surfaces of the head are also mapped. This enables the FARO arm to orient the location of the ports and chambers in relation to the rest of the head.

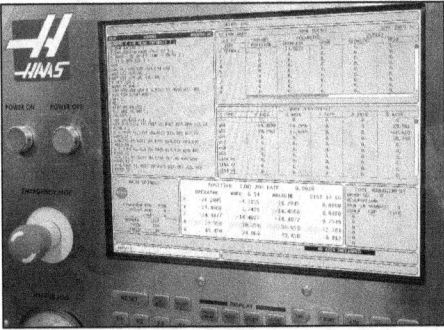

The digitized data from the Verisurf software is run through a post processor to create lines of G-code compatible with the Haas CNC machine. That data is then loaded, via a USB drive, into the CNC machine's control station, which interprets the code, using Mastercam software, to determine the tool path. On a five-axis mill, the place where the A- and B-axes meet is called the point of origin. The final step before machining begins is to make sure that the computer program and the CNC machine have the same point of origin.

Mast Motorsports

Founded in 2007, Mast Motorsports is a newcomer to the performance aftermarket, but the company has already established a reputation for quickly and efficiently developing cutting-edge hardware. Mast developed the industry's first aftermarket rectangle-port Gen III/IV cylinder heads, and it has since expanded its lineup to envelop everything from stock 3.900-inch-bore engines to all-out race motors.

Offered in three basic configurations, for 3.900-, 4.000-, and 4.125-inch bore engines, Mast's rectangle-port LS3 heads flow 353, 370, and 390 cfm, respectively. These 12-degree heads are fully CNC-ported, and they are compatible with the factory LS3 intake manifold and rocker arms. Additionally, the Mast catalog includes an LS7 casting that flows an impressive 395 cfm through a 274-cc intake port that's only a hair larger than stock. For serious race motors, Mast also has a canted-valve LS7 head that flows more than 420 cfm.

To further expand its product line, Mast acquired Performance Induction Specialties. The consolidated resources of both highly respected companies have created a veritable powerhouse in the Gen III/IV cylinder head market. The Mast cylinder head catalog includes a comprehensive lineup of 11-degree cathedral-port castings ranging from 215 to 265 cc. Much like GM's rectangle-port heads, these unique castings incorporate offset intake rocker arms for improved port architecture and a reduced pushrod pinch area, with peak flow numbers ranging between 320 to 370 cfm.

RHS

A circle track and drag racing powerhouse in the 1970s and 1980s, Racing Head Service went on hiatus for several years before reemerging early this millennium. Apparently, RHS hasn't missed a beat, and its cylinder heads are better than ever. For Gen III/IV small-blocks, RHS offers Pro Elite cathedral-port cylinders in 210- and 225-cc configurations. Highlights include an 11-degree valve angle, thick .800-inch deck surfaces, and a taller valve cover rail. The meaty deck surface can be milled to reduce combustion chamber size down to 36 cc, and the extra material between the top of the intake ports and the valve cover rail frees up space for a raised roof port design. Despite these improvements, the Pro Elite heads are fully compatible with standard Gen III valvetrain components and intake manifolds.

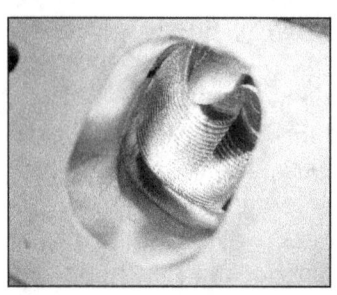

After all programming has been completed, the CNC machine can go to work. The maximum amount of material removed in one pass should be limited to .25 inch. The step-over distance of the tool path determines the size of the ridges that are usually visible with CNC-ported heads. A .100- to .200-inch step-over is typically used when roughing in a port, and a .010- to .020-inch step-over is common on the finishing pass. SAM cut its Edelbrock LSR heads with an ultra-fine .005-inch step-over, which creates a smooth finish that is almost indistinguishable from that on a hand-ported head. Each port flowed within 1 cfm of each other, ranging between 460 to 461 cfm.

Forced induction is a subject that can be an entire book in and of itself, but suffice it to say that turbocharging an LS-series small-block yields stunning performance. Thanks to their high-flow heads, LS-series small-blocks produce outstanding horsepower figures at low boost levels on pump gas. Fastlane's 72-mm turbo system for LS3 Camaros lays down 585 rear-wheel hp at just 7 psi of boost.

Factory GM Cylinder Heads

Type	PN	Minimum Bore	Port Volume	Chamber Volume	Valve Angle	Valve Size
LM7	12563678	3.780	200/70	61.2	15 degrees	1.890/1.550
LQ4/LQ9	12565364	3.898	210/75	71	15 degrees	2.000/1.550
LS1	12559855	3.898	200/70	66.7	15 degrees	2.000/1.550
LS2/LS6	12564824	3.898	210/75	64.5	15 degrees	2.000/1.550
L92/LS3	12615355	4.000	260/90	70	15 degrees	2.165/1.590
LSA	12626958	4.000	260/90	70	15 degrees	2.165/1.590
LS9	12621774	4.000	260/90	70	15 degrees	2.165/1.590
LS7	12578449	4.100	270/85	70	12 degrees	2.200/1.610

RHS's 210-cc heads are designed for engines with a minimum bore of 3.900 inches and feature 2.040/1.570-inch valves. According to RHS, they're good for 320 cfm and can support more than 600 hp. The 225-cc castings are compatible with bore sizes of 4.000 inches and up, and they are fitted with larger 2.080/1.600-inch valves. With an advertised flow rating of 328 cfm, RHS says they'll support in excess of 650 hp. At $1,500 for a set of fully assembled 210-cc castings, RHS's Pro Elite heads are a great value and undercut the price of many ported stock heads.

Trick Flow

Although the company started by manufacturing small-block Ford components, Trick Flow now offers a range of cathedral-port GM Gen III/IV cylinder heads that's one of the most diverse in the industry. All Trick Flow heads have a flatter-than-stock 13.5-degree valve angle, and the company offers a top-notch head for every conceivable application.

Although the smaller-displacement 4.8L and 5.3L LS small-blocks have been widely ignored by most aftermarket manufacturers, Trick Flow recognized they're growing in popularity and created a cylinder head specifically for these applications. The company's GenX Street 205 head is a small-runner casting that works incredibly well on 3.7800-inch-bore engines. The heads feature 58-cc chambers and 2.00-inch intake valves that complement their small 205-cc runner size very nicely and clear the factory bore. All of Trick Flow's 205-cc heads come with fully CNC-machined ports and combustion chambers, and they can also be used on 3.900-inch stock-bore LS1s. According to Trick Flow, a set of its 205-cc castings will out-flow stock LS6 castings, and in-house testing of an otherwise stock 5.3L with a 216/220-at-.050 netted 456 hp and 425 ft-lbs of torque.

CYLINDER HEADS

Moving up the ladder, Trick Flow offers 215-cc heads with 2.040/1.575-inch valves for 3.900-inch-bore engines, and 225-cc heads with 2.055/1.575-inch valves for 4.000-inch-bore applications. Designed for 400-plus, big-bore motors, Trick Flow's 235-cc heads are fitted with 2.080/1.600-inch valves and flow 340 cfm out of the box. For motors displacing upwards of 440 ci, the 245-cc castings utilize 2.100/1.600-inch valves and include provisions for six-bolt blocks. For the truly exotic engine combos that require even more airflow potential, Trick Flow has recently released an unfinished LSX-R casting that can support up to a 265-cc intake runner that pushes preconceived notions of cathedral-port heads to the envelope.

In addition to CNC-ported heads, Trick Flow also offers 220-cc units that incorporate the company's "Fast as Cast" intake and exhaust runners. To create these heads, Trick Flow started with one of its CNC-ported cylinder heads, and then it made intake and exhaust port tooling based off the port shapes. Thanks to modern casting technology that allows locating the intake and exhaust cores to tight tolerances, the port shapes are much more precise than was possible just 10 years ago. With as-cast ports and CNC-machined chambers and bowls, the 220-cc heads flow almost as well as CNC-ported heads for 30 percent less money. Offering 305 cfm of flow for $1,700 in fully assembled trim, the as-cast 220s boast excellent performance for the dollar with plenty of room to grow.

Aftermarket Cylinder Heads

Type	PN	Minimum Bore	Port Volume	Chamber Volume	Valve Angle	Valve Size
AFR 205	1510	3.898	Cathedral	66	15 degrees	2.020/1.600
AFR 215	1530	3.898	Cathedral	64-74	15 degrees	2.020/1.600
AFR 225	1610	3.898	Cathedral	62-72	15 degrees	2.080/1.600
AFR 245	1680	4.060	Cathedral	64-72	15 degrees	2.160/1.600
All Pro 285	LSW	4.100	Rectangle	58-70	12 degrees	2.200/1.600
Dart 205	11011112	3.898	Cathedral	62	15 degrees	2.020/1.600
Dart 225	11021122	3.898	Cathedral	62	15 degrees	2.050/1.600
Dart 250	11071143	4.000	Cathedral	68	15 degrees	2.080/1.600
Edelbrock 203	61969	3.898	Cathedral	65	15 degrees	2.020/1.570
Edelbrock LSR	77049	4.125	Rectangle	N/A	N/A	N/A
GMPP C5R	22534593	4.100	Rectangle	30	11 degrees	N/A
GMPP LSX-L92	19201807	3.890	Rectangle	65	15 degrees	2.000/1.550
GMPP LSX-LS3	19201805	4.000	Rectangle	70	15 degrees	2.165/1.590
GMPP LSX-LS9	19213963	4.000	Rectangle	70	15 degrees	2.165/1.590
GMPP LSX-LS7	19201806	4.100	Rectangle	70	12 degrees	2.200/1.610
GMPP LSX-CT	19166981	4.125	Rectangle	45	11 degrees	2.200/1.610
GMPP LSX-DR	19166979	4.125	Rectangle	50	11 degrees	2.280/1.620
Mast 253	510-301	3.898	Rectangle	62	12 degrees	2.040/1.570
Mast 256	510-302	4.000	Rectangle	69	12 degrees	2.165/1.600
Mast 270	510-304	4.125	Rectangle	70	12 degrees	2.200/1.600
Mast 215	510-320	3.898	Cathedral	63	11 degrees	2.040/1.570
Mast 225	510-321	3.898	Cathedral	62	11 degrees	2.040/1.570
Mast 245	510-322	4.000	Cathedral	70	11 degrees	2.080/1.600
Mast 275	510-324	4.125	Cathedral	70	11 degrees	2.200/1.600
RHS 210	54210-02	3.898	Cathedral	62	11 degrees	2.040/1.570
RHS 225	54225-02	4.000	Cathedral	62	11 degrees	2.040/1.570
TFS 205	30500001-C00	3.780	Cathedral	58	13.5 degrees	2.000/1.575
TFS 215	3060T001-C01	3.898	Cathedral	64	13.5 degrees	2.040/1.57
TFS 220	3060T001	3.898	Cathedral	64	13.5 degrees	2.040/1.575
TFS 220	3060T002	4.000	Cathedral	65	13.5 degrees	2.055/1.575
TFS 225	3060T001-C02	4.000	Cathedral	65	13.5 degrees	2.055/1.575
TFS 235	3060T001-C03	4.000	Cathedral	70	13.5 degrees	2.080/1.600
TFS 245	3061T003-C04	4.000	Cathedral	70	13.5 degrees	2.100/1.600

CHAPTER 10

CAMSHAFTS

The cylinder heads might be the most important part of an engine in terms of producing horsepower, but unless something opens up the valves, the heads will flow no air at all. And zero airflow equals zero horsepower. The responsibility of opening and closing the valves at precise intervals falls on the camshaft, which makes it the second most important component in the overall horsepower equation.

By controlling how much, how long, and when the intake and exhaust valves open and close, the camshaft determines how much horsepower an engine makes and the RPM range in which that power is concentrated. The camshaft also profoundly impacts gas mileage and emissions quality, which probably aren't very high on the priority list for hot rodders, and it also affects idle quality and low-RPM drivability, which are huge concerns for any street-driven vehicle.

What makes proper camshaft selection so critical is that going too big or too small can ruin an otherwise perfect engine combination. Too conservative of a cam won't allow an engine to take full advantage of the cylinder heads' airflow capabilities. Too aggressive of a cam can compromise low-speed drivability so badly that you wonder why you spent so much time and money maximizing the cubic inch total in the first place. As with cylinder head design, camshaft theory is an extremely complex science that involves dozens of inter-related variables. It's quite possible that there are even fewer true camshaft experts than there are cylinder head gurus, and that's really saying something.

The good news is that you don't need to know how to design the perfect lobe profiles in order to pick the ideal camshaft for your stroker motor project. Just learning the basics of camshaft theory will get you in the ballpark, and consulting with camshaft manufacturers and engine builders will get you the rest of the way there.

Camshaft manufacturers have invested thousands of hours into designing hundreds of off-the-shelf cam grinds that complement the vast majority of engine applications. Oftentimes, an off-the-shelf grind out of a catalog works remarkably well, and at roughly $400, it's not terribly expensive to experiment with different camshafts, if necessary. If you do need to spec out a custom cam, chances are its design is based upon an off-the-shelf grind that's been slightly modified to suit the specific demands of your application. Either way, the consumers are the direct beneficiaries of the massive R&D efforts of the major camshaft manufacturers, such as Comp Cams, Lunati, Isky, GMPP, and Edelbrock. Just learn the basics, and you'll be on your way to selecting the perfect camshaft for your stroker buildup.

All LS-series small-blocks come equipped with a hydraulic roller camshaft from the factory. Thanks to improvements in modern valvetrain technology, this combines the convenience and low maintenance of hydraulic lifters with the high-RPM potential once reserved for mechanical lifters.

CAMSHAFTS

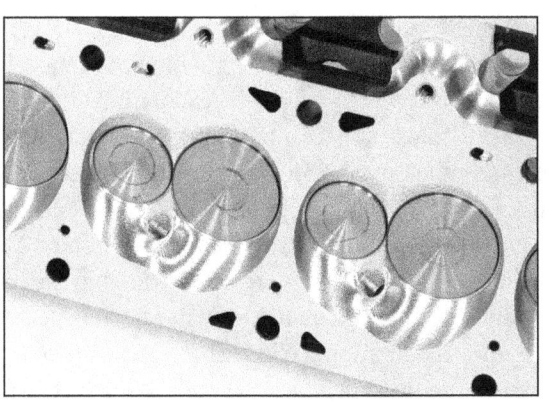

The camshaft determines how long the valves stay open and how far they move off their seats, as well as when these events take place. These factors profoundly impact how much power is produced, in addition to where that power is concentrated in the powerband.

Although LS enthusiasts looking for maximum high-RPM power usually upgrade from a hydraulic roller cam to a solid roller cam, a solid flat-tappet cam is also a very capable performer. It's lighter and offers superior high-RPM valvetrain stability compared to a hydraulic roller cam, which yields greater power potential. Likewise, its flat noses offer quicker initial lift acceleration than a roller design, making it an appealing option for racing classes that place restrictions on maximum duration or lift. (Photo courtesy of Comp Cams)

Dynamic Compression

Compared to production engines, the typical stroker small-block packs a much higher static compression ratio. Of all LS-series motors, the LS7's 11.0:1 squeeze ratio is the greatest, but that still pales in relation to many street/strip combos that exceed 12.0:1.

The reason why this is possible–while still retaining pump-gas compatibility–is due to a product of the dynamic forces at hand during the induction process. Static compression ratio is a useful tool in determining an engine's power potential and fuel-quality requirements, but it doesn't take into account how cam timing and duration affect the actual quantity of air present inside the cylinders. As discussed elsewhere in this chapter, the intake valve stays open even after the piston begins climbing back up the bore during the compression stroke. Therefore, substantial compression of the air/fuel mixture can't be achieved until after the intake valve closes. Recognizing this, engine builders devised a way of determining an engine's dynamic compression ratio to more accurately gauge an engine's peak cylinder pressure and resistance to detonation.

Dynamic compression ratio is an extension of how static is calculated by taking the intake valve closing point into account, as well as where the piston is positioned in the bore at IC. The higher the piston is positioned in the bore at IC, the lower the dynamic compression will be. Furthermore, a longer connecting rod slightly reduces dynamic compression, although its effects are extremely minimal.

Taking both piston position at IC and rod length into account establishes the dynamic stroke length, which is used in place of the actual stroke length to determine the dynamic compression ratio. Unfortunately, calculating dynamic stroke by hand requires complex trigonometry formulas that factor some rather extraneous measurements into account, such as the rod distance below the crankshaft centerline, rod horizontal displacement, and the distance between the piston and the crank centerline. Because most people don't have the desire or dedication to mathematics to calculate dynamic compression by hand, there are dozens of calculators available online to do the number crunching for you.

For example, a 402-ci engine with a 4.000-inch bore, a 4.000-inch stroke, 70-cc combustion chambers, zero deck height, -4-cc valve reliefs, .039-inch-thick head gaskets, and 4.060-inch-bore head gaskets yields a static compression ratio of 11.01:1. If this same motor were equipped with 6.125-inch connecting rods and a Comp Cams 251/256-at-.050 cam with an intake closing point of 74 degrees ABDC, it would have a dynamic compression ratio of 8.16:1. Generally, old-school small-block Chevys with iron heads and carburetors can safely run 8.0:1 points of dynamic compression on pump gas. With newer aluminum-headed EFI small-blocks, such as LS-series motors, dynamic compression ratios of 8.5:1 are common. Consequently, our sample 402 can actually operate at 11.5:1 static compression, thereby raising dynamic compression to 8.5:1 and still running safely on pump gas. Doing so would help minimize the inherent adverse affects of a long-duration cam at low RPM.

CHAPTER 10

Cam Effects

Although camshaft dynamics is an extremely complex subject, a few basic universal truths of cam theory can help simplify understanding the role a cam plays in overall engine performance. Replacing a stock camshaft with a larger aftermarket unit having longer duration and higher lift almost always yields an increase in horsepower. Likewise, the larger the camshaft, the higher in the RPM band an engine produces peak horsepower and torque. And because horsepower is simply torque multiplied by RPM, moving the torque peak higher in the RPM range increases horsepower every single time.

The drawbacks of big camshafts are that they increase emissions output and decrease low-RPM torque, throttle-response, and intake manifold vacuum at idle. Again, tailpipe emissions and gas mileage probably aren't big concerns for the typical hot rodder, but compromised low-speed torque requires shorter gearing, and an engine that doesn't produce adequate idle vacuum won't be able to actuate a power brake system. Furthermore, extremely aggressive camshaft grinds also accelerative wear and tear on the rest of the valvetrain components. Combating this with a heavier-duty valvetrain drives up cost considerably.

That said, like every other aspect of engine building, choosing the right camshaft is all about balance. Having an irrational phobia for duration and lift is a good way to guarantee that an engine never produces respectable power and torque. For instance, it makes no sense whatsoever to invest thousands of dollars in a set of top-notch cylinder heads and a forged rotating assembly capable of handling 9,000 rpm if the parts combination is going to be hampered by a dinky hydraulic roller cam that isn't capable of fully exploiting an engine's airflow and RPM potential. Furthermore, different drivers have different tolerances for low-RPM surge and choppy idle quality, so what's considered an aggressive cam or a tame cam is purely subjective. Although a high school kid may find a lopey 230-at-.050 cam charming and intoxicating in a 346-ci motor, an older and more mature enthusiast might find the same cam unstreetable in a 396.

Varying tastes and tolerances aside, what can't be disputed is that larger-cubic-inch engines reduce the adverse effects of a more aggressive camshaft. For example, a camshaft that struggles to idle and suffers from very poor throttle response in a small-displacement motor idles like stock and yields tire-shredding low-end torque in an engine that's 100 ci larger.

Expanding upon that example, let's say there are two engines, with identical camshafts, cylinder heads, intake manifolds, and compression ratios, but one measures 383 ci and the other measures 427 ci. The peak horsepower output between the two is similar, but the 427 produces far more low- and mid-range torque and manifold vacuum while peaking at a lower RPM. That equates to a far more streetable package that places less stress on the valvetrain components, enhancing durability, and enables running taller gearing for improved gas mileage. Consequently, camshaft selection must be closely matched to an engine's displacement and intended

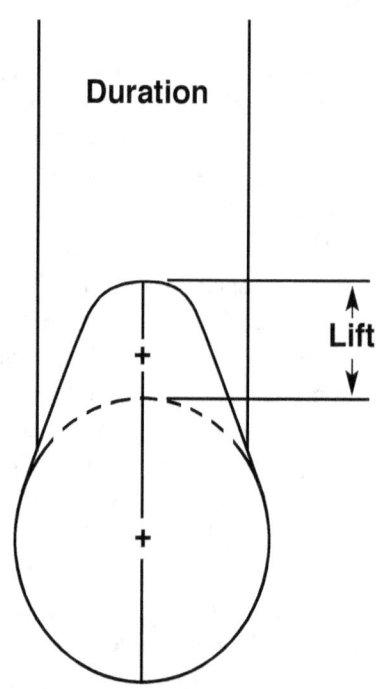

Camshaft grinding is an extremely precise process in which tolerances are held to thousandths of an inch. In order to endure higher valvespring pressures and steeper ramp acceleration rates, solid roller camshafts are usually ground from a durable billet core.

Ideally, the effects of altering duration and lift would be independent from each other, but this isn't possible, because both are determined by the shape of the cam lobe. Increasing lift increases the distance the lifter must travel around the cam lobe, thereby increasing duration. A good rule of thumb is to select duration based on an engine's operating RPM range, and lift should be based on a cylinder head's airflow at high lift.

usage. Simply changing the camshaft can transform driving characteristics from that of a stock-caliber rebuild to a low-RPM street cruiser to a dual-purpose street/strip machine, or a high-RPM race engine.

Lobe Profile

At the risk of pointing out the obvious, a camshaft is a shaft fitted with eccentric cam lobes, and lobe lift is the difference between the radius of the cam lobe's base circle and the height of the eccentric. On an OHV engine like the LS-series small-block, the camshaft is mounted inside the block, and one lobe is designated for each valve, for a total of 16 lobes. The eccentric shape of the cam lobes enables them to convert the rotating motion of the camshaft into reciprocating motion. It's this reciprocating action that pushes up on the lifters, pushrods, and rocker arms, thereby opening and closing the valves. How far the cam lobes push open the valves is referred to as "lift," and the length of time the valves stay open is called "duration."

The shape of the cam lobes establishes lift and duration, and consequently, they are interdependent. For instance, grinding down a cam lobe to reduce lift also reduces duration. Likewise, the maximum amount of lift that can be ground into a cam is ultimately limited by cam duration. That's because increasing lift without increasing duration creates a steeper lobe profile, and there's a physical limit to the rate of ramp acceleration that both the camshaft and lifters can handle. Under ideal circumstances, camshaft design would allow for isolating the effects of duration and lift from each other in terms of how they affect power, but that simply isn't the case. Even so, understanding the relationship between duration and lift is a useful tool in the camshaft selection process.

Duration

Of the multitude of variables that go into designing a camshaft, duration has the most profound impact on power production. Because a camshaft rotates at half the speed of the crank, duration is expressed in degrees of crankshaft rotation. This represents how long the valves stay open in relation to crankshaft rotation. For instance, a cam that has 250 degrees of duration at .050-inch lift stays open for about 250 out of the 360 degrees that it takes the crank to make one complete revolution. At low RPM, when there is plenty of time to fill the cylinders with air, short-duration camshafts perform very well. However, as RPM increase, and the amount of time available to fill the cylinders decreases, a short-duration cam literally chokes off an engine's air supply, and horsepower plummets accordingly.

The concept of time in relation to cylinder filling might seem awkward at first, but it's actually very easy to conceptualize. Consider that at 2,000 rpm, the intake valves open and close roughly 17 times per second. At 6,000 rpm, however, that figure increases to 50, giving the incoming air charge far less time to fill the cylinders with air each time the intake valves open and close. Because longer-duration camshafts hold the intake valve open longer, thus improving cylinder filling, they improve horsepower and torque output at high RPM. Additionally, they also extend the RPM at which peak power is produced. For example, swapping out a 220-at-.050 cam in a 408 stroker motor with a 240-at-.050 cam increases the horsepower peak from about 5,500 rpm to 6,000 rpm.

The distance between the peaks of the intake and exhaust lobes establishes a camshaft's LSA. Although duration and lift dictate how much power an engine will produce, the LSA is a fine-tuning tool that changes where in the RPM range horsepower and torque is concentrated.

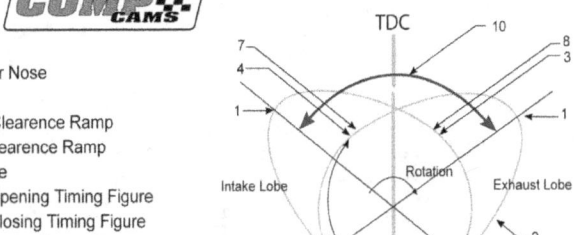

1. Max Lift or Nose
2. Flank
3. Opening Clearence Ramp
4. Closing Clearence Ramp
5. Base Circle
6. Exhaust Opening Timing Figure
7. Exhaust Closing Timing Figure
8. Intake Opening Timing Figure
9. Intake Closing Timing Figure
10. Intake to Exhaust Lobe Separation

If duration, lift, and LSA were the only factors in camshaft dynamics that influenced performance, then one manufacturer could reverse-engineer another company's R&D efforts by simply duplicating their published camshaft specs. The truth of the matter is that there are far more variables involved in designing a camshaft. Two camshafts with identical duration and lift figures can have vastly different acceleration curves. The challenge for manufacturers is figuring out how hard the lobes can push the valvetrain without creating excessive deflection and introducing valve float. (Illustration courtesy of Comp Cams)

On the other hand, the same long-duration camshaft that works so well at 5,000-plus rpm sacrifices low- and mid-range torque compared to a shorter-duration cam. In order to maximize cylinder filling, it's common for the intake valve to stay open even after the piston passes BDC on the intake stroke. As a result, the intake valve doesn't close until after the piston begins traveling back up the bore during the compression stroke. That might sound like a bad idea at first, but at high RPM, the intake air charge packs enough energy and velocity to continue filling the cylinder even after the piston passes BDC.

Unfortunately, that's not the case at low RPM, when the incoming air charge simply lacks adequate velocity to do so. Consequently, a portion of the intake air charge is pushed back past the intake valve and into the intake manifold. The subsequent drop in cylinder pressure accounts for the loss in low-RPM torque in a long-duration camshaft. To compensate for this, it's very common practice to increase the static compression ratio to increase cylinder pressure and minimize low-RPM torque loss. At the end of the day, duration determines both the power potential of an engine and the range of RPM in which it produces that power.

Overlap

During the four-stroke cycle, there is a brief period when both the intake and exhaust valves are open at the same time. As the piston travels up the bore during the exhaust stroke, the intake valve opens before it reaches TDC. This gives the intake charge more time to fill the cylinders at high RPM and increases the scavenging effect imparted by the exiting exhaust gases. At high engine speeds, the inertia of the combustion gases escaping into the exhaust port helps pull additional air through the intake port and into the cylinder.

On the other hand, overlap isn't always a good thing. At low RPM, the scavenging effect of the exhaust is insignificant. Consequently, when the intake valve opens near the end of the exhaust stroke, when residual cylinder pressure is still present in the cylinder, exhaust gas flows past the intake valve and reverts back into the intake manifold. This is what gives performance camshafts a lopey idle.

Overlap is essentially the distance, in cam degrees, between the peaks of the

At maximum valve lift, the piston is nowhere near TDC. With very aggressive cam grinds, the piston often travels halfway down the bore at maximum intake valve lift. As a result, piston-to-valve clearance is more a function of duration than it is maximum lift.

Adjustable timing sets allow altering the installed centerline of a camshaft, thereby advancing or retarding the valve events in relation to crankshaft rotation. Comp Cams' adjustable billet timing set has nine keyway slots in the crank gear for up to 8 degrees of latitude. (Photo courtesy of Comp Cams)

intake lobe and the exhaust lobe. These peaks, known as the intake and exhaust centerlines, are measured in degrees of crankshaft rotation and establish the lobe separation angle (LSA) of the cam. For instance, if a cam has an intake centerline of 108 degrees ATDC and an exhaust centerline of 112 degrees BTDC, averaging the sum of both figures yields an LSA of 110 degrees. In other words, the distance between the peaks of intake and exhaust lobes in such a cam would be 110 degrees of camshaft rotation. Decreasing the lobe separation by moving the intake and exhaust lobe peaks closer together increases overlap. As with duration and lobe lift, the LSA of a camshaft can't be changed without regrinding the lobes.

Although camshaft duration determines the operating RPM of an engine, changing the LSA can be used to further fine-tune the operating characteristics of an engine within its powerband. It seems simple enough, but tightening or widening the LSA as a tuning tool can get tricky, because its effects are dependent upon duration.

On a small cam with roughly 210 degrees of intake duration at .050-inch lift, a tighter LSA improves top-end horsepower at the expense of idle quality and low-end torque. That's because generous overlap improves scavenging at high RPM, but it also increases reversion at low RPM. Conversely, widening the overlap with a short-duration camshaft tends to improve idle quality and low-RPM torque at the expense of top-end power.

However, gauging overlap solely by a cam's LSA can be a bit deceptive. As duration increases, overlap increases, even if the LSA isn't changed. For example, a 260-at-.050 cam has much more overlap than a 225-at-.050 cam, even if both are ground on a 112-degree LSA. In other words, the actual overlap of a camshaft—measured in crankshaft degrees—takes precedence over the lobe separation angle.

This fact is important to remember as duration at .050 inch tappet lift increases. The same 112-degree LSA that idles so smoothly in a 210-at-.050-duration cam will yield a very choppy idle in a 260-at-.050-duration cam. The substantial overlap in the 260-at-.050-duration cam will not only sacrifice low-end torque, it can also dilute the intake charge enough to reduce high-RPM horsepower. Such a cam usually still produces excellent peak horsepower numbers, but the power curve drops off very sharply after that point. Consequently, with long-duration camshafts, a wider LSA can result in a broader, more flexible powerband that drops off much more gradually after peak power. And in competitive racing classes, power after peak is almost as important as peak horsepower.

Between 1997 and 2006, all LS-series small-blocks used cam cores that attached to the timing gear with three bolts. However, GM began phasing in single-bolt camshafts in 2006. Since VVT-equipped Gen IV small-blocks use a single cam bolt that doubles as an oil control valve, GM presumably started phasing in single-bolt cam cores throughout the LS lineup to cut down on production costs. All VVT-equipped LS motors have a single-bolt cam, but not all LS motors with single-bolt cams have VVT. Fortunately, swapping out a three-bolt cam for a single-bolt setup, and vice versa, is as easy as pairing the camshaft with a matching single-bolt timing set.

Studying the specs of factory Gen III/IV camshafts thoroughly reinforces this point. The 5.7L LS1 used in 2001–2002 F-bodies came equipped with a 196/207-at-.050-duration camshaft ground on a 116-degree lobe separation angle. On the other hand, the 7.0L LS7 utilizes a 211/230-at-.050 cam with a 120.5-degree lobe separation angle.

Compared to the typical aftermarket cam, factory LS-series camshafts have far wider lobe separation angles to improve idle quality and clean up emissions output. This is particularly important in the LS7, as its duration specs are quite aggressive in the world of factory cams, which was necessary in order for GM engineers to achieve their target horsepower and operating RPM range. To compensate for the inherent increase in overlap that its longer-duration specs yield, the LS7 cam is ground on a substantially wider LSA than the LS1's. The LS7's wider LSA also helps mask the detrimental effects on idle quality and emissions output that its longer duration naturally creates. Because idle and emissions quality aren't major concerns in a hot rod application, aftermarket cams can get away with much more overlap and tighter lobe separation angles.

Measuring Duration

Camshaft manufacturers publish both advertised duration figures and duration at .050-inch tappet-lift specs. The advertised duration figure is always bigger, and although it seems strange, there's a good reason why two different duration specs are necessary.

Due to the acceleration rate of a cam lobe's ramp, it's difficult to determine the precise moment at which the lifter starts climbing the ramp. As a result, camshaft manufacturers start to measure duration at a predetermined amount of lifter, or tappet, rise. For example, Comp Cams begins measuring duration once the lifter rises .006 inch above the base circle. Obviously, the lower this figure is, the longer the duration specs appear to be, even though the duration hasn't actually changed. This makes the cam look bigger on paper than it is. Because camshaft manufacturers can measure advertised duration at any lift point they choose, it makes it very inaccurate to compare advertised duration specs among different manufacturers. Recognizing this problem, camshaft manufacturers agreed to use duration at .050-inch lifter rise as the industry standard for measuring duration. Doing so allows engine builders and enthusiasts to accurately gauge the duration figures of camshafts among different manufacturers. As a result, it's widely accepted that advertised duration numbers aren't nearly as important as duration at .050 figures.

Although that may be the case, it doesn't mean that the duration figures below .050 inch tappet lift are entirely irrelevant. Low-lift numbers between .001 and .020 inch tell an engine builder a great deal about engine vacuum and throttle response, and high-lift numbers greater than .200 inch are more indicative of power potential. The .050-inch number is relatively easy to measure with a dial indicator and degree wheel, which explains why it's the universal industry standard. Additionally, it does the best job of predicting the operating range of a given lobe in a specified application.

It's important to remember, however, that duration at .050-inch tappet lift isn't the same as the actual amount of time the valve stays open. The actual duration of the intake valve—or how long the valve remains unseated between its opening and closing events—is affected by tappet lift below .050 inch, as well as rocker arm ratio. This is one of the reasons why two camshafts with identical duration, lift, and LSA can perform very differently on the dyno and on the street.

Lift

Compared to duration, cam lift is relatively straightforward. Lobe lift is simply the difference between the radius of the cam's base circle and the height of the eccentric portion of the cam. For example, a factory 2001 LS6 cam has a base circle radius of .760 inch, and the distance between the base circle centerline and the highest point on the intake cam lobe is 1.068 inches. Subtracting the base circle radius of .760 inch from the cam lobe height of 1.068 inches nets .308 inch of lobe lift. This simple illustration explains why high-lift camshafts typically have smaller base circles.

Reducing the size of the base circle while leaving the cam lobe height unchanged increases the lobe lift. That's because decreasing the base circle diameter increases the distance between the top of the cam lobe and the base circle radius. Using this approach, let's imagine that the 2001 LS6 cam's base circle radius was reduced from .760 inch to .720 inch while its 1.068-inch cam lobe height remained unchanged. This would effectively increase lobe lift from .308 inch to .348 inch. Furthermore, smaller base circles are also necessary to prevent the connecting rods from contacting the camshaft in engines with stroker crankshafts.

Single-bolt camshafts are also used in newer non-VVT LS-series engines. Aftermarket companies offer camshafts and timing sets for both three- and single-bolt configurations. An engine equipped with a single-bolt camshaft can be converted to a three-bolt arrangement, and vice versa, by swapping over to a matching timing set. (Photo courtesy of Comp Cams)

In the aforementioned example, marginally increasing lobe lift might seem rather insignificant. However, valvetrain dynamics suggests otherwise. As the cam lobe pushes up on the lifter and pushrod, the rocker arm acts as a see-saw and converts this upward motion into downward motion. During this process, it also multiplies the lobe lift. Consequently, valve lift is the product of lobe lift multiplied by the rocker arm ratio. With the exception of the LS7, all factory Gen III/IV small-blocks utilize a 1.7:1 rocker arm ratio. Therefore, increasing lobe lift from .308 inch to .348 inch increases valve lift from .524 to .591 inches, which is substantial in anyone's book.

While duration specs are based on the target operating RPM range of an engine, lift is based upon airflow through the cylinder heads. This makes it very easy to select the proper amount of lift for a camshaft. For instance, if a cylinder head achieves peak airflow at .650-inch lift, it should be matched with a camshaft that has at least .650-inch valve lift. In extreme applications, however, things can get more complicated. Some engine builders contend that it's sometimes possible to increase horsepower by opening the valves beyond the point where the cylinder heads back up. Such an application might have a .800-inch

Because GM's slick VVT system is hydraulically actuated, it requires channeling oil through the center of the camshaft. To facilitate this, VVT cam cores are drilled hollow.

lift cam even though the cylinder head airflow starts dropping off at .700-inch lift. The justification is that, beyond a certain point, the flowbench can't accurately replicate the operating conditions inside an engine. In other words, in extreme high-airflow, high-RPM conditions, the piston sucks down on the intake charge much harder than the electric motor in a flowbench can draw air in through the ports.

Nonetheless, one aspect of lift that can't be disputed is how much of it can now be packed into a relatively short-duration camshaft. Compared to cams of just 20 years ago, modern bumpsticks allocate much greater lift over much shorter duration cycles. In the past, relatively long-duration camshafts were necessary in order to hit a target valve lift to reduce stress on the valvetrain. That's because steeper lobes place greater loads on the lifters, pushrods, rockers, valvesprings, and the lobes themselves. Cylinder heads of the day rarely flowed well beyond .500-inch lift, so this wasn't a big deal. However, as cylinder head technology improved, as evidenced by factory LS-series castings that flow well past .600-inch lift, it became necessary to improve valvetrain durability. Fortunately, camshaft and valvetrain manufacturers met the demand, and now it's possible to stuff tons of lift over a steep, short-duration lobe. This gives both the drivability that was once missing in large cams and the power that was difficult to achieve with short-lift cams.

Piston-to-Valve Clearance

When planning a new engine build, or upgrading to a larger cam in an existing combo, it's critical to check for adequate piston-to-valve clearance. As the term suggests, there must be enough clearance between the valves and piston crown near TDC in order to prevent severe damage to the valvetrain, cylinder heads, and short-block.

Generally, piston manufacturers recommend a minimum of .080-inch clearance between the intake valves and piston crown and .100-inch clearance for the exhaust valves when using steel connecting rods. Due to the increased stretch of aluminum rods, they require an additional .030 inch of clearance. Hot rodders instinctively examine the maximum lift figures of a cam to try to determine if there will be adequate piston-to-valve clearance, but the issue at hand revolves more around duration than lift. The reason for this is simply because when the piston is at TDC, the intake valve is nowhere near peak lift. In fact, at TDC, the intake valve is just starting to move off its seat.

Verifying this line of thinking is as easy as looking at the intake centerline angle of a cam's published specs. To illustrate the point, let's take a look at one of the most aggressive LS-series camshafts in Comp Cams' catalog, its XFI286R113 grind. This beastly solid roller cam boasts duration specs of 251/256-at-.050 and .660/.655 inch

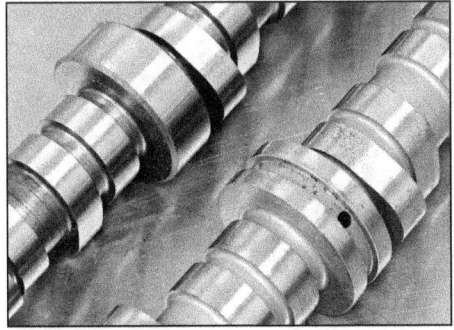

To feed oil to the VVT system's phaser assembly, oil is routed from a groove cut into the number-2 cam journal to the oil control valve that bolts inside the cam snout. This simple arrangement allows supplying hydraulic pressure to actuate the system without any modifications to the block, which makes it very easy to retrofit VVT to non-VVT engines.

valve lift. Despite the fact that it packs a massive amount of lift, especially for a small-block, a quick look at the intake centerline angle reveals that the intake valve doesn't reach peak lift until 110 degrees ATDC. At that point, the piston is nowhere close to TDC and has actually descended about halfway down the bore. That means that even with a stock 3.622-inch LS1 crank, a piston would be nearly 1.811 inches down the bore. Worrying about whether or not the cam's peak lift—in this case .660 inch—is enough to smack into the piston is awfully silly, considering that the piston would be almost 1.811 inches down the bore. And that's before you even take the angularity of the intake valve into account. This resoundingly reinforces the point that piston-to-valve clearance has very little to do with peak valve lift.

On the other hand, it's safe to assume that a cam with 251 degrees of intake duration, regardless of lift, would probably cause piston-to-valve interference issues, unless big valve reliefs were cut into the piston. During the time it takes the crankshaft to make one complete 360-degree revolution, a 251-degree cam leaves the intake valve open for roughly 70 percent of that cycle. That means that the intake valve is closed for just 109 degrees, or 30 percent of time, for each revolution of the crank. Additionally, the actual valve duration is even longer than the duration figure at .050-inch tappet lift.

Unfortunately, although long-duration camshafts increase the potential of piston-to-valve interference, there is no single spec that gives a definitive answer on whether or not it will be an issue. Variations in block deck height, cylinder head casting tolerances, head gasket thickness, combustion chamber depth, and piston shape all affect piston-to-valve clearance. Consequently, the only way to accurately check for it is during

the engine assembly process. A builder checks it by placing a piece of clay on top of the pistons, bolting the cylinder heads down, and then rotating the crank over by hand several times. Removing the cylinder heads and inspecting the clay clearly reveals whether or not piston-to-valve interference is present.

Valve Events

Cam duration and lift determine how long and how much the valves open. Granted they're the two most important variables in the horsepower equation when it comes to camshafts, but they don't offer any insight as to when the valves open and close. In a four-stroke internal-combustion engine, there are four valve events: intake valve opening (IO), intake valve closing (IC), exhaust valve opening (EO), and exhaust valve closing (EC). When each of those events takes place, it is collectively known as valve timing, and each plays a role in the shape of the power curve.

Because lift and duration can't be changed without regrinding a camshaft, the only parameter that can easily be

The phaser assembly in VVT engines replaces the cam gear. It features an internal rotor and stator assembly, which enables the camshaft to be advanced or retarded. An oil control valve that doubles as the cam bolt adjusts hydraulic pressure in the phaser assembly, which advances or retards the camshaft.

tweaked once the lobe profiles have been finalized is the cam timing. Although when the valve events take place in relation to the position of the crankshaft, and therefore pistons, may seem rather inconsequential, engine builders have proven otherwise over the decades. Of the four valve events, intake valve closing most profoundly impacts horsepower output. In fact, some engine builders say that intake closing is more important than the other three valve events combined.

The opening and closing of the intake valves determine how much air can be drawn into the cylinders on the intake stroke. With a typical performance camshaft, it's not uncommon for the intake valve to close up to 60 degrees ABDC. Extremely long-duration cams delay intake closing even farther. This isn't ideal at low RPM, as the pistons push the air/fuel mixture back past the intake valve and into the intake manifold, which hurts low-end torque and idle quality.

On the other hand, delaying the intake closing point is exactly what an engine needs at high RPM, and simple physics dictates why this is the case. Although the piston tries to push the air/fuel mixture back past the intake valve as it travels up the bore, at high RPM the inertia and velocity of the intake charge exceeds the upward pressure exerted by the piston. So even though the piston is moving up the bore after BDC during the intake stroke, the inertia of the intake charge continues filling the cylinder with air. By nature, long-duration camshafts delay the intake valve closing point, which is largely responsible for the increase in horsepower they yield over shorter-duration cams.

To put into perspective how late the intake valve closing point can be delayed in a long-duration camshaft, let's re-examine Comp Cams' XFI286R113 solid roller grind. This 251/256-at-.050 cam has an intake valve closing point of 74 degrees ABDC. That means the intake valve doesn't close until the piston is almost half way up the bore during the compression stroke. Expanding upon this example, many race-only cams have more than 280 degrees of duration at .050-inch tappet lift, pushing the intake valve closing point even farther into the compression stroke. To put it succinctly, with the tremendous airflow potential of modern cylinder heads, and the high-RPM potential of today's short-blocks and valvetrain hardware, never underestimate the effects of inertial charge filling and the dividends in horsepower they offer.

In contrast, the other three valve events also affect power production, but they aren't nearly as important. The exhaust opening point is most commonly accepted as the second most important valve event, as it determines the LSA of a camshaft. Retarding exhaust opening improves bottom-end torque, and advancing it allows spent fumes to exit the cylinders sooner, which generally improves high-RPM power. Because the intake valve opens before TDC during the exhaust stroke, it affects overlap. An earlier IO increases overlap, thereby sacrificing low-end torque for top-end power. Delaying the IO does the exact opposite. Likewise, the exhaust valve closes after TDC during the intake stroke.

One downside to GM's VVT system is that excessive valvespring pressure can overwhelm the hydraulic pressure inside the phaser assembly, sending it into full mechanical retard. To prevent this from happening, Comp Cams and Mast Motorsports offer restrictors that can be fitted into the phaser assembly to limit the movement of its internal rotor to 20 to 30 degrees.

A VVT timing cover is easily identified by the big hump in its upper section, which houses an electric solenoid that controls oil flow through the phaser assembly. The solenoid—which interfaces with the camshaft position sensor—operates via pulse width modulation, since it must react instantaneously to inputs received by the PCM.

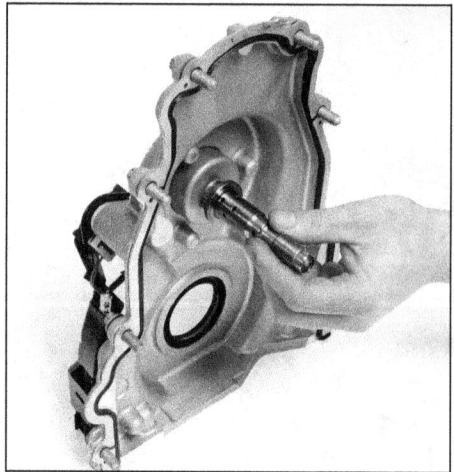

The oil control valve fits behind an electric solenoid mounted in the timing cover. When the solenoid applies pressure to the valve, oil exits out of the valve's multiple orifices and into the phaser assembly. By manipulating pressure, the solenoid can put more pressure on one side of the phaser assembly than the other, causing it to rotate.

CAMSHAFTS

Consequently, an early EC decreases overlap and boosts low-end torque, but it doesn't allow sufficient time for exhaust gases to escape out of the cylinder at high RPM, decreasing top-end power. A late EC has the opposite effect. Although IO, EO, and EC all alter horsepower and torque production in some way, their effects are largely inconsequential compared to IC.

Timing Tricks

As with duration and lift, the four valve events can't be changed independently of each other without regrinding a camshaft. They can, however, be changed at the same time. During engine assembly or dyno tuning, advancing a cam involves turning it a few degrees clockwise in relation to the crankshaft, thereby advancing when the valve events take place; retarding the cam involves turning it a few degrees counterclockwise to delay the valve events. In other words, advancing or retarding the cam simply changes the installed intake centerline in relation to the crank.

For example, if a cam is ground on a 109-degree intake centerline, but it's installed at a 112-degree intake centerline, it has been retarded three degrees. To facilitate quick-and-easy timing adjustments, most aftermarket timing sets have multiple keyway slots ground into the crank sprocket. Advancing the cam generally improves low-end torque and throttle response while sacrificing peak horsepower, and retarding the cam decreases low-end torque while increasing peak power. This is because advancing the cam closes the intake valve sooner, and retarding the cam delays the intake closing point.

In theory, changing all four valve events in unison isn't an ideal situation. Ideally, the intake and exhaust lobes should be phased independently, but that requires either a DOHC valvetrain or a trick cam-in-cam layout like the one in the 2008-and-up Dodge Viper V-10. Fortunately, the other three valve events are so inconsequential compared to intake closing that it's nothing to split hairs over.

For instance, exhaust opening is commonly accepted as the second most important valve event, as it determines the LSA of a camshaft. Retarding the exhaust opening improves bottom-end torque, and advancing it allows spent fumes to exit the cylinders sooner, which generally improves high-RPM power with long-duration camshafts. This is exactly the opposite of what happens when advancing or retarding intake closing, which means that optimizing intake closing actually compromises the exhaust opening point. Nonetheless, the effects of intake closing are so much more profound that it really doesn't matter much at all.

GM's VVT system uses surprisingly few VVT-specific parts. All you need to retrofit VVT onto any Gen III or IV small-block is a timing cover, a phaser assembly, a 58-tooth reluctor wheel, and an oil-control valve from an L92/L99, all of which can be purchased for well under $300. Other requirements include a VVT-specific camshaft and a computer from a factory-equipped VVT car that has the necessary programming tables to control the phaser assembly. A VVT retrofit is quite justifiable if you're building an LS motor from scratch to drop into a muscle car, since most of the retrofit-specific hardware is stuff you'd have to buy anyway.

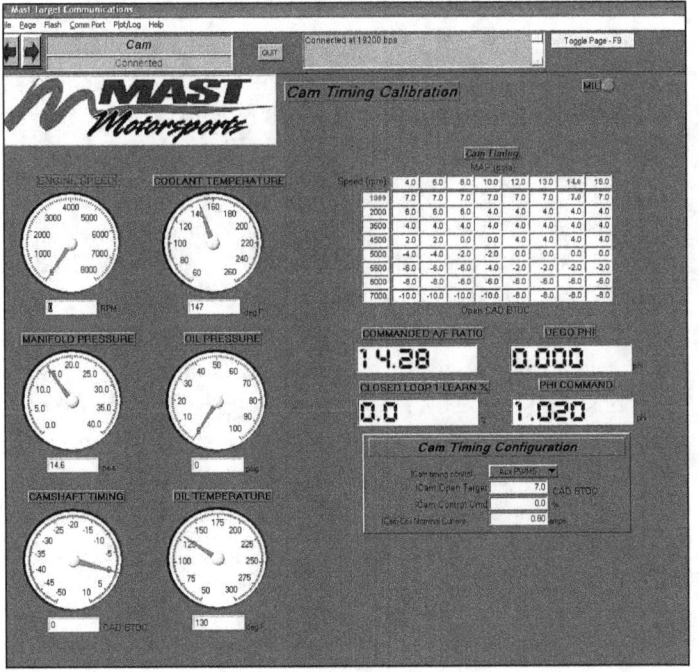

Programming the VVT system requires obtaining a PCM from a VVT-equipped car and reprogramming it with software from HP Tuners or EFI Live. Another alternative is to use Mast Motorsports' stand-alone M-90 PCM and wiring harness, which has the necessary tables to control the factory VVT system.

HOW TO BUILD BIG-INCH GM LS-SERIES ENGINES

CHAPTER 10

Variable Valve Timing

The obvious limitation of valve timing adjustments is that after an engine is built and installed into a car, the only way to make addition adjustments is to tear into the motor again. Furthermore, aftermarket timing sets typically limit the latitude of adjustment to roughly six degrees. New car manufacturers recognized this problem long ago, and as a result, variable valve timing (VVT) systems have been used in production cars for more than 20 years. GM got in on the action, too, with the Gen IV L92 small-block in 2007. The L92 was the first production GM small-block to utilize variable valve timing, and the system has since been installed on the L99 and LY6.

The beauty of the system is its simplicity. GM's VVT setup features a hydraulically actuated phaser assembly that's integrated into the cam gear. Essentially a rotor that rotates inside of a stator, the phaser assembly uses oil pressure to move the camshaft in relation to the timing chain and crankshaft. Using instructions from the engine management computer and cam position sensor, an electric solenoid mounted inside the timing cover presses upon a hydraulic valve bolted into the nose of the cam. This manipulates oil flow into the phaser assembly to advance or retard the cam. GM's VVT system is very flexible, and it allows advancing the cam 7 degrees and retarding it up to 45 degrees, for a total of 52 degrees of latitude.

Although GM uses VVT technology as a means of boosting fuel economy and cleaning up emissions, in performance applications, its primary purpose is to optimize the intake closing point. This allows advancing the cam at low RPM to boost torque and retarding it at high RPM to increase top-end horsepower for tremendous flexibility in broadening up the power and torque curves.

Perhaps the key to the system's seamless performance is advances in modern electronics that make its technology possible. Because the phaser assembly is essentially a rotor that moves inside of a stator, hydraulic pressure

Variable Valve Timing Dyno Test

The merits of variable valve timing technology sure look promising in theory, but do they hold up in real-world dyno testing? To find out, let's take a look at some revealing dyno tests conducted on one of Mast Motorsports' 416-ci L99 crate motors.

Dubbed the L99 416 SS, Mast's combo features a 6.2L aluminum block bored to 4.070 inches, a Callies 4.000-inch steel crank and rods, Mahle 11.4:1 pistons, a custom Mast 236/250-at-.050 hydraulic roller cam with .603/.618-inch lift, CNC-ported factory LS3 cylinder heads, and a stock L99 intake manifold. Mast rates the 416 at 595 hp, and to test the virtues of the VVT system, we made several pulls on Mast's Superflow 902 dyno. For this test, the cam was phased in three different positions: advanced for maximum torque, retarded for maximum hp, and with the VVT system engaged. Timing changes were performed in real time using Mast's stand-alone M-90 ECM. The results were quite impressive, to say the least.

Advancing the cam 5 degrees achieved maximum torque. In this configuration, the L99 produced 591 hp at 6,100 rpm and 563 ft-lbs at 5,000 rpm. In search of maximum peak horsepower in the following test, the 416 responded best to 4 degrees of retard. This yielded peak output of 609 hp at 6,400 rpm and 553 ft-lbs of torque at 5,400 rpm. The results are precisely what you'd expect, with the L99 adding 10 ft-lbs of torque at 400 rpm lower with the cam advanced and adding 18 hp at 300 rpm higher in the powerband with the cam retarded. In a standard non-VVT motor, this would typically be the point where an engine builder has to make the painful decision to either sacrifice low-end for top-end, top-end for low-end, or shoot for a happy medium between the two extremes.

This is the sort of compromise VVT promises to eliminate in theory, and on Mast's dyno, it did just that. With the VVT system switched on, and continually phasing the cam throughout the dyno pull, the L99 cranked out 608 hp at 6,400 rpm and 563 ft-lbs at 5,000 rpm. These dyno runs prove that VVT is quite literally the best of both worlds. Engaging the VVT system yielded horsepower and torque output that was spot on to the prior tests in which the cam was retarded for max power and advanced for max torque. Granted the motor made 1 hp less on the VVT dyno pull, but that's well within the .5-percent run-to-run variation limit of what's considered acceptable for even a very consistent dyno cell. More impressive is the difference in the all-important power after peak metric when comparing the dyno numbers with the cam advanced versus the dyno numbers with VVT enabled. At 6,900 rpm, the advanced dyno pull netted 556 hp, and the VVT run produced 597 hp. That 41-hp difference is staggering.

CAMSHAFTS

When installing a camshaft, it's a good idea to cover it with a liberal coating of assembly lube. Although roller cams do not require a break-in period, the lube helps keep friction in check until oil starts to flow through the engine during the initial start-up period.

is the only thing preventing the cam from twitching around erratically. Even when the cam phasing is locked in one position, the engine management software is constantly adjusting oil pressure into the phaser to keep the cam in a fixed position. Otherwise, the pressure exerted on the phaser from the valvesprings could force it into full mechanical retard, as the system relies on hydraulic pressure to overcome the force exerted by the valvesprings. In fact, once valvespring pressure exceeds 380 pounds of open pressure, the VVT systems starts losing control of the cam phasing beyond 5,000 rpm. Consequently, there is a practical limit to how aggressive cam duration and valvespring pressure can be when using GM's VVT system in a performance engine build.

Nonetheless, hot rodders have already used the factory VVT system in stroker builds, producing well in excess of 600 hp with ultra-broad powerbands that non-VVT motors can only dream of.

Single- vs. Dual-Pattern

With production cylinder heads, the exhaust ports always flow less than the intake ports. Unlike the intake ports, which rely on the pressure differential created by the piston to draw in air during the intake stroke, the exhaust ports benefit from the pistons physically pushing exhaust gases out of the cylinders during the exhaust stroke. Consequently, it simply isn't necessary for the exhaust ports to flow as well as the intake ports. Nonetheless, to compensate for this disparity in airflow, engine builders often use camshafts with more exhaust duration than intake duration. These are referred to as dual-pattern cams, and bumpsticks that have the same duration and lift specs on both the intake and exhaust lobes are known as single-pattern cams.

As no surprise, GM uses dual-pattern cams on all LS-series small-blocks. However, there is a big difference between the amount of duration split used on GM's cathedral-port and rectangle-port heads. For example, a stock LS2 features a 204/211-at-.050 cam, and a stock LS7 cam measures 211/230-at-.050. The reason why the LS7 needs 19 degrees of intake/exhaust split compared to the LS2's meager 7 degrees of split is because the LS7's exhaust is relatively weak. A stock LS2/LS6 cylinder head flows roughly 183 cfm on the exhaust side and 260 cfm on the intake side for an exhaust/intake ratio of 70 percent. In comparison, a stock LS7 head flows about 220 cfm through the exhaust ports and 370 cfm through the intake ports for an exhaust/intake ratio of 60 percent. As the two heads illustrate, the amount of duration split in a dual-pattern must always be matched to the flow rate of both the intake and exhaust ports.

VVT Swap Parts List

Component	PN
VVT camshaft	N/A
L92/L99 timing cover	12616491
Phaser assembly	12585994
Cam bolt/oil valve	12588151
58-tooth reluctor wheel	12586768
Mast M-90 computer and harness	M-90DBW

Cam Bolt Configurations

Engine Type	Displacement	Cam Core
LR4	4.8L	Three-bolt
LY2	4.8L	Single-bolt
LS4, LY5, LMG, LC9, LH8	5.3L	Single-bolt
LM7, LM4, L33, L59, LH6	5.3L	Three-bolt
LS1, LS6	5.7L	Three-bolt
LS2, LQ4, LQ9	6.0L	Three-bolt
L76, LY6	6.0L	Single-bolt
LS3, LS3, LSA, L92, L9H	6.2L	Single-bolt
LS9	6.2L	Three-bolt
LS7	7.0L	Three-bolt

CHAPTER 11

VALVETRAIN

Just 20 years ago, the prospect of a production pushrod engine turning 7,000 rpm—while being backed by a 100,000-mile factory warranty—seemed absolutely preposterous. Nonetheless, that's exactly what GM did with the LS7, which it introduced in the 2006 Corvette Z06. Needless to say, valvetrain technology has elevated the OHV platform far beyond what anyone dreamed of just a few short years ago.

As is often the case, the push to improve valvetrain durability starts at the highest levels of professional motorsports. Most sanctioning bodies limit maximum displacement as a means of trying to regulate horsepower levels, and teams inevitably reach a point where maximum RPM, rather than cylinder head airflow, is the limiting factor in power output. Consequently, he who turns the most RPM stands the best chance of winning the race, which explains why NHRA Pro Stock motors are now turning more than 11,000 rpm. Perhaps even more impressive are NASCAR Sprint Cup engines, which turn 9,500-plus rpm reliably for 500 to 600 miles each race. As the lessons learned on track have trickled down into the hot rod market, RPM is now limited more by the size of an enthusiast's bank account than by the durability of the valvetrain components. The good news is that valvetrain hardware is more durable and affordable than ever.

Just a few decades ago, a pushrod V-8 capable of turning 7,000-plus rpm required a full-race valvetrain that would never survive the rigors of daily driving duty. Thanks to dramatic improvements in valvetrain technology, the LS7 small-block offers peak engine speeds on par with DOHC motors and is backed by a 100,000-mile warranty. (© GM Corp.)

Valvetrain Dynamics

In essence, the valvetrain is the link between the camshaft and the cylinder heads. Without the valvetrain, there is no valve actuation, and without valve actuation, there is no horsepower. This simple truth helps put the importance of the valvetrain into perspective. The more precisely the valvetrain translates the motion of the camshaft to the valves, the more horsepower it produces. In addition to precision, an optimized valvetrain must perform reliably over extended periods of time. This is far easier said than done, as the valve actuation process is nothing short of violent.

It all starts at the crankshaft, which transfers rotational motion to the camshaft through a crank gear, cam gear, and timing chain. As the camshaft turns, its eccentric lobes push up on the lifters. The reciprocating motion of the lifters then pushes upward on the pushrods and rocker arms, which then pivot like a see-saw to push open the valves. All the while, the entire valvetrain is working against the force of the valvesprings, which attach to the valves with spring retainers and locks.

VALVETRAIN

All of these moving parts make precise and reliable valve actuation extremely challenging, especially when the cumulative mass and deflection of all the components are taken into account. The more the valvetrain deflects, the smaller the cam appears to the engine, as the motion of the cam lobe isn't precisely transferred to the valve. Consequently, camshaft manufacturers must consider the valvetrain mass and inertia as a whole when designing cam lobe profiles, as the entire valvetrain must work as a single system.

The goal is to get the valve motion to match the designed cam motion. During the initial opening of the valve, the lifter, pushrod, rocker arm, and valvespring are compressed into action. The lobe design has to be quick yet smooth to prevent transferring bad harmonics into the system, which causes springs to surge and potentially destroy them. As the lifter runs up the ramp to the peak of the lobe, the valve is opening farther, the parts are compressing more, and the dynamic loads are getting higher, placing tremendous stress on the system. At maximum lift, the valvetrain is fully compressed and struggling to rebound against the force imparted on it.

At high RPM, the inertia of the entire valvetrain going over the nose of the lobe resists the return spring force, and the lifter tries to hang in the air instead of following the cam profile. To prevent this, the mass of the valvetrain and spring pressure must be sufficient enough to allow the lifter to follow the cam all the way down the ramp. If not, the lifter bounces, which damages the valve seat and sends harmonics through the system that destroy the springs as well as the needles in the roller lifters. This reduces the volumetric efficiency of the engine, as the valve doesn't seat properly and robs horsepower.

As daunting as all that may seem, selecting the right valvetrain components for a stroker motor is rather straightforward, because camshaft manufacturers have already done most of the homework for you. A cam's duration and lift specs determine the type of valvesprings that will need to be used. After spring pressure and max valve lift

All LS-series small-blocks use beehive-style valvesprings, units in which the upper coils are wound in a smaller diameter than the bottom coils. This arrangement removes weight from the area of the valvespring that experiences the fastest acceleration and moves the farthest distance. The result is a substantial reduction in active mass and superior high-RPM valvetrain control while using lower pressure. Beehive springs are naturally progressive in rate, and each coil vibrates at a slightly different frequency. This prevents the springs from going into resonance and provides a self-dampening effect. (Photo courtesy of Comp Cams)

The key to eliminating valve float is to reduce valvetrain mass and deflection. Durable springs, lightweight valves, and lightweight retainers go a long way in promoting valvetrain stability and extending the RPM range of an engine.

A hydraulic roller lifter has an internal piston assembly that pushes up against a cushion of oil stored inside the lifter body. This deflection allows a hydraulic lifter to absorb the expansion of the valvetrain components as they heat, but it also increases mass and the lifter's tendency to pump up at high RPM.

Not only are solid roller lifters lighter than their hydraulic counterparts, they can endure far steeper cam lobe profiles to open and close the valves more quickly. Furthermore, they can handle higher spring pressures for improved high-RPM stability. For sustained 7,500-plus-rpm operation, using a solid lifter valvetrain is a must. Their only downsides are cost, noise, and routine lash adjustments.

have been established, the balance of the valvetrain components can be selected based on durability and the target RPM range of the engine combo. If that's not easy enough, cam manufacturers often publish a list of matching valvesprings, retainers, locks, rocker arms, pushrods, lifters, and timing sets to go along with their off-the-shelf camshafts.

Fighting Float

The inherent challenge of designing valvetrain components is trying to make them as light as possible to reduce valvetrain inertia while also making them as stiff as possible to reduce deflection. Unlike an overhead cam engine that positions the camshafts on top of the cylinder heads for a more direct actuation of the valvetrain, an OHV motor must transfer the reciprocating motion of the cam lobes from the center of the block all the way up to the cylinder heads by using lifters, pushrods, and rocker arms. More moving parts means more weight, which is a big problem when the entire valvetrain must reverse its direction of travel every time the valves open and close.

By nature, aggressive cam lobe profiles require stiffer spring pressure to keep the lifter seated, but this also increases stress on the valvetrain. That, in turn, increases the potential for deflection, and the stiffer valvetrain hardware required to resist this deflection can increase mass. It's an ugly cycle, but having too much valvetrain deflection and mass leads to valve float, a condition where the valvetrain can no longer control the motion of the valves. When this happens, the valves open and close erratically, crash into the valve seats, and limit how many RPM an engine can turn. In extreme cases, the valves can slam into the pistons and destroy an entire engine.

In order to prevent valve floating, taking a single-system approach to valvetrain setup works best. For example, because installing stiffer valvesprings increases the loads placed on the rocker arms, pushrods, and lifters, it's imperative to make sure the rest of the valvetrain is up to par when upgrading just one of the components in the entire system.

Lifters

The cylindrical slugs of metal that ride the surface of the cam lobes are called lifters, tappets, or followers. They're retained inside recesses, known as the lifter bores, in the block. Regardless of what you call them, lifters can be classified into four groups: hydraulic flat tappets, hydraulic rollers, mechanical flat tappets, and mechanical rollers. Unlike their flat-tappet counterparts, roller lifters have a roller wheel assembly integrated into the base of their bodies. This substantially reduces friction and allows for much steeper cam lobe profiles. In other words, for any given amount of duration, a roller lifter can handle much more lobe lift. This allows camshaft designers to lift the valves high enough to take advantage of the high-lift flow potential of modern cylinder heads while keeping duration short enough to retain excellent drivability.

All LS-series small-blocks are equipped with hydraulic roller lifters from the factory, and in fact, GM hasn't installed flat-tappet cams in a production small-block in decades. In the distant past, roller lifters were more prone to failure, as the allocated valvespring pressure loads onto a smaller surface area. Additionally, the roller wheels ride on needle bearings, which present another area of potential failure. Nonetheless, roller lifter technology has improved to the point that these drawbacks have been mostly eliminated. For proof, look no further than any production GM small-block built today, whose roller lifters often last for 200,000 miles. Unless an engine is being built for an obscure racing class that bans roller lifters, LS-series small-blocks are rarely built with flat-tappet lifters.

That said, both mechanical and hydraulic roller lifters are used in the vast majority of stroker Gen III/IV engine combos. Mechanical lifters, or solid lifters, as they are sometimes called, are solid pieces of metal. Because the valvetrain components expand as they heat up, a valvetrain utilizing mechanical lifters must be set up with some slack to accommodate this growth. This clearance, or lash, is measured between the rocker arm and valve stem tip using a feeler gauge. Naturally, this slack makes for noisier valvetrain operation. Conversely, hydraulic lifters incorporate an internal cavity filled with oil and a piston. This hydraulic assembly enables much of the lash to be removed from the valvetrain, because the piston inside the lifter compresses as the valvetrain expands, which

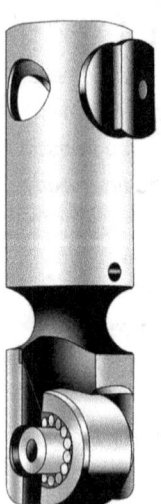

Early solid roller lifters were plagued by reliability issues in street applications. That's because they were used mainly in race engines where lifters relied solely on oil thrown up by the crankshaft for lubrication. That works fine in high-RPM race conditions, but not so much for street cars that spend lots of time at idle. To solve this problem, valvetrain manufacturers, such as Comp Cams and Isky, have developed street solid roller lifters that feature oil passages to the needle bearings. This provides a steady supply of oil, regardless of engine speed. (Photo courtesy of Comp Cams)

VALVETRAIN

eliminates the clatter associated with mechanical lifters. In addition to quieter operation, hydraulic lifters eliminate the need for periodic lash adjustments that mechanical lifters require.

The reduced maintenance and quieter operation offered by hydraulic lifters are the primary reasons why GM uses them in all LS-series small-blocks. Those benefits aside, solid roller lifters offer clear performance advantages, particularly at high RPM. On a typical street/strip engine, a hydraulic roller system often experiences valve float between 6,500 and 7,000 rpm. Hydraulic lifters are more prone to valve float, due to their greater mass and tendency to pump up at high-RPM. Furthermore, higher valvespring pressure goes a long way in reducing valve float, but there is only so much pressure the piston assembly of a hydraulic lifter can handle.

When replacing a valvespring with the cylinder head still on a motor, compressed air must be injected into the spark plug hole to prevent the valve from dropping into the cylinder. The other option is to rotate the crank until the piston in the cylinder you're working on is at TDC. That way, the valve only drops a fraction of an inch and rests on top of the piston.

By comparison, a solid roller lifter's lower mass and ability to manage greater valvespring pressure make it the clear victor in applications exceeding 6,500 rpm. Although the performance difference between a hydraulic roller system and a solid roller application with similar camshaft specs might be marginal up to about 6,000 rpm, beyond that point the horsepower advantages of a solid roller lifter can easily exceed 50 hp.

When it comes to valvetrain hardware, RPM usually costs money, and that's definitely the case with a mechanical roller valvetrain. Not only are the stiffer valvesprings necessary to run a solid roller valvetrain more expensive, the rocker arms and the lifters themselves also cost more. Additionally a solid roller valvetrain's steeper cam lobes and stiffer valvesprings increase the stress on the entire valvetrain, so stronger rocker arms are required, which adds cost.

For example, a set of mild beehive valvesprings for a hydraulic roller cam costs about $200, and super-stiff dual springs for a solid roller cam cost $400. Likewise, a set of $150 stock GM rocker arms will work fine in a hydraulic cam application, but a high-RPM solid roller combo often requires a $1,500 shaft-mount rocker arm setup. At the end of

When assembling a set of cylinder heads, it's always a good idea to pressure-test the valvesprings. This ensures that pressure is uniform across all 16 valves. Pressure-testing used springs is the best way to determine whether or not a set of used springs needs to be replaced.

Valvespring pressure is dependent upon how much the spring is compressed, so a spring's installed height must be adjusted to make sure that the spring is neither too soft nor too stiff. This is accomplished by placing the necessary number of shims beneath the spring, then slipping a height mic over the spring to measure the installed height.

the day, solid roller lifters offer irrefutable advantages over their hydraulic counterparts, but they require much more expensive valvetrain hardware.

Although flat-tappet lifters aren't common in Gen III/IV engine builds, it's worth noting that a solid flat-tappet lifter system can sometimes outperform a solid roller setup. These instances aren't common, but certain race classes, such as in circle track, sometimes impose limits on valve lift or duration. In such a scenario, solid flat-tappet lifters can be advantageous over solid roller lifters, because they offer quicker initial lobe acceleration very early in the lift curve. Roller lifters can, indeed, handle higher peak ramp acceleration rates, but solid flat-tappets have the advantage very early in the lift curve. And, if a racing class limits peak valve lift to, say, .500 inch, then a solid flat-tappet cam might actually perform better than a roller cam.

Solid Rollers for the Street

In many hot rodding circles, solid roller camshafts and street cars don't mix, and that reputation is well earned. Decades ago, solid roller lifters were plagued with reliability issues, as they were originally designed for high-RPM race use. The only way their needle bearings could be lubricated was from oil thrown up by the crank. Because race cars spend very little time at idle and low RPM, that oiling method worked just fine. However, when people tried to use the lifters on the street, the same lifters that lasted for several seasons in race cars were failing more quickly. Compounding the problem of using solid roller lifters in a street car was that most old roller cams were designed for very high spring loads. This kept everything under control at high RPM with an aggressive cam, but it greatly increased valvetrain load at low speed.

Camshaft manufacturers recognized these problems and pioneered several effective solutions. First, mechanical roller lifters were completely redesigned to include an integrated oil band with a small hole to feed oil down to the needle bearings. Furthermore, the steel used for the axle was greatly increased in strength and redesigned to distribute load more efficiently. Second, new lobe profiles and valvesprings were developed specifically for street use. These new profiles perform very well in the 2,000- to 7,000-rpm range while requiring far less spring pressure than older race profiles. Together, these changes make it possible to now run a solid roller cam in a street car without any of the past reliability issues. Although it is recommended to check valve lash every 5,000 to 6,000 miles with solid lifters, the need to do so is greatly reduced with rocker arms that have poly locks.

Valvesprings

The valvesprings sit in recesses, or pockets, machined into the cylinder heads and provide tension upon the valves. Valvesprings force the valves shut against the seats until they're compressed by the rocker arms, at which point the valves open. Valvesprings attach to the valves with retainers and locks, which center the springs around the valves and keep them in a slightly preloaded state. This load is known as the spring's seat pressure, and the load the spring provides at maximum valve lift is called open pressure.

Retainers prevent the valvesprings from shooting off the heads, but because they're positioned at the very top of the springs, they must accelerate and change directions rapidly while traveling a long distance. In an effort to reduce mass, high-end street and race engines often employ titanium retainers, which can extended an engine's operating range by 200 to 300 rpm before valve float sets in.

All Gen III/IV small-blocks feature stamped-steel rocker arms with roller trunions. LS7s utilize a 1.8:1 ratio, and all other LS motors have a 1.7:1 ratio. The rocker arms are extremely durable and capable of handling 7,000 rpm.

Aftermarket rocker arms have trunions that are beefier than those on factory units in order to handle higher valvespring loads. Additionally, their bodies are contoured for additional clearance for larger-diameter springs. They're constructed from both aluminum and steel. Aluminum rockers are lighter, easier to manufacture, and provide a dampening effect on the valvetrain. However, they have a more limited life cycle. (Photo courtesy of Comp Cams)

The position of the valvesprings in relation to the rest of the valvetrain helps put their importance into perspective. During compression, the springs are responsible for keeping the lifters in contact with the cam lobes so they can precisely follow the contour of the ramps. As the springs rebound after the point of maximum valve lift, their job is to close the valves in a controlled fashion while preventing them from bouncing off their seats. Accomplishing both of these functions requires having just enough spring pressure.

Valvespring pressure is determined by several factors, chief among them are spring rate and load. The rate of a valvespring is simply the force required to compress it 1 inch. For instance, a spring that compress 1 inch under 100 pounds of force has a spring rate of 100 pounds per inch. The spring rate, combined with how much the spring is compressed (load), determines valvespring pressure. For illustrative purposes, let's take a look at a set of Comp Cams springs designed specifically for LS-series small-blocks, part number 26921. They feature a spring rate of 408 pounds per inch, which, at an installed height of 1.770 inches, yields 135 pounds of seat pressure. Compressed to a height of 1.120 inches, the spring load increases to 400 pounds of open pressure.

Because spring diameter, wire thickness, and the number of active coils affect the spring rate and, therefore, pressure, aftermarket manufacturers are constantly juggling these variables around to establish a wide variety of pressures for a diverse range of applications. Nevertheless, because wire diameter and the number of coils are built into a spring and can't be changed, the only two factors relevant to engine builders are the diameter of the spring and how much the spring is compressed after installation. That's because spring compression, or installed height, can be adjusted after the spring has been installed on the cylinder head. Using shims to adjust the installed height serves as a handy fine-tuning tool in achieving target spring pressure. As for spring diameter, the size of the valvespring pocket determines the maximum-diameter spring that can be used. Larger-diameter springs provide more pressure, but they also require the spring pockets to be machined wider, and there's a physical limit to how much the pockets can be opened up.

With stock Gen III cathedral-port cylinder heads, a 1.250-inch-outside-diameter valvespring is as large as you can go. The valvespring pocket can safely be machined to about 1.450 inches, but anything larger runs the risk of breaking into the ports. Factory rectangle-port castings have more commodious pockets and can be enlarged safely to approximately 1.550 inches. Even so, with the very heavy-duty spring pressures that aggressive camshafts require, sometimes running a larger-diameter valvespring just isn't enough. Consequently, aftermarket manufacturers offer dual valvesprings that feature a small inner spring that fits inside the primary spring to increase pressure.

Ultimately, optimizing valvespring pressure is a delicate balancing act, as too much pressure will place undue stress on the valvetrain, and not enough pressure will compromise valvetrain stability. Load is just one of the many factors that needs to be addressed when selecting valvesprings, and more isn't always better. A lower-mass spring with less load often performs far better than a fat spring with more load. The trick is to use a spring that offers just enough pressure to get the job done, and not a pound more.

As with camshaft selection, there is no universal rule of thumb to follow

Compared to aluminum units, steel rocker arms are heavier, but that extra mass provides an increase in durability and life cycle. Conversely, they're more difficult to manufacture and harder on the rest of the valvetrain. (Photo courtesy of Comp Cams)

In a stud-mount rocker arm arrangement, the stud bears the brunt of the load imparted by the valvespring and pushrod. In a shaft-mount rocker system, the rocker pivots around a central shaft that's bolted to the cylinder head. With this setup, the shaft absorbs most of the valvetrain load, reducing deflection and increasing durability and high-RPM stability. (Photo courtesy of Comp Cams)

A shaft-mount rocker arm system makes it easy to compensate for pushrod offset, because a rocker can easily be moved onto different parts of the shaft. Additionally, they're available in just about every ratio imaginable.

when it comes to choosing the right valvesprings. Instead, opting for springs that are proven performers in applications similar to yours will usually suffice. On the other hand, if your combo isn't exactly mainstream, it's not a bad idea to seek expert advice to avert potentially catastrophic engine failure. Camshaft manufacturers have thousands of hours invested into developing valvesprings, so it makes sense to tap into their expertise.

Retainers

Even on a head as mild as a stock LS6 cylinder head, the valvesprings exert 90 pounds of seat pressure. So even at 0 rpm, the valvespring needs to be cinched tightly in place to prevent it from launching off the cylinder head. That's the job of the retainer, which sits on top of the valvespring and locks into a notch machined into the valvestem with a set of valve locks. Like most production engines, the LS-series small-block utilizes steel retainers that do a fine job in the 6,000 to 7,000 peak RPM that they're designed for. Beyond that point, however, reducing retainer mass just a few grams can extend an engine's peak RPM dramatically.

Titanium is the most commonly used material for lightweight retainers, and they weigh roughly 40 percent less than standard steel retainers. This decrease in mass alone is enough to add up to 200 rpm before an engine starts floating the valves. Although that can be the difference between winning and losing in a competitive racing class, the increased cost of titanium retainers makes them cost-prohibitive for most street/strip motors. A set of standard steel retainers can be had for $50, while equivalent titanium units ring up a $250 tab.

To bridge that gap, Comp Cams has recently introduced a new line of lightweight tool steel retainers that offer the best of both worlds. These retainers tap into the company's NASCAR connections, and according to Comp, each one weighs just 2 to 4 grams more than a titanium retainer. Furthermore, extensive testing has revealed that they are just as durable. The best news is the price, as Comp's tool steel retainers cost $150 for a set of 16.

Rocker Arms

A rocker arm is responsible for converting the upward motion of the pushrod into the downward motion that pushes the valve open. To accomplish this, a rocker pivots like a see-saw on a trunion, which acts as a fulcrum. The stiff valvespring pressure and high RPM associated with aggressive camshaft grinds place tremendous loads on the rocker arms. The upward force of the lifters and pushrods works against the pressure of the valvesprings, and steeper cam lobe profiles and stiffer springs only compound the situation.

Fortunately, the factory GM rocker arms are excellent pieces of hardware. All LS-series small-blocks come equipped with 1.7:1 roller rocker arms from the factory. The only exception is the LS7, which uses 1.8:1 roller rockers. Compared to those of the Gen I small-block Chevys, most of which were equipped with stamped 1.5:1 rockers, Gen III/IV rocker arms are more like race hardware than typical factory equipment.

Stock LS rockers perform extremely well at engine speeds up to 7,000 rpm. For many stroker combinations, it's not even necessary to replace the stock rockers with aftermarket units. They do have their limits, however, and with elevated

Mast Motorsports offers drop-in, shaft-mount rocker arms that are direct replacements for the factory units. Instead of having eight rocker arms riding on a central shaft, the Mast design features a shared shaft for each pair of rockers. The design is compact enough to fit under stock valve covers.

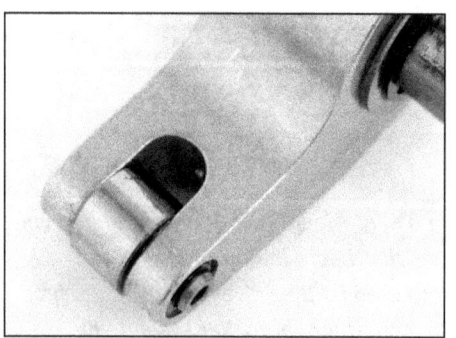

Most aftermarket and factory LS rocker arms incorporate a roller tip that presses down on the valvestem. At high lift, a plain tip has a tendency to place unwanted side loads on the valvestem, and a roller tip helps alleviate this effect.

The pushrods represent one of the biggest areas for potential deflection, because they bear the opposing forces imparted by the valvesprings and cam lobes. If a pushrod isn't stiff enough, reciprocating motion that should be transferred to the rocker arm instead flexes the pushrod, thereby reducing the effective valve lift and duration. Stiffer pushrods feature thicker walls, which increases weight, but the benefits in valvetrain stiffness are worth the tradeoff.

VALVETRAIN

valvespring pressures and sustained 7,000-plus-rpm operation, aftermarket rocker arms are a wise investment. Another drawback of stock rocker arms is that they are not adjustable. That's great for reducing manufacturing costs in a high-production, volume environment, but in performance applications where the valvetrain geometry has been altered, the only way to adjust the stock rockers is by changing pushrod length and the rocker stand height.

The three primary advantages that aftermarket rockers offer over their stock counterparts are reduced deflection, lower mass, and a higher multiplication ratio. Deflection can be reduced using several different methods. Aftermarket rocker arms are built using stronger alloys than those in production units, which reduces flex. Also, production and entry-level aftermarket rocker arms are pedestal-mount designs that attach to the cylinder heads using bolts or studs. In this type of arrangement, the stud is often the area of the valvetrain that's most prone to flex. The aftermarket offers several solutions, with companies, such as Comp Cams and ARP, offering stiffer 3/8-inch rocker studs that replace the factory bolts.

A decades-old technique is to bolt a girdle on top of the rocker arm assembly. This dramatically reduces deflection and stabilizes the valvetrain. With quality aftermarket rocker arms, studs, and a girdle, a pedestal-mount rocker system can operate safely at 8,000 rpm. Even so, such an arrangement is fairly uncommon in a typical LS stroker build, because, in recent years, more cost-effective shaft-mount rocker arm systems have entered the market.

Shaft-mount rockers pivot on a centrally mounted shaft that's bolted to the cylinder head. The body of the rockers actually slides around the shaft, decreasing friction and increasing mounting stiffness. Although shaft-mount rockers don't make horsepower in and of themselves, they allow an engine builder to make more power by providing a stable, high-RPM valvetrain platform to work with. An entry-level shaft-mount rocker system costs about $800 to $1,000, which is only marginally more than the combined cost of pedestal-mount rockers, aftermarket studs, and a girdle. Furthermore, stud girdles also require using a valve cover spacer, which is another strike against a pedestal-mount rocker system in a high-RPM application.

Rocker Ratio

Because valve lift is simply lobe lift multiplied by the rocker arm ratio, there are several lobe-and-rocker ratio combinations that can be used to achieve a target valve lift figure. Some engine combinations utilize lots of lobe lift with a relatively conservative rocker arm ratio, and others feature conservative lobe lift and a very aggressive rocker arm ratio. One combo isn't necessarily better than another, and there is a time and place for each. Adding the acceleration speed with the rocker is easier on harmonics and valvetrain stability in relation to RPM. With a higher ratio, the rocker is responsible for valvetrain acceleration, which allows for a gentler cam lobe ramp design. Generally, high ratios can be used to open the valve off the seat more quickly, and lower ratios can be used to stabilize a valvetrain that is out of control. Using a lower rocker ratio reduces the load on the pushrod and thereby helps increase stiffness. Ultimately, cam manufacturers design their lobe profiles around specific rocker ratios in mind, so for the average hot rodder, the issue isn't worth splitting hairs over.

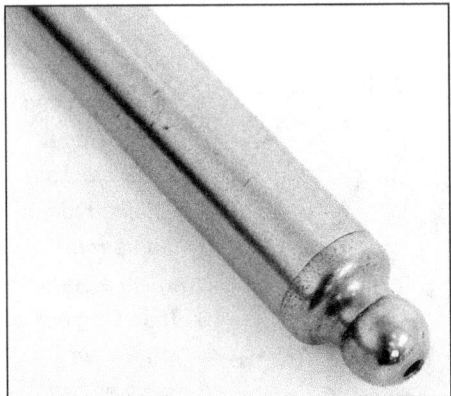

Most pushrods have a standard 180-degree radius on each end. In applications exceeding .750-inch lift, it's sometimes necessary to upgrade to pushrods with a 270-degree radius to prevent interference between the pushrod end and the pushrod cup in the rocker arm.

Any time the lifter height, block deck height, gasket thickness, cylinder head deck thickness, or valvestem length is altered, the pushrod length must also be changed. Pushrod length determines the rocker-tip-to-valvestem geometry. The ideal pushrod length places the rocker tip at the center of the valvestem tip at mid lift.

HOW TO BUILD BIG-INCH GM LS-SERIES ENGINES

CHAPTER 11

Pushrods

In some respects, pushrods represent the inherent inefficiency of mounting a camshaft in the middle of the block and having it transfer the reciprocating motion of the cam lobes and lifters all the way to the top of the cylinder heads. Breakthroughs in valvetrain technology have helped overcome this setback, and improvements to the pushrod itself are part of that equation. As with the rest of the valvetrain, pushrods must be stiff to resist deflection and accurately translate cam motion to the valves, but they also need to be lightweight to reduce inertia.

To accomplish this, pushrods come in a dizzying array of steel alloys, such as 1010, 4130, and 4340. The other two ingredients to pushrod stiffness are diameter and wall thickness. All stock LS-series small-blocks come equipped with 5/16-inch pushrods, except for the LS7, which has 3/8-inch pushrods. Although factory pushrods work fine under normal operating conditions, sustained high-RPM operation and a few missed shifts can bend them up rather quicker. Consequently, aftermarket pushrods from companies, such as Comp Cams, Manley, Trick Flow, and Isky, are highly recommended in all stroker motor combinations. In addition to using superior alloys, aftermarket pushrods are offered in both 5/16- and 3/8-inch diameters with wall thicknesses ranging from .080 to .125 inch.

Because the length of the pushrod determines the rocker-arm-to-valve-tip geometry, a pushrod's length is just as important as its stiffness and mass. Block deck height, cylinder head deck thickness, rocker arm design, camshaft base circle size, lifter design, and valve stem length all affect the correct pushrod length of an engine combo. Optimizing pushrod length allows the rocker arm tip to press on the center of the valve stem, and aftermarket manufacturers sell tools that make it easy to measure for the proper length. Tools to check pushrod length are basically threaded rod assemblies that can be varied in height until the correct pushrod length has been determined. Most of the time, the correct-length pushrods are offered as off-the-shelf items, but when they aren't, manufacturers offer custom-length units at a very reasonable price.

The single-roller factory LS2 timing chain offers outstanding performance at a dirt-cheap price. It can handle more than 400 pounds of open valvespring pressure and has proven to be reliable beyond 7,000 rpm.

The cam phaser assembly used in VVT Gen IV small-blocks is nothing more than a rotor within a stator. The cam gear rotates via chain as usual, but the rotor and vanes don't physically come into contact with it. Instead, a cushion of oil on both sides of the rotor determines where the camshaft will be positioned in relation to the crankshaft. (© GM Corp.)

VALVETRAIN

Timing Sets

In order for an engine to operate properly, the camshaft's rotation must be perfectly synchronized with the crankshaft. It's up to the timing set to get the job done, but the stiffer valvesprings used in high-performance engine combinations increase load and, therefore, the potential for deflection. The good news is that there are dozens of factory and aftermarket timing set options that can easily handle the most demanding of engine combinations.

On the factory front, GM redesigned the timing chain assembly with the introduction of the LS2 in 2005. The single-roller LS2 unit features a stronger alloy steel and thicker sideplates for significant improvements in strength over the Gen III design. This chain has proven reliable in applications having slightly more than 400 pounds of valvespring open pressure.

At anything beyond 400 pounds, an aftermarket timing set buys cheap insurance. They're offered from companies, such as Comp Cams, Trick Flow, SLP, Manley, and Katech, in both single- and double-roller applications. Generally, double-roller sets are more durable, but some single-roller timing sets are also extremely durable. Aftermarket timing sets have adjustable cam and/or crank gears, making it possible to advance or retard the cam manually.

In addition to offering them as a traditional timing chain setup, aftermarket companies also offer timing sets as belt drives and gear drives. Belt drives are usually mounted outside of the timing cover, which allows for quick and easy timing changes without removing the timing cover or water pump. Also, this feature greatly simplifies the cam swap process. Additionally, belt drives reduce frictional losses and oil windage while helping to dampen engine harmonics. Their biggest downside is that they cost two to three times as much as a chain-drive setup. Gear drive timing sets use a series of gears between the cam and crank sprockets to synchronize them. They offer the ultimate in durability and timing precision, but they also generate lots of noise.

Timing Covers

From the factory, LS-series small-blocks come with four different types of timing covers. The Gen III timing cover, also known as the LS1/LS6 cover, is the most basic and has no provisions for a cam sensor. The standard Gen IV timing cover, which is used on most non-VVT Gen IV engines, is similar to the Gen III unit but with an integrated cam sensor. The LS7's dry sump oiling system uses a larger pump assembly, and it requires its own timing cover for extra clearance. The VVT-equipped Gen IV timing cover has an electric solenoid assembly built in that actuates the oil control valve in the camshaft.

All factory timing covers are durable cast-aluminum units, and there's no real performance advantage to upgrading them. However, with some aftermarket double-roller timing sets, it's necessary to grind down the factory timing cover for additional clearance. Two-piece aftermarket timing covers don't offer much in the way of performance gains, but they do make swapping out cams much easier.

Although it's possible to calculate spring pressure by hand using simple arithmetic, it's far more practical to simply look up a manufacturer's published valvesprings specs or to measure spring pressure in a testing tool.

The purpose of the valvetrain is to open and close the valves, but the valves themselves must also be lightweight to avert valve float. To accomplish this, valves are built with hollow stems, and in extreme cases, they are whittled into shape out of a slab of titanium. (© GM Corp.)

When setting the installed height of a valvespring, it's important to check the valve-seal-to-retainer clearance. Not doing so can cause the retainer to smack into the seal and destroy it. At maximum valve lift, there should be a minimum of .050 inch of clearance. (© GM Corp.)

CHAPTER 12

INDUCTION

Cylinders heads are sometimes referred to as an engine's lungs. That being the case, the intake manifold can accurately be described as an engine's nostrils. As important as airflow through the cylinder heads is, it's ultimately limited by the efficiency of the intake manifold. In fact, the only way an engine can use all of the cfm potential the cylinder heads have to offer is if they're bolted to an intake manifold that operates at 100-percent efficiency. Realistically, that's nearly impossible to achieve, so the goal when designing an intake manifold isn't so much to improve airflow, but rather to minimize the loss in airflow the cylinder heads will experience once the intake manifold is bolted to them.

Intake manifold design is always a compromise. That's because a manifold designed with airflow as the top priority would never fit under the hood of a car. Underhood installation constraints are the biggest obstacles to overcome during the R&D process of intake manifold design.

Intake Dynamics

At its core, the purpose of the intake manifold is to distribute air evenly to all eight intake ports. Unlike cylinder head and camshaft dynamics, which most enthusiasts find quite fascinating, intake manifold design is very boring in comparison. That's because the most important, yet least interesting, aspect of manifold design is hood clearance.

As with the location of the cylinder head's intake ports in relation to the valves, a runner design with the highest, most direct approach into the intake ports will usually produce the most horsepower. In essence, the intake manifold's runners are an extension of the cylinder head's intake ports, and the cross-sectional area of the manifold's runners determines the power potential of an intake. Establishing the proper cross-sectional area of the runners is a balance between airflow and air velocity.

Unlike a cylinder head, whose intake port lengths can't be changed, the length of the runners on an intake manifold can easily be tweaked, provided there's adequate underhood space. Changing runner length affects the RPM at which pressure waves inside the manifold best promote cylinder filling. Longer runners increase low- and mid-range torque, and shorter runners promote improved high-RPM horsepower. That's because longer runners increase the distance the air must travel, which promotes increased air velocity at low RPM. However, longer runners become restrictive at high RPM.

Plenum size and shape are other factors that impact intake manifold design. The plenum is the central chamber inside the manifold positioned directly ahead of the intake runners. A larger plenum promotes top-end power production, and a smaller plenum has the opposite effect. The shape of the plenum, incidentally, greatly affects cylinder-to-cylinder air distribution.

Because EFI intake manifolds are designed to fit under very low hood profiles, most of the important elements of an intake's design—such as runner length, cross-sectional area, and plenum volume—can't be measured without cutting the manifold in half. Consequently, the only way to gauge an intake manifold's airflow potential is through reading the manufacturer's published specs or by studying the performance of various intakes on combinations similar to your own. It's certainly not the most

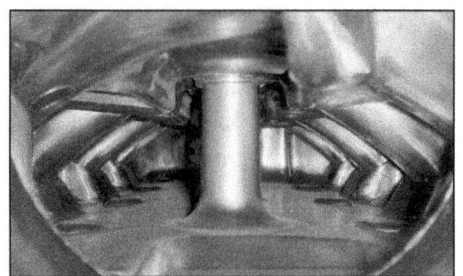
Unlike those of a carbureted intake manifold, the inner workings of an EFI manifold can't be seen without cutting it in half. To maximize runner length under a steeply sloped hood, the driver-side intake ports draw air from the passenger side of the plenum, and the passenger-side ports draw air from the driver side of the plenum.

scientific approach, but it's by far the most effective.

Early Stock Intakes

The early days of modifying the Gen III small-block's induction system were simpler times, as the LS1, LS6, and truck intake manifolds were the only choices available. With the high-flow potential of the LS cylinder heads, enthusiasts quickly reached the limit of these factory manifolds. Nonetheless, certain situa-

Dollar for dollar, it's tough to beat the performance of the GM LS3 and L92/L76 intake manifolds. Both designs are nearly identical, and each manifold can feed plenty of air for a 600- to 650-hp stroker combo. The cost for that caliber of performance is just $250 through GMPP.

The production LS6 intake manifold is an excellent choice for an engine with cathedral-port heads producing up to 600 hp. GM installed it on all 5.7L LS1 and LS6 engines from 2001 onward, so they're plentiful on the used market.

tions still warrant their use, so it certainly doesn't hurt to examine their virtues and drawbacks.

All factory GM Gen III/IV intake manifolds are built from nylon, not of aluminum or iron as in small-blocks of generations past. This not only reduces weight, but it helps minimize heat absorption from the lifter valley into the intake manifold. Unfortunately, the nylon material is more difficult to port

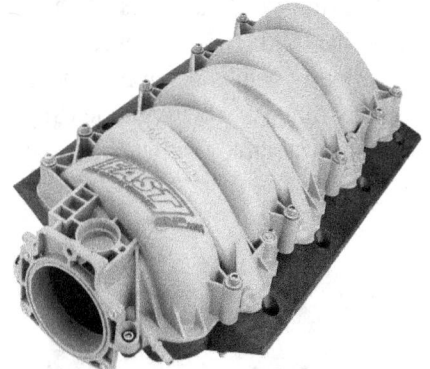
Fuel Air Spark Technology was one of the first companies to come to market with an aftermarket LS-style intake manifold. The design has since been superseded by FAST's LSX_R line of intakes, but there are a fair number of the old-school units floating around on the used market. Gains of 20 to 30 hp over the stock LS6 intake manifold are common. (Photo courtesy of Comp Cams)

The stock LS7 intake manifold is quite possibly the best-flowing small-block manifold GM has ever built. It can easily support 650 to 700 hp, and it provides more than enough airflow for the vast majority of street engines.

than metal, especially because it's just 3 mm thick. With the assortment of factory and aftermarket intake manifolds on the market, it often makes much more sense to upgrade to a higher-flowing unit rather than to port a stock intake.

The intake manifold found on the original 5.7L LS1 is best suited for mild, stock-displacement engine combinations. Although the manifold performs well in the 350-hp applications it was designed to support, simply porting the heads and installing a mild hydraulic roller camshaft in an otherwise stock 346 can leave it gasping for breath. The manifold's biggest flaw is its lack of plenum volume that can't provide enough airflow when matched with a set of quality cylinder heads. In fact, very early aftermarket LS1 camshafts relied on reverse-split patterns—with more intake duration than exhaust duration—to make up the deficiencies of the stock LS1 intake. At anything beyond 500 hp, the LS1 intake is a poor choice. Throw extra cubic inches and cylinder head airflow into the mix, and the LS1 intake is an even less appealing option.

Realizing the limitations of the LS1 intake manifold, GM improved upon it tremendously while designing the LS6. The main difference between the LS1 and LS6 intake manifolds is that the LS6 unit incorporates a dropped-floor design. This adds much-needed plenum volume and boosts airflow significantly. Additionally, the throttle body opening on the LS6 intake is enlarged from 75 to 80 mm. These changes enable the stock LS6 intake to easily support 600 hp, and at roughly $500, it's a much more reasonably priced alternative to many aftermarket units. From 2001 onward, the LS6 intake was used on all LS1 engines, as well as the LS6, which means finding a good deal on a used unit isn't that difficult.

GM originally planned on using a common intake manifold on all early LS-series small-blocks, but installation constraints forced engineers to raise the throttle body inlet 3 inches in order to clear the cooling fan in truck applications. This led to the development of a truck-specific intake manifold, used on 4.8L, 5.3L, and 6.0L Vortec truck engines. The truck manifold's long runners should hint at poor high-RPM performance, but that simply isn't the case. In back-to-back dyno testing, the truck manifold often produces even more power than the LS6 intake while boosting low-end torque. The downside is that its taller design requires more hood clearance.

The black sheep of the factory cathedral-port intake manifolds is the LS2 unit. Because the LS2 small-block uses LS6 cylinder heads, the LS2 intake manifold is very similar in design to the LS6 unit. The LS2 manifold features a larger 90-mm throttle body opening, re-contoured runners, and slightly more plenum volume than the LS6 unit, but it actually flows less air. So, unless you can find a very good deal on a used LS2 intake manifold, in the wake of stock intakes, the LS6 unit is a better option.

Stock Rectangle-Port Intakes

Perhaps the greatest asset of the LS-series small-block is the outstanding performance capabilities of its stock components. GM added to this mystique by creating the rectangle-port cylinder heads that made their debut in the LS7 and L92. Aware that these new head castings would flow substantially more air than their cathedral-port forebears, GM went to work and created intake

Edelbrock's Pro-Flow XT intake manifold for cathedral-port heads does away with the factory-style, cross-ram setup for a more conventional runner design. The result is a manifold with copious plenum volume and long tapered runners for a broad powerband. Provided enough hood clearance, Edelbrock advertises a 30-hp gain over a stock LS6 intake. (Photo courtesy of Edelbrock)

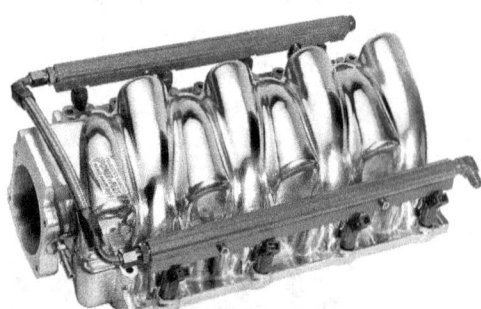

Professional Products' Power Plus Typhoon intake manifold for cathedral-port heads is available with 85- and 96-mm throttle body openings. It boasts a removable bottom cover for easy runner access and includes a set of fuel rails. In forced-induction and nitrous applications, aftermarket intakes are less prone to blowing apart compared to their factory GM counterparts.

The Weiand Air Ram intake manifold features a removable bottom panel for access to the runners and extra-thick walls for porting. According to the manufacturer, it's good for 25 hp over a stock intake.

INDUCTION

If the stock LS7 intake manifold isn't enough, FAST offers its LSX$_R$ unit as an upgrade. Independent dyno testing has proven that the FAST LS7 intake is good for an additional 25 to 30 hp over the stock unit.

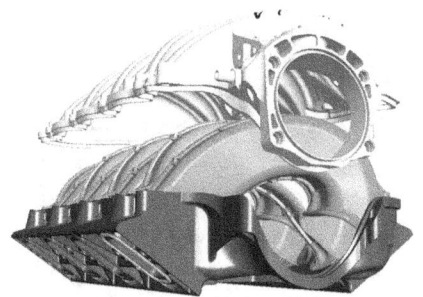

A unique feature of the FAST LSX$_R$ intake is that the top cover and runners can be disassembled from the base of the intake manifold. This provides tremendous flexibility for porting. (Photo courtesy of Comp Cams)

FAST's new LSX$_R$ intake manifolds feature several improvements over the models they replace, such as longer runners, increased plenum volume, and larger throttle body openings. They're available for both cathedral- and rectangle-port cylinder heads. In applications that have enough hood clearance for an LSX$_{RT}$ manifold, the unit's additional plenum volume and runner length have the potential to produce an extremely flexible powerband throughout the RPM range. (Photo courtesy of Comp Cams)

manifolds that could keep pace. The result is a family of state-of-the-art intake manifolds that pack tons of performance for the dollar. These intake manifolds share the same nylon construction as previous LS-style units, but they have larger 90-mm throttle body openings that hint at their high-flow potential.

The production LS7 intake manifold was the first of the factory rectangle-port units, and considering that it was designed to feed a 427-ci engine that turns 7,000 rpm, it's a very impressive piece of engineering. The LS7 intake has proven to be extremely effective in stroker combos putting out 650 to 700 hp. Just as impressive is its ability to deliver a very broad torque curve from idle to peak power. Available for less than $400 through GMPP, the LS7 intake manifold is a raging bargain. In reality, very few stroker combos need more airflow than the LS7 intake can provide.

Just as the LS7 cylinder heads inspired the design of the L92 heads, Gen IV small-blocks equipped with the L92 castings feature an intake manifold that doesn't flow quite as well as the LS7 unit, but it is an exceptional performer in its own right. The LS3, L92, L99, and L76 all share a common intake manifold. Although there are very subtle variations between the LS3 and L92/L76 units, such as the use of noise-reduction covers on the LS3 intake and the mounting of the MAP sensor, the basic design and performance of both manifolds are virtually identical. Compared to the LS7 intake, the LS3 and L92 manifolds have runner and plenum designs better suited for the smaller-displacement short-blocks they're bolted to. Providing enough flow to support 600 to 650 hp, at just $250 through GMPP, the LS3 and L92 intake manifolds are great values.

Designed for factory hydraulic roller small-blocks, it's not surprising that both the LS7 and LS3 intake manifolds are very well matched to the RPM range associated with the hydraulic roller stroker small-block. The LS7 intake provides

Thanks to Edelbrock and MSD, it's now possible to run a carburetor on an LS-series small-block. Edelbrock's carbureted LS intake manifolds feature an integrated MAP sensor. When a manifold is combined with the MSD ignition box, which has a harness that plugs into the factory coil packs and camshaft and crankshaft position sensors, the result is an LS small-block that doesn't need a factory computer. (Photo courtesy of Edelbrock)

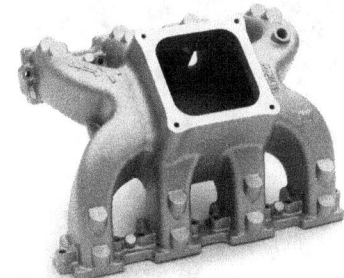

Like Edelbrock, GMPP offers a full line of carbureted LS-style intake manifolds. The LSX-DR intake loudly broadcasts its high-winding intentions with enormous runners and a mounting pad for 4500-series Holley carburetors.

CHAPTER 12

Just because you bolt a carbureted intake to an LS small-block doesn't mean you have to run a carburetor. Mast Motorsports' Retro LS intake manifold includes an adapter that allows for the mounting of a throttle body onto the carburetor pad. The single-plane intake comes with runners drilled for fuel injectors. Mast offers the complete kit with the manifold, adapter, injectors, and fuel rails.

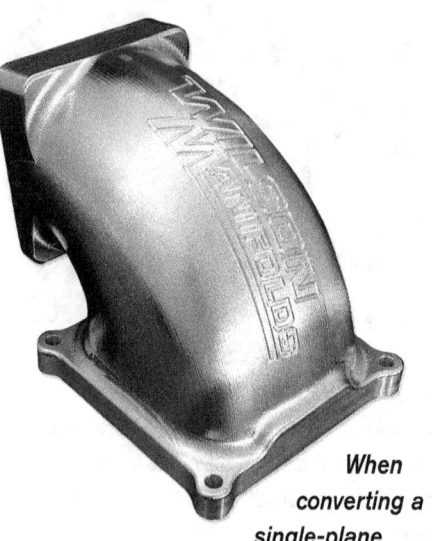

When converting a single-plane intake for EFI duty, there are two options for mounting a throttle body. Companies, such as FAST and Wilson Manifolds, offer carb-style throttle bodies that mount directly to the carb pad. Wilson also offers 90- and 100-degree elbow adapters that mount to the carb pad. This allows for the attachment of a conventional forward-facing EFI throttle body, which is often necessary for hood clearance concerns.

enough air for 427- to 454-ci motors to pull up to 6,500 to 7,000 rpm, and the LS3 intake works well in 396- to 416-ci motors in the same RPM range. Because the ports on the LS7 head and LS3/L92 heads are shaped differently, intake manifolds must be matched up accordingly. For instance, the LS3 intake manifold isn't compatible with LS7 heads, and the LS7 intake won't work on LS3 heads. Furthermore, even though the L92/L76 intake manifold is used in truck applications, it has a low-profile design that fits under steeply sloped car hoods.

LS6-Style Aftermarket Intakes

Whether it's a solid roller screamer that turns 8,000 rpm or a 500-ci hydraulic roller behemoth that makes more than 725 hp, there comes a point where even the high-flow factory intake manifolds run out of breath. Fortunately, companies, such as FAST, Holley, Wilson, Weiand, BBK, Professional Products, and Edelbrock, offer an assortment of intake manifolds for both cathedral- and rectangle-port cylinder heads. Early aftermarket intake manifolds were based on the stock LS6 design. Because of that, they offer slight improvements in airflow and horsepower, but exactly how much is debatable. Holley, Weiand, BBK, and Professional Products all offer aluminum intake manifolds that fall within this design category, and independent dyno testing results on both 5.7L and stroker motor combos are all over the map. Performance gains over the stock LS6 range anywhere from 10 to 25 hp.

Raising the carburetor allows for much more flexibility when designing a single-plane intake manifold. The runners can be made very large for high-RPM breathing, but they can also be made very long to promote low-RPM torque production. Tapering down the cross-sectional area of the runner also helps enhance this dual-purpose effect.

By raising the carburetor or throttle body, air can travel in a direct path into the intake ports. Air doesn't like to bend or change directions, so this arrangement yields dividends in airflow and power. Hood clearance is the only problem.

INDUCTION

Common features among these LS6-style intake manifolds include aluminum construction, thicker runner walls, and larger throttle body openings. Compared to the plastic factory manifolds, plumbing in nitrous injection nozzles and porting the runner is much easier on the cast-aluminum units. Furthermore, they're more durable under high-boost, forced-induction applications. Considering that these manifolds were designed before aftermarket blocks enabled the huge displacement figures that are common today, they're best suited for smaller engines between 346 and 396 ci. Even so, LS6-style aftermarket intakes only cost $100 to $200 more than a stock LS6 intake, so they can work quite well on a smaller-displacement stroker combination.

Without question, Fuel Air Spark Technology's (FAST) cathedral-port intake manifolds have set the performance benchmark for LS6-style intakes. FAST was the first to release an aftermarket LS intake, and its manifolds have a consistent track record of proven performance in a diverse range of applications. They feature high-strength polymer construction that's 30 percent stronger than stock and a unique three-piece design that allows engine builders to disassemble the intake for easy access to the runners should porting be necessary. The runners on the FAST manifold have a large cross-sectional area that tapers as the runners approach the cylinder heads. This affords excellent top-end power while retaining air velocity to preserve low-end torque. Gains of 20 to 30 hp are common over a stock LS6 intake in hydraulic roller stroker combinations. Furthermore, the FAST intake is offered with 78-, 90-, 92-, and 102-mm throttle body openings.

FAST's 102-mm LSX_R intakes are the latest units in the company's original LS manifold design evolution. It would be somewhat inaccurate to call them LS6-style intakes, because their design has several significant improvements over the standard LS6 architecture. In addition to their larger throttle body openings, they feature an increase in plenum volume and longer runners. Additionally, all eight runners can be removed individually for greater porting flexibility. Building upon these improvements, FAST's 102-mm LSX_{RT} intake offers the same basic improvements as the LSX_R, but with even more plenum volume and runner length. Given enough hood clearance, the LSX_{RT} is tough to beat in high-end street/strip or race applications that require a broad powerband with outstanding high-RPM airflow.

Aftermarket Rectangle-Port Intakes

The factory LS7 intake is an exceptional piece of engineering, but it was never intended to be pushed beyond the

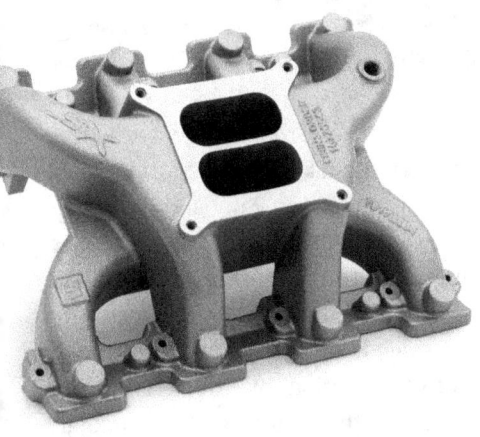

A dual-plane intake manifold produces more low-end torque than a single-plane intake, at the expense of high-RPM power. They're best suited for heavy street cars that will rarely exceed 6,500 rpm.

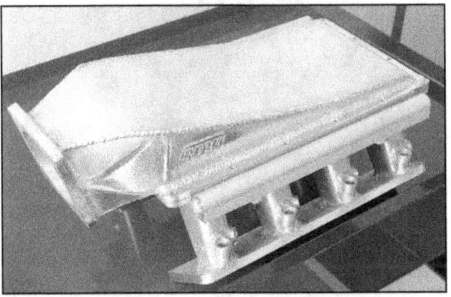

If readily available factory or aftermarket intake manifolds are deemed unsuitable for an application, there's always the option of stepping up to a custom sheet-metal intake. Each one is custom fabricated for a specific application, so although a custom intake is extremely expensive at $1,500 to $2,000, it's capable of performing extremely well.

As a company famous for its diverse range of intake manifolds, it's hardly surprising that Edelbrock offers a full line of dual- and single-plane LS-style intake manifolds, as well as EFI intakes. Edelbrock's Super Victor intake manifolds are famous for their high-RPM breathing capabilities. (Photo courtesy of Edelbrock)

CHAPTER 12

Since cylinder heads are only part of the induction equation, GMPP released a new line of LSX intake manifolds to go along with its LSX-LS3, LSX-LS7, LSX-CT, and LSX-DR heads. As with most carbureted LS-style intakes, they can also be drilled for fuel injectors. (© GM Corp.)

Factory throttle bodies are either actuated by a throttle cable or an electric motor. A drive-by-wire throttle body can be used in an engine swap application, but it must interface with a matching computer and a stock gas pedal.

700-hp mark that's becoming more common with 450-plus-ci short-blocks and serious cylinder heads that now define stroker Gen III/IV small-blocks. Furthermore, because the stock LS7 intake isn't compatible with L92/LS3 cylinder heads, enthusiasts opting for these castings needed a quality aftermarket intake manifold. FAST responded again with its 102-mm LSX_R intakes, which are designed specifically for rectangle-port cylinder heads. Two versions are offered, one for LS7 cylinder heads and another for L92/LS3 heads. Independent third-party dyno testing of the LS7 LSX_R intake on a 500-ci hydraulic roller small-block showed an increased output from 720 to 750 hp over a factory LS7 manifold.

Carbureted Intakes

Edelbrock stunned the hot rodding community when it released a dual-plane carbureted intake manifold for the LS1 in 2003. The Performer RPM LS1 intake manifold, designed for cathedral-port heads, works in conjunction with an MSD ignition control module that replaces the stock computer; the manifold also allows replacing the factory EFI system with a carburetor. As with most dual-plane intakes, the Performer RPM places a priority on low- and mid-range torque over top-end power, with an operating range from idle to 6,500 rpm. More importantly, however, the success of the Performer RPM and its overwhelmingly positive reception by the hot rodding public set the quintessential paradigm shift in motion.

Shortly after the launch of Edelbrock's ground-breaking carbureted intake, companies, such as GM Performance Parts and

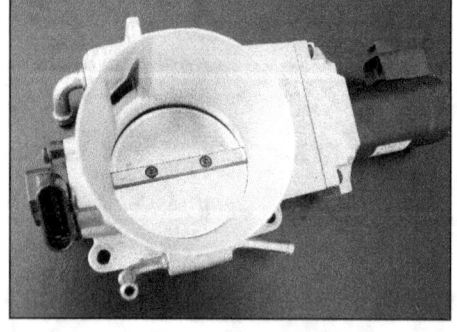

Porting the stock throttle body is a common trick that yields noticeable improvements in airflow. Katech's LS1 units feature a smoothed throttle body radius, and the company claims that they flow an additional 5 to 10 percent of air over stock units.

Almost all aftermarket throttle bodies are cable-actuated, which explains their popularity in engine swap applications. FAST's billet Big Mouth units are available in 92- and 102-mm diameters. (Photo courtesy of Comp Cams)

Professional Products' 80- and 85-mm throttle bodies for early Gen III engines are budget priced at $190. Each one includes an adapter plate that fits between the intake manifold and throttle body. This is said to smooth the throttle-body-to-manifold transition for improved airflow.

INDUCTION

Ideally, the diameter of the throttle body and the intake manifold opening should be the same. Not surprisingly, FAST offers 102-mm throttle bodies to go along with its 102-mm LSX_R intake manifolds. (Photo courtesy of Comp Cams)

If using a 90-degree adapter on a single-plane intake, it must be matched with a throttle body recommended by the manufacturer. Wilson Manifolds' square-flange throttle bodies bolt to the company's elbows, but they aren't necessarily LS-specific parts.

Performance Induction, got in on the action with carbureted manifolds of their own. From these companies, there are now dozens of carbureted intakes in single-plane and dual-plane configurations for everything from stock-displacement motors all the way up to 10,000-rpm full-race applications.

The significance of these intakes is two-fold. Not only do they enable hot rodders to enjoy the simplicity of carburetors on late-model LS engines, but they also allow EFI to be retrofitted onto these carb-style intakes. This is easily accomplished by drilling holes into the intake runners for fuel injectors and bolting a throttle body onto the carburetor pad. A conventional forward-facing throttle body can also be used by holding a 90-degree elbow adapter to the carburetor pad.

For high-end street or race applications where hood clearance isn't an issue, a single-plane intake offers irrefutable advantages in horsepower. They typically have very large plenum volumes and generous cross-sectional area to assist with high-RPM breathing, as well as long runners to help minimize low-RPM power loss. In the average 440- to 460-ci hydraulic roller stroker combo with 250 to 260 degrees of duration at .050 inch, a single-plane intake usually sacrifices 20 to 30 ft-lbs of torque in the mid-range, compared to an EFI intake, but it makes up for it with an additional 50 to 60 hp beyond 6,500 rpm. Furthermore, single-plane intakes extend the useable powerband by as much as 500 rpm. So, in applications with lots of hood clearance where giving up some low- and mid-range torque isn't a big deal, a single-plane intake manifold offers huge dividends in horsepower.

Throttle Bodies

As GM continually upped the horsepower ante with successive iterations of the LS-series small-block, throttle body diameters increased accordingly. The original 5.7L LS1 came equipped with a 75-mm throttle body, and the LS6, LQ4, and LQ9 received 80-mm units. By the time the 6.0L, 6.2L, and 7.0L Gen IV small-blocks entered production, the factory throttle bodies had grown to 90 mm.

GM stepped up to a larger 90-mm throttle body in the 6.0L, 6.2L, and 7.0L Gen IV small-blocks. These units are capable of moving lots of air, and they can support more than 700 hp.

FAST and Wilson Manifolds both offer throttle bodies that bolt directly to the carb pad on a single-plane intake. Naturally, they resemble a carburetor without a base plate. (Photo courtesy of Comp Cams)

Popular LS-Series Intake Manifolds

Type	PN	Runner Shape	Throttle Body Opening/Type	Material
BBK	5004	Cathedral	82 mm	Aluminum
Edelbrock Performer RPM	71187	Cathedral	Dual-Plane	Aluminum
Edelbrock Super Victor	28095	Cathedral	Single-Plane	Aluminum
Edelbrock Victor Jr. L76	28455	Rectangle	Single-Plane	Aluminum
Edelbrock Victor Jr.	29085	Cathedral	Single-Plane	Aluminum
FAST	5038	Cathedral	78 mm	Plastic
FAST	5039	Cathedral	90 mm	Plastic
FAST LS3	146102	Rectangle	102 mm	Plastic
FAST LS6	146302	Cathedral	102 mm	Plastic
FAST LS7	146202	Rectangle	102 mm	Plastic
FAST LSXRT	146602	Rectangle	102 mm	Plastic
GM L92/L76	12590124	Rectangle	90 mm	Plastic
GM LS3	12602477	Rectangle	90 mm	Plastic
GM LS6	88894339	Cathedral	80 mm	Plastic
GM LS7	12569011	Rectangle	90 mm	Plastic
GMPP 4BBL LS2	89958675	Cathedral	Single-Plane	Aluminum
GMPP 4BBL LS7	25534394	Rectangle	Single-Plane	Aluminum
GMPP 4BBL L92	25534401	Rectangle	Single-Plane	Aluminum
GMPP LSX-CT	19166950	Rectangle	Single-Plane	Aluminum
GMPP LSX-DR	1916654	Rectangle	Single-Plane	Aluminum
GMPP LSX-LS3	19244035	Rectangle	Dual-Plane	Aluminum
GMPP LSX-LS3	19244037	Rectangle	Dual-Plane	Aluminum
GMPP LSX-LS7	19244038	Rectangle	Single-Plane	Aluminum
Professional Products	52060	Cathedral	85 mm	Aluminum
Weiand	300-111C	Cathedral	85 mm	Aluminum
Wilson LS6	210001	Cathedral	85 mm	Aluminum
Wilson LS7	210002	Rectangle	90 mm	Aluminum

Additionally, aftermarket companies, such as Edelbrock, BBK, Wilson, FAST, Holley, and Summit, offer aftermarket units ranging from 80 to 102 mm.

Unlike a carburetor, the throttle body in an EFI engine doesn't directly impact the amount of fuel that's metered into the air intake charge. Consequently, EFI motors aren't nearly as sensitive to changes in throttle plate diameter. A good rule of thumb to follow is that the throttle body diameter should match the inlet opening of the intake manifold. For example, if you are installing a factory LS3 intake manifold on a stroker engine buildup, its 90-mm inlet opening should be paired with a 90-mm throttle body. There aren't any adverse affects of installing a throttle body that's slightly larger than the inlet opening of the intake manifold, but it won't improve performance, either.

Almost all aftermarket throttle bodies are cable-driven, whereas GM installed both cable-actuated and drive-by-wire units in production cars. For stroker engine builds utilizing a cable-actuated throttle body, switching to an aftermarket unit is a bolt-in affair. Alternately, a factory GM drive-by-wire unit can be retrofitted by installing a GM gas pedal that interfaces with the throttle body. For stroker LS buildups destined to power GM vehicles originally equipped with drive-by-wire throttle bodies, the stock 90-mm unit is the best option. This factory throttle body provides plenty of airflow, and it has proven to be effective beyond 700 hp. Other alternatives include converting to a cable-actuated throttle body or porting the stock unit. Smoothing out the throttle body radius and putting a bullnose finish on the leading edge of the throttle blades can boost airflow by 5 to 10 percent.

CHAPTER 13

FUEL AND SPARK

With the short-block, cylinder heads, valvetrain, and induction installation sorted out, the last step before hitting the throttle is feeding that new LS stroker motor some fuel and spark. This can be achieved by using the factory EFI system, an aftermarket EFI system, or by converting over to a carbureted induction setup. All three methods have their pros and cons, and there are dozens of different options among the three arrangements.

For instance, GM used several different types of factory powertrain control modules, which must be matched with specific engines and wiring harnesses. Furthermore, the stock PCM can be tuned by using specialized programs and a laptop computer, or a simpler hand-held device. Stand-alone aftermarket EFI systems eliminate much of the application-specific minutia associated with running a factory PCM, but they're generally more expensive; however, there are several different manufacturers to choose from.

If simplicity is the primary objective, a carbureted induction system is the easiest to install and tune. Thanks to stand-alone ignition systems from companies such as MSD and GMPP, LS-series small-blocks can have their timing maps tuned with a laptop while still relying on a venerable carburetor for fuel delivery. Although space limitations here prevent breaking down every single option on the market, here's a run-down of some of the most popular engine management systems available.

Electronic Fuel Injection

Part of the appeal of building an LS-series small-block for any project car is its high-tech credentials. Electronic fuel injection (EFI) adds to this mystique, and it offers irrefutable advantages over a carburetor in cars that see an appreciable amount of street duty. EFI-equipped motors start up reliably—even in cold weather—and offer improved fuel mileage, cleaner emissions, and superior drivability.

Options abound when it comes to feeding that freshly built LS stroker combo fuel and spark. Choices include running a stock PCM, using a stand-alone aftermarket EFI system, or even bolting on a carburetor. Stand-alone aftermarket systems represent the pinnacle of EFI tuning flexibility and power potential. (Photo courtesy of Comp Cams)

CHAPTER 13

EFI has the edge over a carburetor in every single category except power and cost. Although fuel injection offers unparalleled benefits in streetability, fuel mileage, emissions output, and cold startup ability, the venerable carburetor almost always makes more horsepower. Additionally, the cost of a carburetor is far less than the total tally of eight injectors, a computer, and tuning hardware and software.

On the other hand, EFI's impact on horsepower output is a topic of much debate. In numerous back-to-back, EFI-vs.-carburetor dyno tests conducted by several highly respected engine builders, a fuel-injection system rarely produces more power than a carburetor. Usually, it's the other way around, with the carb taking top power honors. That's because carburetors atomize fuel very high in the intake manifold, which increases charge density and the inertial ram effect of the incoming air/fuel charge.

In fact, this is why Formula One engines have their fuel injectors positioned at the top of the intake manifold runners. In contrast, production engines, including the Gen III/IV small-block, have injectors placed at the very end of the intake runners. Additionally, EFI systems tend to be more temperamental and difficult to tune. These inconveniences aside, no carb can touch the versatility and streetability of a well-tuned EFI system. So although it may take more initial effort to dial in, a properly tuned fuel injection system offers the best balance of all-around performance and economy.

Stock Powertrain Control Modules

The LS-series small-block has only been in production since the late 1990s, but GM has matched it with a dizzying array of powertrain control modules (PCM). Nevertheless, when matched with software programs, such as those from HP Tuners or EFI Live, the factory computer is an incredibly powerful tuning device that can tame even the most radical engine combinations. These software programs offer levels of tuning flexibility similar to that of an aftermarket stand-alone system, and at a fraction of the cost. Just a few years ago, this type of technology was unheard of.

If you are opting for a used-core engine as the basis of a stroker LS project, know that they're often sold with a matching PCM and wiring harness. This ensures that the engine and PCM are compatible with each other. However, with the increasing availability of aftermarket blocks, not all engine builds start with a used-core engine. If you are electing to run a stock PCM-based engine management system, it's imperative to choose the right computer. Factory GM computers can be broken down into two basic groups: those designed for 24-tooth reluctor wheels and those designed for 58-tooth reluctor wheels.

Engines equipped with 24-tooth wheels include 1997–2004 LS1s, 2001–2004 LS6s, 2005 and 2006 LS2s, and 1999–2006 Vortec truck motors. Gen IV small-blocks—including the LS3, LS7, LS9, LSA, L76, L99, and 2007-and-later Vortec truck engines—come equipped with 58-tooth reluctor wheels. Generally, either style PCM can be used to operate any LS-series small-block, as long as it's matched with the correct reluctor wheel and wiring harness. For instance, if you're using an LS3 core as the basis of a stroker built, it can be paired with a PCM designed to work with a 24-tooth reluctor wheel, as long

Factory 1999-and-later PCMs used with 24-tooth reluctor wheels are the most popular units with engine swappers. They can be used for both cable-actuated and drive-by-wire throttle bodies, and they are very inexpensive at $50 to $100.

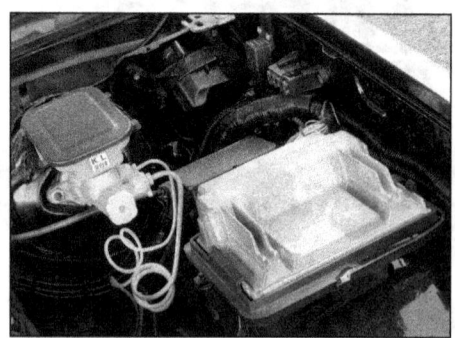

Early Gen III PCMs that came equipped on 1997 and 1998 F-bodies and Corvettes have a different pin-out configuration and require an application-specific wiring harness. Because of that, they're not very popular in retrofit applications.

HOW TO BUILD BIG-INCH GM LS-SERIES ENGINES

FUEL AND SPARK

as a 24-tooth reluctor wheel is installed on the crankshaft.

A major difference between the two is that 24-tooth reluctor wheel PCMs can be programmed to operate both drive-by-cable and drive-by-wire throttle bodies, and 58-tooth reluctor wheel PCMs are only compatible with drive-by-wire throttle bodies. Because PCMs designed for 58-tooth reluctor wheels have been produced in much lower quantities thus far, they tend to be harder to find and

Powerful software programs, such as those from EFI Live and HP Tuners, enable hot rodders to manipulate all of the factory tuning parameters. In addition to modifying the fuel and spark maps, these programs can adjust an automatic transmission's shift points and firmness, and they can also disable the factory Vehicle Anti-Theft System, which is very handy in engine swap applications.

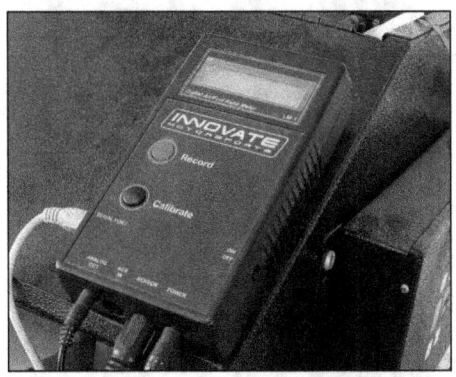

A wideband oxygen sensor is a critical tool for properly tuning the air/fuel mixture. Naturally aspirated engines typically produce the most power with the air/fuel ratio locked in at 11.5 to 12.5:1. Innovate Motorsports offers several affordable and easy-to-use wideband sensors, which feature data logging for enhanced flexibility and control.

The race track is the ultimate tuning venue, but a chassis dyno provides an excellent test bed for getting an engine's baseline fuel and spark curves dialed-in. Mustang and Superflow dynos can load the drive wheels to simulate wind resistance and the vehicle's weight. One great benefit of EFI is that it can automatically account for differences in air quality and density. By comparison, carburetors must be re-jetted constantly to account for changing ambient air conditions.

Stock EFI Basics

In contrast to a carburetor, which meters fuel, based on changing engine loads, via mechanical means, EFI relies on a slew of sensors strategically positioned throughout an engine. Although these sensors add to EFI's complexity, these same sensors equate to extra precision. At the heart of every EFI system is the PCM, which interprets signals from the sensors and relays instructions to various engine components, such as the fuel injectors, coil packs, and throttle body. To calculate engine load, the PCM receives manifold pressure readings from a manifold absolute pressure (MAP) sensor. Additionally, factory EFI systems also employ a mass airflow (MAF) sensor to calculate the volume of air entering the engine. The PCM then uses the engine load reading from the MAP sensor and airflow reading from the MAF sensor and matches them up with the corresponding fuel and ignition maps for the RPM the engine is turning to provide the proper amount of fuel and timing advance.

Perhaps the biggest benefit of EFI is that it can automatically compensate for changing atmospheric conditions. Should an EFI system's knock sensors and crankshaft position sensors detect vibrations that indicate detonation, the PCM automatically retards timing a specified amount. If the system's oxygen sensors detect an overly rich or lean air/fuel mixture, the system shortens or lengthens the injectors' pulse width to adjust the air/fuel ratio. Furthermore, the inlet air temperature (IAT) sensor, positioned in the air induction stream, and the engine coolant temperature (ECT) sensor help the PCM compensate for changes in ambient air and coolant temperature. Of course, there is a functional limit to the self-calibrating ability of factory computers. Although stock programming typically has no problem adjusting for basic bolt-on modifications, the mass influx of airflow associated with larger camshafts and ported cylinder heads can give it fits. That's why when building a stroker LS small-block, reprogramming the factory computer is mandatory.

CHAPTER 13

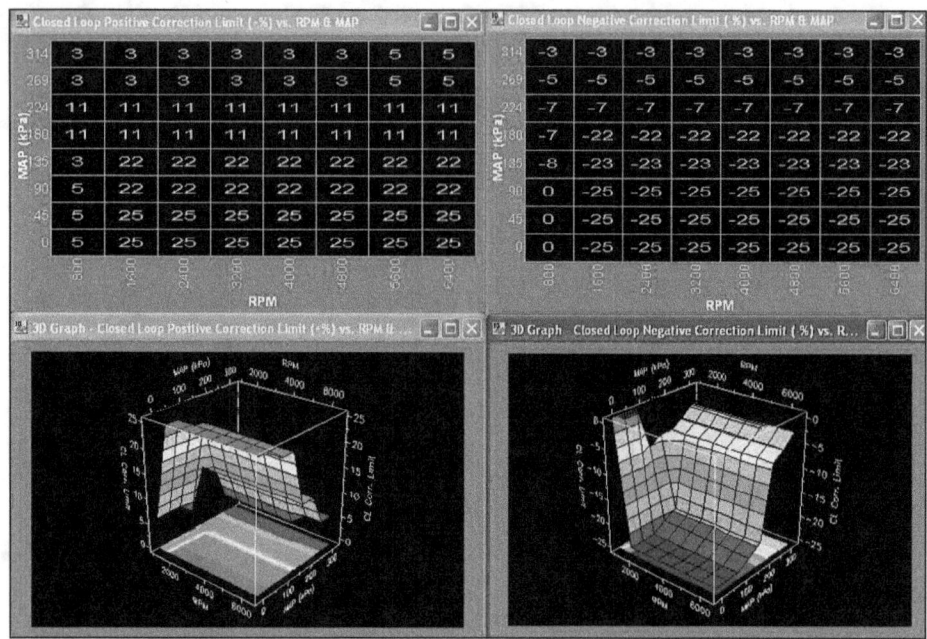

Perhaps the biggest drawback of both stock and aftermarket tuning platforms is that the dizzying array of tuning parameters makes it easy to get lost. Fortunately, there are myriad online forums where enthusiasts can seek help and even specialty training programs that you can enroll in to seek additional assistance. If that's still too intimidating, many speed shops offer their own tuning services. (Photo courtesy of Comp Cams)

The FAST XIM ignition controller was originally designed to work in conjunction with the FAST EFI computer. With the growing popularity of carbureted LS engines, hot rodders are now using the XIM to take over the factory ignition control functions. The XIM is compatible with both 24- and 58-tooth reluctor wheels. (Photo courtesy of Comp Cams)

A standalone aftermarket computer box is built from a durable aluminum housing and resembles a heat sink. Because low-impedance injectors force the computer to endure high electrical loads, the box must be able to efficiently dissipate heat to prevent its internals from cooking. The lack of heat capacity is why low-impedance injectors can't be used with stock PCMs. This is one major reason why extremely high-horsepower applications almost always run aftermarket computers. (Photo courtesy of Comp Cams)

more expensive. Consequently, the 24-tooth reluctor wheel PCMs are far more popular with LS enthusiasts. They're plentiful and can be purchased for as little as $50 to $100. One caveat is that the PCMs used on 1997 and 1998 LS1-powered F-bodies and Y-bodies have a different pin-out configuration, which requires a different wiring harness, so they are less common for engine swap applications.

PCM Tuning

For decades, the only way to comprehensively reprogram a fuel-injected engine was to bypass the stock PCM entirely with a stand-alone aftermarket computer. That all changed in the late 1990s, when computer-savvy hot rodders figured out how to hack into the factory computer codes and fully unlock the

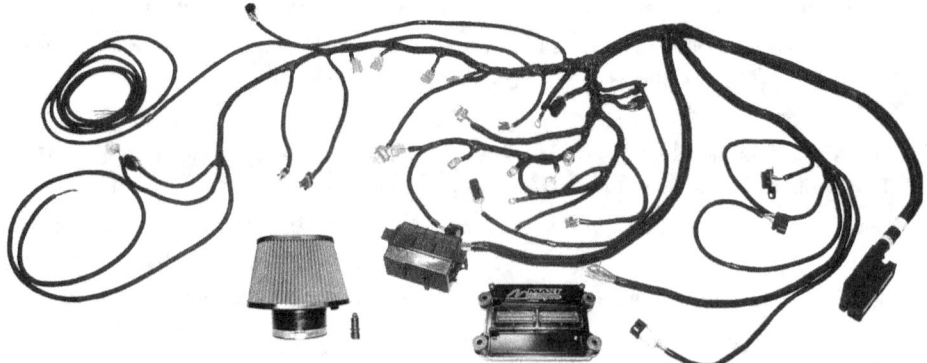

If you scored a Gen III/IV small-block to drop into your project car but don't have a computer, Mast Motorsports' M-90 PCM is the perfect solution. It offers all of the tuning power of a typical stand-alone EFI system, but it includes an idiot-proof wiring harness. After plugging all of the connectors onto the engine, all you have to do is hook up the power wire, ground wire, and fuel pump wire before firing up the motor.

FUEL AND SPARK

tuning potential of stock PCMs. In the LS camp, tuning software from HP Tuners and EFI Live has set the standard for flexibility and ease of use. These systems are essentially software programs that are downloaded to a laptop computer, and they interface with the factory PCM through the diagnostic port. The versatility of these programs is truly impressive, as they allow modifications of the fuel injector pulse widths, ignition timing, rev limits, knock retard, transmission shift points, cooling fan thresholds, speed limiters, final drive ratios, idle speed, and data logging. Additionally, the compatibility with two- and three-bar MAP sensors allows control over extreme-horsepower, forced-induction applications.

Because reprogramming the stock PCM can be intimidating, both HP Tuners and EFI Live offer comprehensive support forums on their websites, as well as a stockpile of various tunes users can download to use as a solid baseline program instead of trying to create one from scratch. Prices range from $400 to $800.

The factory PCM can also be tuned using hand-held devices from companies such as Superchips, Granatelli, Jet, and Diablosport. These hand-held units plug into the PCM's diagnostic port, but they do not require a laptop to operate. Most offer generic tunes that alter the fuel and spark maps based on fuel octane ratings, and some allow alterations of shift points, rev limits, and shift firmness. Due to their limited range of flexibility, hand-held tuners are best suited for stock or near-stock engines, but not for a heavily modified stroker combination.

Aftermarket EFI Systems

Without question, tuning software, like that from HP Tuners and EFI Live, has pushed the stock PCM beyond what anyone could have imagined just a decade ago. In fact, it's not unheard of anymore for a 1,000-hp forced-induction engine to make do with a factory computer. Even so, there's a limit to the stock PCM's capabilities, which is why you won't find a single Outlaw drag car running anything but a standalone aftermarket EFI system.

Once eclipsing the 1,000-hp mark, where heavy doses of boost and multiple stages of nitrous are the norm, an aftermarket EFI system offers a level of precision and versatility that a stock computer just can't match. Obviously, these systems are geared more toward race cars

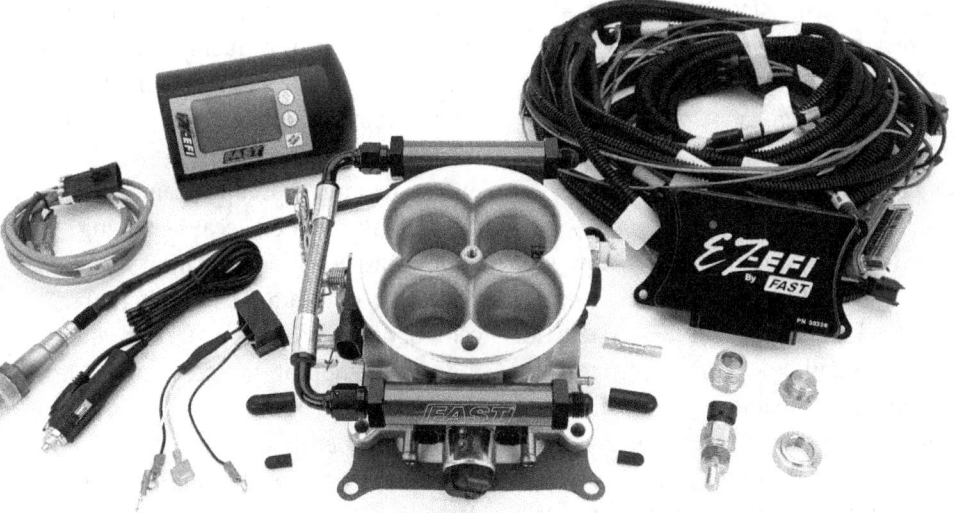

Self-learning aftermarket EFI systems, such as FAST's EZ-EFI, have just recently hit the market. Using feedback from the oxygen sensors at wide open throttle, EZ-EFI can create a custom fuel map within two dyno pulls. (Photo courtesy of Comp Cams)

Compared to a carbureted fuel system, EFI operates at much higher fuel pressures of 40 to 60 psi. For any given horsepower output, EFI requires a larger-capacity fuel pump. Aeromotive and FAST sell complete fuel systems that include an external pump, filters, a pressure regulator, and hoses. (Photo courtesy of Comp Cams)

CHAPTER 13

Holley is getting in the self-learning EFI segment, too, with its new Dominator standalone system. It features dual-channel wideband oxygen sensors, 12-channel distributorless ignition system outputs, and control of up to four stages of nitrous. As with competing systems, the Holley Dominator EFI unit creates a custom fuel curve within a couple of wide open throttle dyno pulls.

Fuel injectors may look similar from afar, but they come in various shapes, sizes, and spray patterns. Injectors must fit snugly into the intake manifold and fuel rail to prevent leaks. (Photo courtesy of Comp Cams)

and extremely high-end street cars, but with the tremendous horsepower potential of the LS platform, street cars equipped with aftermarket EFI systems are becoming more common.

There are literally dozens of standalone EFI systems on the market, but the most popular units with LS enthusiasts are offered by FAST, BigStuff3, and Accel. Compared to their stock-based counterparts, aftermarket systems offer more durable injector drivers, traction control, individual cylinder tuning, wideband oxygen sensor compatibility, multiple stage boost and nitrous controls, and data-loggers featuring accelerometers and blazing sampling rates. The biggest downside to these systems is cost, as they ring up a bill between $2,000 and $3,000. That price includes an aftermarket computer, wiring harness, engine sensors, and computer software. For the ultimate in tuning flexibility and horsepower potential, an aftermarket EFI system offers limitless possibilities.

Self-Learning EFI Systems

As computer technology continues to evolve at an alarming rate, it has enabled the automotive aftermarket to develop EFI systems that can now program themselves. Holley has recently launched its Dominator EFI system for LS-series small-blocks, and it offers many of the same flexible tuning features as competing systems. The ace up its sleeve, however, is a self-tuning fuel table that greatly simplifies the tuning process. By utilizing dual-channel wideband oxygen sensors, the Dominator EFI system can precisely create a fuel map based on an engine's fueling needs within a couple of wide-open-throttle (WOT) dyno pulls. From there, the end user can fine-tune the programming. It's very impressive technology, for sure, and it offers a glimpse into the future of aftermarket EFI systems.

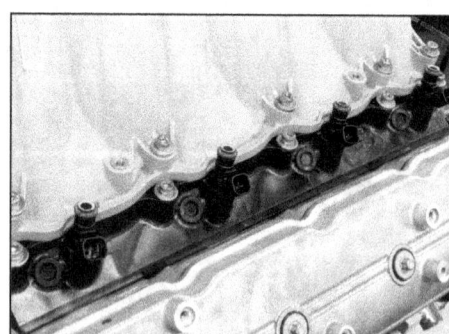

Certain fuel injectors are taller than others, but that's not too big of a deal. Spacers can be placed between the fuel rail stands and the intake manifold to account for taller injectors.

Fuel Pump and Injector Sizing

Of the multitude of decisions that go into properly planning and building a stroker LS small-block, choosing an appropriately sized fuel pump and injectors is relatively easy. For naturally aspirated combinations, a good rule of thumb to follow is to use a fuel pump that flows .5 lb/hr of fuel for every 1 hp. For example, a 1,000-hp naturally aspirated combination needs a pump that can flow 500 lb/hr of fuel, and a 500-hp engine requires a pump capable of flowing 250 lb/hr of fuel. Because maxing out a fuel system leaves no margin for error, it's not a bad idea to add another 10 percent of flow as a safety factor. Forced-induction applications tend to be less efficient, so fuel pump flow rates of .60 to .65 lb/hr per hp are ideal.

Once proper fuel pump size has been determined, selecting the right injectors can be calculated in a similar fashion. A 1,000-hp naturally aspirated engine that requires a 500-lb/hr fuel pump would need 62.5 lb/hr injectors. That's because 500 pounds of fuel divided by eight injectors yields 62.5 lb/hr per injector. That said, fuel injectors are all rated at a certain fuel pressure, and increasing fuel pressure can bump up the flow rate of an injector. Therefore, it's important to

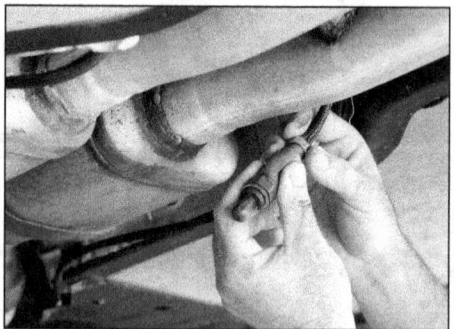

When installing a wideband oxygen sensor in a car, it must be positioned in front of the catalytic converters. Placing it behind the converters will skew the air/fuel ratio readings.

FUEL AND SPARK

compare the pressure an injector is rated at to the fuel pressure you will be running in your engine combo when selecting fuel injectors.

Carburetors

Although the Gen I small-block Chevy was built in both carbureted and fuel-injected configurations from the factory, all LS-series motors came equipped with EFI. This presented a problem for traditionalists, as they recognized the horsepower potential of the LS platform, but they didn't care for the complexity of EFI.

Edelbrock and MSD teamed up to create an ingenious solution in 2003 that allowed a person to bolt a carburetor to the Gen III small-block. Edelbrock got things rolling by creating a series of carbureted intake manifolds for LS-series small-blocks that could accommodate a MAP sensor. MSD then developed a revolutionary new ignition controller that took care of the spark side of the equation. The MSD 6LS controller looks like any other MSD ignition box, but it features a wiring harness that plugs into the coil packs and crankshaft and camshaft position sensors of the LS small-block. That and the MAP sensor integrated into the Edelbrock intake manifold are all that's needed to manipulate the factory ignition system. The MSD box allows creating custom timing advance maps with a laptop computer and has controls for vacuum advance, rev limits, and a step retard for nitrous use. Furthermore, MSD has two versions of its LS ignition box that will work with both 24- and 58-tooth reluctor wheels. With a carburetor administering fuel, and the MSD box controlling the electronics, for traditionalists, this combo is the best of both worlds.

Ignition

For good reason, when the topic at hand is the phenomenal performance of the Gen III/IV small-block, most of the talk revolves around the cylinder heads. However, the cast of supporting components, such as the ignition system, shouldn't be overlooked. As with many modern cars, the LS-series small-block utilizes crankshaft and camshaft position sensors to precisely measure the location of each piston. This allows the ignition system to fire each cylinder at exactly the right moment to maximize power and reduce emissions. Another benefit is that the system eliminates the need for a conventional distributor. In its place are eight coil packs, one for each cylinder, that bolt on top of the valve covers.

With one coil pack dedicated to each cylinder, this coil-on-plug arrangement results in a tremendous amount of spark energy. In fact, the stock ignition system performs reliably in engines producing well in excess of 1,000 hp. The only reason to replace a factory coil pack is if it's stopped working, due to age. Otherwise, the stock coils can handle just about anything an engine can throw at them. Over the years, GM has produced five different types of coils. Although they look different externally, due to the fact that they're made by different suppliers, GM says that the performance among them is identical. MSD also offers stock replacement coil packs, which are said to produce three times the spark energy.

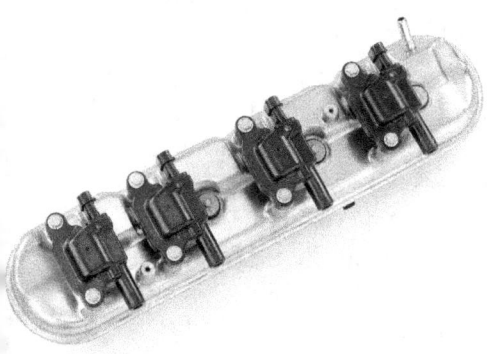

The coil-on-plug ignition system used on all LS-series small-blocks features one coil pack for each cylinder. This yields an extremely powerful spark that's capable of supporting well over 1,000 hp without any modifications. GM used several different styles of coils and brackets over the years, but, performance-wise, they are all nearly identical. (© GM Corp.)

Another benefit of the Gen III/IV small-block's coil-on-plug arrangement is that it significantly cuts down on the length of the plug wires. Not only does this make it easier to route them away from the headers, it also reduces the potential for electrical interference. With the LS small-block, burning spark-plug wires is a thing of the past.

Functionally, the factory coil-on-plug system offers outstanding performance. Unfortunately, it's not very aesthetic. Mast Motorsports offers coil brackets that relocate the coils to the side of the valvecovers. This cleans up the engine compartment and allows accessing the valvecover bolts without removing the coil brackets.

CHAPTER 14

PROVEN STROKER COMBINATIONS

Nothing illustrates the power potential of a stroker Gen III/IV small-block better than a real-world engine strapped to the dyno. Thus far, the prior chapters have outlined how to select the myriad components necessary to assemble a stroker LS-series small-block. However, there are literally thousands of ways in which those components can be mixed and matched. Different horsepower goals, displacement targets, rules restrictions, budgets, and intended uses mean that diversity is just part of the engine-building game. Even so, some stroker combinations stand out from the crowd, due to their raw power output, simplicity, sheer size, low cost, or efficiency. This chapter lists several exceptionally designed LS stroker combinations, ranging from affordable street motors to 500-ci thumpers to all-out 9,600-rpm race engines.

Full-Race Screamer LSX

Simply put, this 429-ci race engine is one of the meanest LS small-blocks ever built. Without the assistance of nitrous or forced induction, it kicks out a staggering 1,002 hp and 663 ft-lbs of torque. At 2.34 hp per ci, its specific output is

Full-Race Screamer LSX Specifications

Output: 1,002 hp at 9,000 rpm; 663 ft-lbs at 7,500 rpm; 2.34 hp/ci
Displacement: 429 ci
Bore/stroke: 4.132 x 4.000 inches
Block: GMPP LSX
Deck height: 9.240 inches
Crankshaft: Bryant billet steel
Rods: GRP 6.125-inch aluminum
Pistons: Wiseco 15.4:1 domed
Piston dome volume: -15.2 cc
Oiling system: Barnes dry sump
Cylinder heads: C5R
Combustion chamber volume: 44.2 cc
Valves: 2.180/1.625-inch intake/exhaust
Camshaft: Comp Cams 285/302-at-.050 solid roller; .969/.897-inch lift; 115-degree LSA
Intake manifold: Custom Beck sheet metal
Throttle body: Accufab Dominator-style
EFI: BigStuff3

PROVEN STROKER COMBINATIONS

right on par with that of a NASCAR Sprint Cup motor.

Built by the School of Automotive Machinists, the 429 powers a 3,500-pound 1999 Camaro down the quarter-mile in 8.52 seconds at 158 mph. Producing that kind of power in naturally aspirated trim requires a meticulously thought-out and executed combination that's extreme in every regard. Based on a GMPP LSX block, the engine not only boasts a healthy dose of displacement, but it turns 9,600 rpm and breathes through a set of heavily massaged C5R cylinder heads that flow 430 cfm. To get the most out of those cfm, the 429 utilizes a Comp Cams 285/302-at-.050 solid roller cam that boasts nearly a full inch of valve lift. Obviously, this isn't the kind of engine that will ever see street duty, as evidenced by its 7,500- to 9,600-rpm powerband. Because the Camaro that it powers is equipped with a Liberty's clutchless 5-speed manual transmission, and the motor never turns less than 8,000 rpm at the track, the 429's tight RPM band suits it perfectly.

Interestingly, SAM students and instructors built this monster small-block as part of a class project. The school operates one of the most respected vocational programs in the performance industry. Its unique curriculum covers short-block machining and assembly, cylinder head porting, CNC programming and operation, and race engine design. Between classes, SAM students work on the school's various race cars, and they are actively involved in the design and testing process of engines, such as this 1,002-hp small-block. Many of SAM's graduates go on to build race motors for some of the top names in racing, such as Hendrick Motorsports, John Force Racing, Warren Johnson Enterprises, Roush-Fenway Racing, McLaren Engines, and Honda IRL. For more information on SAM's unique program, visit www.samracing.com.

Wee Beast LS1

In the realm of stroker Gen III/IV small-blocks, a 383-ci motor is a bit on the small side. Proving that a well-executed parts combination can sometimes overcome a displacement handicap, this 383 produces horsepower and torque figures on par with those of many 408- and 427-ci stroker motors, all while burning 91-octane pump gas. It churns out 535 hp and 508 ft-lbs of torque on a Dynojet chassis dyno. Using the accepted figure of 15-percent drivetrain power loss, that equates to roughly 629 hp and 598 ft-lbs of torque. Trying to extrapolate horsepower at the crankshaft from rear-wheel horsepower isn't an exact science, but, needless to say, this 383 is one stout package (designed and built by Tony Mamo of Airflow Research).

It's equipped with an Eagle crank and rods, Wiseco 11.35:1 pistons, lightly ported Air Flow Research 205-cc cylinder heads, and a mild Comp Cams 234/238-at-.050 hydraulic roller camshaft. Peak horsepower figures aside, what makes this 383 truly impressive is its broad powerband. It produces nearly 550 ft-lbs

Full-Race Screamer LSX Dyno Data

RPM	TQ	HP
7,500	663	947
7,600	659	954
7,700	655	960
7,800	651	967
7,900	646	972
8,000	642	978
8,100	637	982
8,200	632	987
8,300	627	991
8,400	623	995
8,500	616	997
8,600	610	999
8,700	604	1,000
8,800	598	1,001
8,900	591	1,001
9,000	584	1,002
9,100	578	1,001
9,200	570	999
9,300	562	995
9,400	554	992
9,500	545	986
9,600	536	980

CHAPTER 14

Wee Beast LS1 Specifications

Output: 535 rear-wheel hp at 6,500 rpm; 508 rear-wheel ft-lbs at 4,700 rpm
Displacement: 383 ci
Bore/stroke: 3.905 x 4.000 inches
Block: GM LS1
Deck height: 9.240 inches
Crankshaft: Eagle forged steel
Rods: Eagle 6.125-inch steel
Pistons: Wiseco 11.35:1 flat-top
Piston dome volume: 5 cc
Oiling system: Stock
Cylinder heads: AFR 205 cc
Combustion chamber volume: 65 cc
Valves: 2.020/1.600-inch intake/exhaust
Camshaft: Comp Cams 234/238-at-.050 hydraulic roller; .595/.605-inch lift; 112-degree LSA
Intake manifold: FAST 90 mm
Throttle body: FAST 90 mm
EFI: Stock

Wee Beast LS1 Dyno Data

RPM	TQ	HP
4,000	462	352
4,100	465	363
4,200	475	380
4,300	488	400
4,400	498	417
4,500	500	428
4,600	505	442
4,700	508	454
4,800	507	463
4,900	504	470
5,000	502	478
5,100	500	486
5,200	499	494
5,300	495	499
5,400	492	506
5,500	489	512
5,600	484	516
5,700	479	520
5,800	473	522
5,900	466	523
6,000	460	525
6,100	454	527
6,200	450	531
6,300	445	534
6,400	439	534
6,500	432	535
6,600	420	529
6,700	410	523

of torque at 4,000 rpm, and it carries most of it through the entire RPM range. This kind of low- and mid-range torque makes for an outstanding street/strip motor with explosive throttle response at all RPM.

For enthusiasts on a tight budget, a 383 makes a lot of sense, as the largest bore a 5.7L aluminum or 5.3L iron block can handle is approximately 3.905 inches. When you match that bore size with a 4.000-inch crank that requires minimal clearancing, the end product is an easy-to-build and affordable 383-ci short-block. As this wee beast illustrates, big performance can come in small packages.

Big Daddy LS2

There was a time when even big-blocks couldn't crack 500 ci, but now small-blocks can reach that massive displacement total. Add that to the astounding airflow potential of the Gen III/IV cylinder heads, and it's a match made in horsepower heaven. Few engine combinations illustrate the benefits of massive cubic inches better than the SAM 500-ci LS2 small-block.

It's based on an ERL Super Deck II block that boasts a towering 10.200-inch deck height, and it can accommodate a 4.500-inch Callies stroker crank. When that's combined with Darton sleeves that allow for a 4.202-inch bore, the result is a 500-ci monster. To feed all those hungry cubes, the LS2 relies on a stock LS7 intake manifold and a set of ported LS7 cylinder heads that flow 390 cfm. Actuating the valves is a modestly sized Comp Cams 248/254-at-.050 hydraulic roller cam that many people would consider conservative in an engine 50 ci smaller.

As no surprise, SAM's 500-ci LS2 produces an incredibly stout torque curve that peaks at 630 ft-lbs at 5,100 rpm. Even more impressive is the fact that the 500 dishes out 600-or-more ft-lbs of torque from 4,500 to 6,200 rpm. Of course, torque is useless without horsepower, and the 500 doesn't disappoint in that department, either. The motor posts a total of 717 hp, thanks to its generous displacement, and peak power arrives at a leisurely 6,500 rpm. If the same heads and camshaft were installed on a 427, it would have to turn at least 500 rpm more to produce the same peak horsepower.

As with all of its project engines, the SAM 500 was put through its paces at the race track. Installed in the school's 1998 Camaro project car, the motor was good for a 9.96-at-135-mph pass in the quarter-mile. That's not too shabby at all for a 3,700-pound car running on 93-octane pump gas.

Welterweight Brawler LS3

Measuring right in the middle of the displacement spectrum, this 417-ci small-block strikes a sweet balance of affordability and size. By pairing a factory 6.2L aluminum block's 4.065-inch bore—cleanup-honed to 4.071 inches—with a 4.000-inch stroke, the result is a healthy

PROVEN STROKER COMBINATIONS

Big Daddy LS2 Dyno Data

RPM	TQ	HP
4,200	564	451
4,300	570	466
4,400	582	488
4,500	600	514
4,600	615	538
4,700	622	557
4,800	626	572
4,900	628	586
5,000	629	599
5,100	630	612
5,200	629	623
5,300	627	633
5,400	625	643
5,500	622	651
5,600	618	659
5,700	614	667
5,800	611	675
5,900	609	684
6,000	608	694
6,100	605	703
6,200	601	709
6,300	595	713
6,400	588	716
6,500	579	717

Big Daddy LS2 Specifications

Output: 717 hp at 6,500 rpm; 630 ft-lbs at 5,100 rpm; 1.43 hp/ci
Displacement: 500 ci
Bore/stroke: 4.202 x 4.500 inches
Block: ERL Super Deck II
Deck height: 10.200 inches
Crankshaft: Callies forged steel
Rods: Carrillo 6.800-inch steel
Pistons: Wiseco 10.8:1 dished
Piston dome volume: 28 cc
Oiling system: Stock pump, Moroso pan
Cylinder heads: GM LS7
Combustion chamber volume: 66 cc
Valves: 2.200/1.615-inch intake/exhaust
Camshaft: Comp Cams 248/254-at-.050 hydraulic roller; .647/.647-inch lift; 114-degree LSA
Intake manifold: GM LS7
Throttle body: Nick Williams 92 mm
EFI: Stock

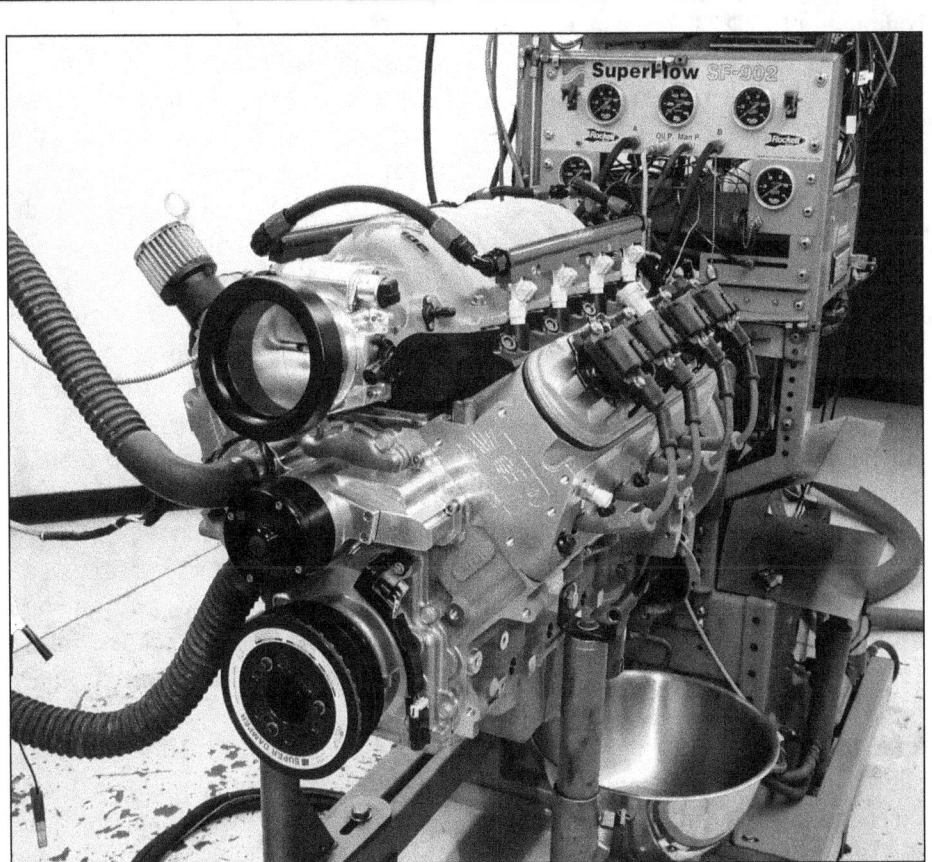

CHAPTER 14

Welterweight Brawler LS3 Specifications

Output: 663 hp at 6,600 rpm; 579 ft-lbs at 5,500 rpm; 1.59 hp/ci
Displacement: 417 ci
Bore/stroke: 4.071 x 4.000 inches
Block: GM LS3
Deck height: 9.240 inches
Crankshaft: Compstar forged steel
Rods: Compstar 6.125-inch steel
Pistons: Wiseco 11.4:1 flat-top
Piston dome volume: 5 cc
Oiling system: Stock
Cylinder heads: AFR 230 cc
Combustion chamber volume: 65 cc
Valves: 2.080/1.600-inch intake/exhaust
Camshaft: Comp Cams 243/247-at-.050 hydraulic roller; .624/.624-inch lift; 112-degree LSA
Intake manifold: FAST 102 mm
Throttle body: FAST 102 mm
EFI: Stock

Welterweight Brawler LS3 Dyno Data

RPM	TQ	HP
3,400	510	330
3,500	508	339
3,600	512	351
3,700	518	365
3,800	525	380
3,900	531	394
4,000	538	410
4,100	544	425
4,200	550	440
4,300	555	455
4,400	559	469
4,500	564	484
4,600	571	500
4,700	574	514
4,800	575	525
4,900	574	536
5,000	574	547
5,100	575	558
5,200	576	570
5,300	577	583
5,400	579	595
5,500	579	606
5,600	578	616
5,700	576	625
5,800	574	634
5,900	570	641
6,000	565	646
6,100	560	651
6,200	555	655
6,300	549	658
6,400	542	661
6,500	535	662
6,600	528	663
6,700	519	662
6,800	510	661
6,900	499	657
7,000	488	651

dose of displacement without the need for a costly re-sleeving procedure. For hot rodders looking to build a budget-priced aluminum Gen III/IV motor without breaking the bank, the 417 is an extremely popular displacement combination. This particular 417 (designed and built by Tony Mamo of Airflow Research) ups the ante with a Compstar rotating assembly and a heavy-breathing top end comprised of AFR 230-cc cylinder heads and a FAST 102-mm intake manifold and throttle body. When they're all matched with a Comp Cams 243/247-at-.050 hydraulic roller cam, the result is 663 hp and 579 ft-lbs of torque on 91-octane pump gas.

Peak output, however, is the least impressive aspect of this potent combination. The 417 produces more than 500 ft-lbs of torque from 3,400 to 6,900 rpm. Furthermore, the 417 kicks out more than 570 ft-lbs from 4,600 to 5,900 rpm, and it peaks 579 ft-lbs at 5,500 rpm. The beauty of a highly optimized combination like this is that it combines outstanding peak horsepower with an incredibly flexible torque curve. That means it will pull all the way to 7,000 rpm when called upon, yet easily roast the hides anywhere in the low- and mid-RPM range. Further enhancing its street credentials, the 417 idles smoothly at 900 rpm, and it also boasts a hydraulic roller cam valvetrain that requires minimal maintenance. With its blend of power and streetability, the 417 treads on turf that only big-blocks could touch just a few years ago.

Brazilian Stock Car LS3 Motor

A budget race engine is somewhat of an oxymoron, but Mast Motorsports' 416-ci LS3 is the exception to the rule. Because the engine had to be designed and built as a spec motor for Brazil's Copa Nextel stock car road racing series, Mast had to stick with a strict $15,000 budget. Making the task that much more difficult, the motor has to last for a full 12-race season, which equates to roughly 2,800 hard racing miles. Nonetheless, the 416 produces 617 hp and 568 ft-lbs of torque.

To pull off this impressive feat of dollar-stretching performance and durability, Mast relies heavily upon production GM components. A testament to the race-bred nature of modern LS-series small-blocks, the Mast 416 utilizes a factory 6.2L aluminum block, finish-honed to 4.070 inches, and a stock LS3 intake manifold, throttle body, and cylinder heads. With a mild 240/256-at-.050 hydraulic roller cam actuating the valves, the 416 produces peak power at a modest 6,300 rpm, which greatly improves overall engine durability. Holding the short-block together are a Compstar 4.000-inch forged crank and rods and Mahle 11.3:1 pistons.

In contrast to the high-octane gasoline used in NASCAR Sprint Cup engines, the Brazilian Copa Nextel stock car series mandates an E98 fuel that's 98

PROVEN STROKER COMBINATIONS

percent ethanol. Interestingly, the Mast 416 produced an additional 26 hp (617 vs. 591) on ethanol compared to 93-octane gasoline. Although ethanol has less BTUs of energy than gasoline, Mast says that its greater heat of vaporization enables it to pack a denser air/fuel mixture into the cylinders for an increase in power. The downside is that it takes 1.5 times as much ethanol to make similar power as gasoline, dramatically reducing fuel mileage. Nonetheless, considering that this 416 is a bona-fide race engine, the fact that it's based heavily on production GM components is simply amazing.

Brazilian Stock Car LS3 Motor Specifications

Output: 617 hp at 6,300 rpm; 568 ft-lbs at 5,100 rpm; 1.48 hp/ci
Displacement: 416 ci
Bore/stroke: 4.070 x 4.000 inches
Block: GM LS3
Deck height: 9.230 inches
Crankshaft: Compstar forged steel
Rods: Compstar 6.125-inch steel
Pistons: Mahle 11.3:1 flat-top
Piston dome volume: 4 cc
Oiling system: Armstrong dry sump
Cylinder heads: GM LS3/L92
Combustion chamber volume: 70 cc
Valves: 2.165/1.590-inch intake/exhaust
Camshaft: Comp Cams 240/256-at-.050 hydraulic roller; .610/.634-inch lift; 114-degree LSA
Intake manifold: GM LS3
  Throttle body: GM 90-mm LS3
EFI: Stock

Brazilian Stock Car LS3 Motor Dyno Data (Gasoline)

RPM	TQ	HP	RPM	TQ	HP
2,000	351	134	4,300	507	417
2,200	343	142	4,600	526	456
2,400	370	168	4,800	534	486
2,600	394	198	5,000	538	517
2,900	412	228	5,300	537	544
3,100	439	259	5,600	531	567
3,400	461	297	5,900	520	580
3,600	475	327	6,100	505	588
3,800	479	351	6,400	487	591
4,100	485	378	6,600	467	588
			6,900	443	578

Brazilian Stock Car LS3 Motor Dyno Data (Ethanol)

RPM	TQ	HP	RPM	TQ	HP
2,000	381	145	4,400	548	456
2,100	380	154	4,600	562	494
2,400	380	175	4,900	567	525
2,600	420	211	5,100	568	554
2,900	450	246	5,400	566	578
3,100	475	283	5,600	560	597
3,400	494	318	5,900	547	609
3,600	506	349	6,100	529	614
3,900	507	375	6,300	511	617
4,100	521	410	6,600	490	614
			6,800	465	605

CHAPTER 14

What's a Dyno?

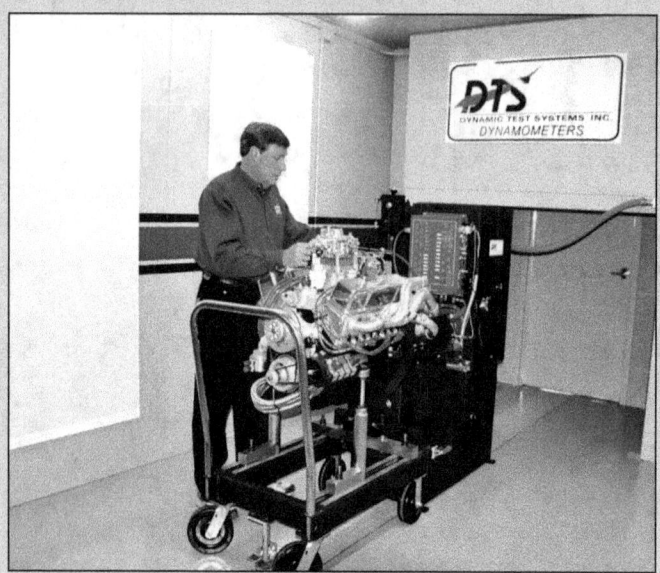

An engine dynamometer, commonly known as a dyno, is an excellent tuning tool for testing various parts combinations. Although few hot rodders will ever strap their engines to a dyno, a dyno allows for the precise measuring of the horsepower and torque of a motor in a controlled environment. This begs the question, "What exactly is a dyno, and how does it work?"

By far, water brake dynos–manufactured by companies such as Superflow and Dynamic Test Systems–are the most popular in performance automotive applications. A power absorption unit is at the heart of the dyno, and it attaches directly to an engine's crankshaft or flywheel. As an engine is accelerated on the dyno, the absorption unit's rotational element, or rotor, spins inside its stationary housing, called the stator. It functions much like a torque converter, but it uses water instead of transmission fluid. Consequently, although the rotor and stator are not physically connected, as the rotor starts to spin, the stator tries to rotate with it in the same direction. Attached to the stator housing on one end and to the dyno's steel frame on the other, a strain gauge prevents the absorption unit from spinning and measures torque. In essence, dynos actually measure torque, not horsepower. Because horsepower is a mathematical equation, the dyno measures torque and calculates horsepower.

Eddy current dynos operate on a similar principle, but with electrical current providing load in lieu of water. A steel rotating element spins through an electromagnetic field, and load is increased by cranking up the magnetism. The benefit of eddy current dynos is their precise load control. In steady-state testing, they can control an engine within 1 to 2 rpm, as opposed to the 5- to 10-rpm range of a water brake dyno. However, they're not very practical or appropriate for most engine builders. Although they're very precise, eddy current dynos are extremely expensive to set up and operate and have less dynamic operating range in terms of calculating horsepower. That's why they're better suited for R&D labs at the OEMs.

The most sophisticated, yet least common, type of dyno is the alternating current (AC) dyno. Essentially a large AC motor, this dyno, in addition to absorbing power, can also power an engine. This allows AC dynos to replicate any on-track condition–such as coasting, upshifting, and downshifting–and simulate an entire race in a test cell. Expensive even by Nextel Cup standards, AC dynos are typically reserved for mega-buck racing operations, such as Formula One. In contrast, due to their affordability and accuracy, water brake dynos are the most prevalent in performance engine shops.

The typical dyno test cell has its own fuel and water supplies to feed to the test engine, as well as a ventilation system designed to route exhaust to the outside of the building. Because weather conditions can dramatically impact horsepower and torque readings, dyno cells utilize correction factors for improved accuracy. Without correction factors, it would be impossible to accurately compare horsepower numbers from one test facility to another.

In theory, correction factors produce numbers that reflect an engine running at sea level, but not all are created equal. There are many SAE correction factors, which are known in the industry as J codes. The current standard is J1349, which corrects to 29.23 inches of Hg at 77 degrees F and 0-percent humidity. However, in the automotive aftermarket, it's very common to correct to 29.92 inches of Hg at 60 degrees F and 0-percent humidity. The difference between the two, in terms of horsepower calculations, is about 4 percent. Furthermore, in order to gather pertinent atmospheric conditions, a dyno facility's weather station should be located in the test cell itself. Although it shouldn't interfere with an engine's airflow, the weather station, ideally, should hang from the ceiling and be positioned near the carburetor or throttle body to most precisely measure the air the engine is ingesting.

Source Guide

Air Flow Research
28611 West Industry Drive
Valencia, CA 91355
877-892-8844
www.airflowresearch.com

Automotive Racing Products
531 Spectrum Circle
Oxnard, CA 93030
800-826-3045
www.arp-bolts.com

ATI Performance Products
6747 Whitestone Road
Baltimore, MD 21207
410-298-4343
www.performanceproducts.com

B&M Racing & Performance Products
9142 Independence Avenue
Chatsworth, CA 91311
818-882-6422
www.bmracing.com

BBK Performance Parts
27440 Bostik Court
Temecula, CA 92590
951-296-1711
www.bbkperformance.com

Big Stuff 3
4352 Fenton Road
Harland, MI 48353
248-329-7000
www.bigstuff3.com

Callies Performance Products
202 South Main Street
Fostoria, OH 44830
419-435-2711
www.callies.com

Canton Racing Products
14 Commerce Drive
North Branford, CT 06471
203-481-9460
www.cantonracingproducts.com

Competition Cams
3406 Democrat Road
Memphis, TN 38118
800-999-0853
www.compcams.com

CP-Carrillo
1902 McGaw Avenue
Irvine, CA 92614
949-567-9000
www.cp-carrillo.com

Crower Cams & Equipment
3333 Main Street
Chula Vista, CA 91911
619-661-6477
www.crower.com

Dart Machinery
353 Oliver Street
Troy, MI 48084
248-362-1188
www.dartheads.com

Diamond Pistons
23003 Diamond Drive
Clinton Township, MI 48035
877-552-2112
www.diamondracing.net

Eagle Specialty Products
8530 Aaron Lane
Southaven, MS 38671
662-796-7373
www.eaglerod.com

Edelbrock
2700 California Street
Torrance, CA 90503
800-416-8628
www.edelbrock.com

EFI Live
121 Elliot Street, Unit 2
Howick Auckland, 2014
New Zealand
www.efilive.com

ERL Performance
2560 Charlestown Road
New Albany, IN 47150
877-815-3434
www.erlperformance.com

Fuel Air Spark Technology
3400 Democrat Road
Memphis, TN 38118
877-334-8355
www.fuelairspark.com

GM Performance Parts
800-577-6888

Holley Performance Products
Earl's, Holley, Hooker, NOS
1801 Russellville Road
Bowling Green, KY 42102
270-782-2900
www.holley.com

HP Tuners
725 Hastings Lane
Buffalo Grove, IL 60089
www.hptuners.com

Isky Racing Cams
16020 South Broadway Street
Gardena, CA 90248
323-770-0930
www.iskycams.com

SOURCE GUIDE

JE-SRP Pistons
15312 Connector Lane
Huntington Beach, CA 92649
714-898-9763
www.jepistons.com

KB Pistons
4909 Goni Road
Carson City, NV 89706
702-882-7790
www.kb-silvolite.com

Lingenfelter Performance Engineering
1557 Winchester Road
Decatur, IN 46733
260-724-2552
www.lingenfelter.com

Lunati
11126 Willow Ridge Drive
Olive Branch, MS 38654
662-892-1500
www.lunatipower.com

Mahle Clevite
1240 Eisenhower Place
Ann Arbor, MI 48108
800-338-8786
www.mahleclevite.com

Manley Performance Products, Inc.
1960 Swarthmore Avenue
Lakewood, NJ 08701
732-905-3366
www.manleyperformance.com

Mast Motorsports
330 Northwest Stallings Drive
Nacogdoches, TX 75964
888-417-5407
www.mastmotorsports.com

Melling Automotive Products
2620 Saradan Drive
Jackson, MI 49204
517-787-8172
www.melling.com

Milodon
2250 Agate Court
Simi Valley, CA 93065
805-577-5950
www.milodon.com

Moroso Performance Products
80 Carter Drive
Guilford, CT 06437
203-453-6571
www.moroso.com

Mr. Gasket Company
Accel, Erson Cams, Mallory
10601 Memphis Avenue, #12
Cleveland, OH 44144
216-688-8300
www.mrgasket.com

Oliver Racing Parts
1025 Clancy Avenue Northeast
Grand Rapids, MI 49503
800-253-8108
www.oliver-rods.com

Professional Products
12705 South Van Ness Avenue
Hawthorne, CA 90250
323-779-2020
www.professional-products.com

Pro-Filer Performance Products
P.O. Box 217
New Carlisle, OH 45344
937-846-1333
www.profilerperformance.com

Quick Fuel Technologies
2352 Russellville Road
Bowling Green, KY 42101
270-793-0900
www.quickfueltechnology.com

Racing Head Service
3406 Democrat Road
Memphis, TN 38118
877-776-4323
www.racingheadservice.com

Reher-Morrison
1120 Enterprise Place
Arlington, TX 76001
817-467-7171
www.rehermorrison.com

Ross Racing Pistons
625 South Douglas Street
El Segundo, CA 90245
310-536-0100
www.rosspistons.com

Scat Enterprises
1400 Kingsdale Avenue
Redondo Beach, CA 90278
310-370-5501
www.scatcrankshafts.com

School of Automotive Machinists
1911 Antoine
Houston, TX 77055
713-683-3817
www.samracing.com

Scoggin-Dickey Performance Center
5901 Spur 327
Lubbock, TX 79424
800-456-0211
www.sdpc2000.com

SLP Performance Parts
1501 Industrial Way North
Toms River, NJ 08755
732-349-2109
www.slponline.com

Summit Racing Equipment
1200 Southeast Avenue
Tallmadge, OH 44278
800-230-3030
www.summitracing.com

T&D Machine
4859 Convair Drive
Carson City, NV 89706
702-884-2292
www.tdmach.com

TCI Automotive
151 Industrial Drive
Ashland, MS 38603
888-776-9824
www.tciauto.com

Trick Flow Specialties
1248 Southeast Avenue
Tallmadge, OH 44278
330-630-1555
www.trickflow.com

Wilson Manifolds
4700 Northeast 11th Avenue
Fort Lauderdale, FL 33334
954-771-6216
www.wilsonmanifolds.com

Wiseco Pistons
7201 Industrial Park Boulevard
Mentor, OH 44060
800-321-1364
www.wiseco.com

World Products
51 Trade Zone Court
Ronkonkoma, NY 11779
631-981-1918
www.worldcastings.com